PARADISE LOST

Eve Offering Adam the Forbidden Fruit

PARADISE LOST

An Account of Its Growth and Major

Origins, with a Discussion of Milton's

Use of Sources and Literary Patterns

By GRANT McCOLLEY

Illinois Institute of Technology

NEW YORK

RUSSELL & RUSSELL · INC

1963

To

ALICE ELIZABETH McCOLLEY

I SHALL emphasize in this volume the ancient and power-ful tradition which gave birth to *Paradise Lost*. By so doing, I shall hope to deepen both the intuitive and intellec-tual comprehension so essential to appreciation of Milton's greatest poem. Enjoyment is the companion of compre-hension, and varies with our understanding of the themes, the values, and the motives which vitalize a book. To enjoy *Paradise Lost* means no less than walking at ease among the conceptions which make dynamic its rolling verse.

For some years I have thought of relating Milton's epic to the literature from which it sprang. It remained however for Albert Croll Baugh to provide the impetus which made the idea an actuality. He will not, I trust, find misplaced his suggestion that readers of *Paradise Lost* become ac-quainted with my studies. To Arthur O. Lovejoy, Marjorie Hope Nicolson, and George Coffin Taylor, I owe a debt as varied as it is fundamental. Equally immeasurable is my obligation to Henry Todd and subsequent Miltonic schol-arship.

During the preparatory period of this discussion, George R. Coffman repeatedly gave indispensable advice and en-couragement. I have benefited much from the generous criticism of Charles G. Osgood, Ronald S. Crane, and Douglas Bush. Other friends whose assistance has proved more than incidental are A. C. L. Brown, W. F. Bryan, Margaret B. Crook, Walter Clyde Curry, Harris F. Fletcher, J. Milton French, William Haller, Raymond D. Havens, James Holly Hanford, Virgil L. Jones, T. O. Mabbott, William R. Parker, Richard A. Rice, Arnold Williams, and Robert Withington. Walter Hendricks, S. I. Hayakawa, Elder Olson, and Robert Sanford, colleagues at

Illinois Institute, made further essential contributions. My Mother and Father, ably assisted by Margaret and Carolyn McColley, have aided substantially in the reading of proof. Allan H. Gilbert, Lawrence and Carolyn Hout-chens have joined with this courtesy, that of numerous helpful suggestions.

I have made no attempt completely to normalize capital-ization, spelling, and punctuation. In citing quotations, the general criterion has been to effect such a compromise as retained some flavor of the period without too greatly handicapping the rapid reader. On occasion, extended sentences have been broken up. In accord with the style of Scripture, and of Milton and his age, pronouns referring to Deity generally are not capitalized, the major exceptions falling within quotations either from early writers or mod-ern translators who used our conventional method. Biblical texts are those of the King James Version.

The conventional dots which represent gaps within a quotation not infrequently are omitted. In general, either the citation indicates clearly that the quotation consists of fragmentary material, or the omissions are such as should preclude misinterpretation. Documentation is provided in the *Index of Writers and Books,* and the interested reader will find additional citations in the several articles by the writer listed in the *Bibliography.*

The introductory chapter which follows will discuss briefly the growth and influence of the hexameral tradition, with some remarks on its relation to *Paradise Lost.* Within the chapter, I occasionally quote illustrative material which complements the analogues given in Part I. Concluding paragraphs of this limited introduction will outline the scope of Parts I and II.

30 July, 1940   GRANT McCOLLEY

CONTENTS

CONTENTS

ILLUSTRATIONS

INTRODUCTION

Chapter I

THE HEXAMERAL TRADITION

WE long have known the Seventeenth Century as the Century of Genius. With equal truth we may name it the century of the Roman god Janus, for no period so unmistakably looked backward and forward. Within its years the scientific movement laid the foundations of modern technology. Societies devoted to dissemination of the 'new philosophy' began stated meetings which since have continued without serious interruption. In England, economic and political leadership passed gradually into the hands of the mercantile and industrial middle class. Democracy and the sanctity of the individual became increasingly more than a theory, and definite progress was made in the separation of Church and State. The nationalistic spirit, whose present manifestations threaten the best achievements of the period, reached some maturity and a new height of influence. Theology slowly became more liberal, and not a few divines praised the virtues of Natural Religion.

The second face of the century looked steadily toward the past. Without any awareness of inconsistency, such an enlightened individual as Joseph Glanvill supported on the one hand the claims of the new science, and on the other defended vehemently the existence of witches. In art, in treatises on ethics and government, and above all in literature, the ancients stood supreme. Those who advocated 'new' scientific and philosophic conceptions stressed the point that these doctrines had descended from antiquity. Precisely as we today turn unconsciously to 'the latest

1

thing,' so the Seventeenth Century sought first the oldest
and the longest tried.

As a man who lived much with his age, Milton necessarily
proved an individual Janus. In his conception of government, of education, and of the relations of Church and State,
he anticipated the future. He looked forward in defending
freedom of speech, of conscience, and of intimate personal
relationships. The divine right of monarchy he challenged.
With these and other advanced beliefs the poet joined
much that belonged to the past. He could write of visiting
Galileo and of the telescope, but attack mercilessly the
scientific investigations which Galileo defended and the
telescope in part made possible. He preached human liberty, but retained toward children the most repressive of
antiquated views. Not unappreciative of modern literature,
yet it was the ancient which chiefly developed and sustained him.

Among ancient books sacred to Milton, Scripture stood
first. Vitally important, especially in the formation of his
style and conception of literary art, were the Classics.
Equally basic proved the vast body of religious literature
which Christendom had slowly accumulated for sixteen
centuries. It is with the last of these living influences that
I am now concerned. However, lest the first dominant
force seem neglected, I may mention the notes of Newton
and Todd, together with such studies as Mr. Harris F.
Fletcher's *Use of the Bible in Milton's Prose*. In addition
to Newton and Todd, the poet's debt to the Classics is interestingly revealed by Mr. Charles Grosvenor Osgood in
his *Classical Mythology of Milton's English Poems*; by
Gilbert Murray, *The Classical Tradition in Poetry*; and
Douglas Bush, *Mythology and the Renaissance Tradition
in English Poetry*.

Among the varied religious writings to which Milton frequently turned, the most important for *Paradise Lost* fall within the somewhat amorphous genre known as hexameral literature. As Mr. Frank E. Robbins, Maury Thibaut de Maisières, and George Coffin Taylor have shown with such illumination, it is this genre which the epic chiefly follows in general scope and major divisions. Defined strictly, the hexameral literature consisted of the poems or treatises on the days of Creation, based primarily upon the first chapter of Genesis. Highly expanded paraphrases of subsequent chapters, together with similar expansions from other books of Scripture, became in time a vital part of the hexameral literature.

The genre had begun development as early as Philo (A. D. 40), and grew both in popularity and diversity of treatment until some decades after 1600. Largely the creation of early Christian Fathers, it remained a favorite with medieval writers, who frequently included discussion of the attributes of God, of the angels and the fall of the apostates, the restoration of man through the Incarnation, and of the last Judgment. The Fifteenth, Sixteenth, and early Seventeenth Centuries brought to it a new wave of popularity, with further expansion and diversification. Among its important forms was that which Thibaut termed 'the celestial cycle,' a trilogy which described the rebellion and battle in heaven, creation of the world, and the fall of man. To the last, numerous writers appended a paraphrase of subsequent Biblical history. A further practice described Satan in hell following his overthrow, plotting revenge on God by the seduction of man.

From Philo and doubtless other writers of his era, the hexameral literature continued a progressive development. The second century brought the contributions of Candidus,

Justin Martyr, and Rhodon; the third, those of Caius, Hippolytus, Methodius, and Origen. With the fourth century, the tradition burst into full flower, and, as I shall reiterate, produced the hexamera which largely set the pattern for many subsequent works. The greatest single *Hexameron* from the point of view of the writers influenced by it, probably was that composed by Basil. Ambrose, himself of Basil's school, perhaps held second place during the Renaissance. Other illustrious names include Ephraem, from whom Basil borrowed and repeated a number of ideas; and Gregory Nazianzen, principal source of Pisidias. We might easily develop an epic catalog for the many exegetes of this and the next century who added both to the prestige and content of the hexameral literature. However, it may be preferable merely to list by name the more outstanding: Augustine, Athanasius of Alexandria, Avitus, Chrysostom, the two Cyrils of Alexandria and Jerusalem, Dracontius, Eusebius of Emesius, Gregory of Nyssa, Jerome, Hilary of Poitiers, Juvencus Hispanus, Lactantius, Marius Victor, Theodoret, and Theophile.

We find among subsequent contributors to the tradition, the influential Gregorius Magnus, Cosmas of Alexandria, Junilius Africanus and Zacharius. About the year 700, Anastasius of Sinai composed an *Introduction to the Hexameron* in twelve books, eleven of which are extant in Latin translation. During these centuries, expanded paraphrases of Genesis had entered poetry as well as prose, and seemingly enjoyed equal prestige. The most extended, and perhaps the best known of the metrical versions is that at times attributed to Caedmon. This early English poet, said the venerable Bede, was an illiterate laborer who lived near Whitby during the closing decades of the Seventh Century. The Caedmonian *Genesis* shows, however, an acquaintance with the hexameral tradition distinctly unusual for such a character. Be that as it may, the work displays clearly the conversion into poetry of the prose expansions of Genesis.

More than a century ago, Henry Todd remarked that the Caedmonian poem is 'a *Paradise Lost* in rude miniature. It contains the fall of the angels, the Creation, the temptation of Eve, and the expulsion from Paradise.' Among many other interesting analogues, I may add that Caedmon included a paraphrase of such events from Biblical history as Milton narrated in Books XI-XII. Not only is the Caedmonian *Genesis* illustrative of the tradition which chiefly nourished *Paradise Lost*, but it was known in London during the decade when Milton set seriously to work upon his epic. Such circumstances make doubly significant this early poem. Of the following excerpts from the *Genesis*, given in partially modernized prose, the first describes the rebellion and fall of Satan and his legions:

> The hosts of angels had joy and splendor from their original beginning; glorious bliss was their great fruit. The glory-fast thanes praised the King; they uttered willingly praise to their Life-Lord, and obeyed his dominion with virtuous acts. They lived very happily, knowing neither sins nor the framing of crimes, and existed in peace with their eternal Elder. Before the Ruler of the angels they did not begin to raise in the sky anything other than right and truth, until pride divided them in error.
>
> They would not continue for themselves the heavenly council, but from self-love threw off the love of God. So great was their pride that they sought, against the Lord, to divide the glory-fast place, the majesty of their hosts, and the wide and bright sky. To the mind of the angel [Satan] that first began to cast, to weave and frame this bad counsel, there came grief, envy, and

pride. He then uttered words blackened with iniquity, and declared he would possess in the north part of heaven's kingdom a home and a high seat.

In keeping with the tradition which Milton later followed, the Satan of Caedmon had stood in heaven next to God. Among all angels the highest, he also was the brightest and most beautiful. Despite these gifts from his Creator, he rebelled:

One He had made so strong, so mighty in his mind's thought, that he permitted him to govern much, and be the highest in heaven's kingdom. So splendid had God created him, and so beautiful was his fruit in heaven which came to him from the Lord of hosts, that he resembled the brilliant stars. This angel should have voiced praise to his Lord; he should have valued dear his joy in heaven. He should have thanked his Lord for the bounty which he shared in that brightness, when God so long permitted him to govern in heaven.

But the angel departed from this to evil action. He began to raise strife against the Governor of the highest heaven who sits on the holy seat. Precious he was to our Lord, from whom it could not be concealed that his chief angel grew over-proud. He turned against his Master; he uttered vainglorious words and inflammatory speeches. He refused to serve God, declaring he was God's equal in light and brilliance, and possessed a hue as white and bright.

Nor could he accept the thought of giving obedience to his God and King. His plan was to obtain subjects of greater might and skill than those who served the holy God. This angel of pride spoke many words, and believed through his own cunning he might erect in the heavens a seat stronger and higher than that of God's.

The Satan or Lucifer of Caedmon voiced a soliloquy loosely comparable to portions of the address which Milton's Apostate subsequently delivered in the closing lines of Book V. Said the angel of the early *Genesis:*

> I may many wonders work with my hands, and I must possess great power to acquire a more godlike seat, one higher in the heavens. Yet why should I sue for His grace, or bend before Him with obedience? I may well be a god such as He. Stand with me, strong companions, who will prove faithful in this battle. These warriors of hardy mind, illustrious soldiers, they have chosen me for their ruler. With such, indeed, one may take counsel; with them one may seize a station. My earnest friends they are, and faithful in declaring their minds. As their leader, I may govern in this kingdom. So I believe it not just, nor need I bring flattery, as though I were a god inferior to any god. I no longer will remain His subject.

Omniscient God, aware of Satan's evil designs, created hell for the rebel host, and drove them from heaven:

> Then God waxed angry and wrathful at the angels he earlier had esteemed illustrious and glorious. For those perfidious spirits he made a home of exile, a work of retribution—hell's groans and hard hatreds. Our Lord, the Ruler of spirits, ordered a house of punishment for the home of the exiles, a place deep and joyless. When God knew the house ready with foul perpetual night, containing sulphur, and filled with fire, smoke and red flame, and extensive cold; he commanded those set over this house, without debate, to increase the horror-punishment. . . . Then was he angry. With judgment and might, with power and victorious arm, he struck his enemies; and from them took all pleasure, joy, and peace. The illustrious Lord brought greatly on the enemies his anger, and deprived their power of strength. Grimly provoked, the Lord was stern of mind, and in his wrath seized the limbs of his enemies, and broke them

in pieces. His adversaries he deprived of their country; our Creator cut off from the stations of glory the proud race of angels, the faithless host.

As Scripture had suggested and the hexameral tradition demanded, the defeated host of Satan dropped from heaven into hell:

The Fiend with all his followers then fell from heaven for the space of three nights and days—this long they spent falling from heaven into hell. They would not reverence the word and deed of God. For this sin the Almighty placed them, broken, in the black hell under the earth. There each of the fiends shall have forever, for an immeasurable length of time, a fire always renewed. At last will come to mingle with the fire, the cold frost and the eastern wind. . . . They suffer punishment for their battle against the Ruler, imprisoned within fierce torrents of fire in the midst of hell. Likewise came bitter smoke, vapor, and darkness.

Again in keeping with the pattern of thought which Milton was later to follow, the Satan of Caedmon stood undaunted by defeat. Bound in hell, he planned immediately to obtain revenge by seducing Adam and Eve:

Then spoke the too proud king, that once was the most shining of angels and the brightest in heaven—beloved by his Master and endeared to his Lord until he turned to evil. With sorrowful speech, Satan said: 'Is this the narrow place that my Master puts me in, one unlike the others which we knew before, high in the kingdom of heaven? . . . Oh that I had free the power of my hands, and might for a time escape, I and my host, but for a winter's space. But iron bonds encompass me; knots of chains press me down. . . . God has now marked out a middle region, wherein he has created man after his own likeness. From the race of mankind, the Lord again will populate with pure souls the kingdom of heaven. If possible, we must labor diligently to this end—that on Adam and his offspring we achieve some revenge.

For an extended period following the Eighth Century, commentaries on the early chapters of Genesis made little apparent contribution to hexameral literature. There were of course such notable exceptions as the *Paradise* (*De Paradiso*), and perhaps the *Hexameron* written by the ninth-century Syrian Bishop, Moses Bar Cepha. The major increments seemingly came through the *Speculum* or Mirror literature, together with the equally popular digest known both as a *Summa* or Sum, and as a Book of Sentences. On occasion, as in the *Summa Sententiarum* of Hugo of St. Victor, the two titles coalesced. By virtue of its nature, this type of theological encyclopedia developed among its many readers a common body of historical information, and, on the whole, tended to so standardize and unify religious knowledge as to make it easily utilized for literary purposes. Because various passages in Job, Isaiah, Ezekiel, and Revelation were thought descriptive of Satan, commentaries on these books either added to or consolidated the tradition of the rebellion and battle in heaven. Such works as *The Victory of Christ* (*De Victoria Verbi Dei*) of Rupert definitely prepared the way for literary versions of the conflict which described Christ as the conqueror of Satan.

For the sufficient reason that much Medieval literature either has been lost or remains untouched in manuscript, it is difficult to determine the extent to which this literature utilized the hexameral tradition. Thibaut found the tradition inactive in Italy and Spain, but frequently employed in France. Its high place in medieval England, Mr. P. E. Dustoor proved beyond question in his 'Legends of Lucifer in Early English and in Milton.' Among twelfth-century

French works, we find the drama *Adam* of particular significance, in part because its closing lines stressed the hope of redemption. The fifteenth-century *Mistère du Viel Testament* included *The Overthrow of Lucifer*, together with *The Creation of the Angels*, and *The Creation of Adam and Eve*.

Despite a sustained interest in hexameral literature from the Sixth to the Fifteenth Century, its second great period was yet to come. The harbinger of this era proved the invention of printing, which spread abroad throughout Christian Europe many early hexamera. Various works by Chrysostom, Gregory the Great, Lactantius and Origen appeared during the Fifteenth Century, as well as the *Hexameron* of Ambrose and that of Juvencus Hispanus. *The Origin of the World* (*De Initio Mundi*) of Avitus was published at Paris both in 1508 and 1545; the *Carmen Heroicum* of Hilary in 1510. During 1527 and 1532, editions of Ambrose and Basil merited prefaces by Erasmus. Four years after the second of these editions came the work of Marius Victor, and in 1558 the hexameron of Justinus, with a French translation. A single volume brought together in 1560 Avitus, Cyprian, Dracontius, Hilary, and Marius Victor. By the first decades of the Seventeenth Century, educated Europe had before it, and had turned to literary use, the bulk of the important early hexamera.

With major themes of the early hexamera, Christian writers of the Sixteenth and Seventeenth Centuries joined a variety of conceptions and episodes. The additions came chiefly from medieval theology, but the contributions from literary and other works seem more than negligible. By the end of the Sixteenth Century a flood of dramas and poems brought the hexameral tradition to all parts of Europe. In general, these representatives of the tradition were built around one or more of four distinct but related subjects:

(1) Satan's rebellion and the battle in heaven; (2) the basic hexameral theme of the days of Creation; (3) the temptation and fall of man; and (4) paraphrases of Biblical history. Such classification is extremely loose, and normally can only indicate the subject which received the greater emphasis—or, noticeable emphasis being absent, which subject was given the more extended treatment. On occasion, as in the *Second Week* of Du Bartas, a classification with pretentions toward accuracy must place the work under both the third and the fourth subjects. Again, the major stress of *Paradise Lost* falls on the first and third; its minor emphasis upon the second and fourth.

However, the differentiation is not unserviceable. Among examples of works which stress or chiefly were built around Satan's rebellion, we may include Agnifilo, *La Caduta di Lucifero;* Alfano, *La Battaglia Celeste;* Heywood, *The Fall of Lucifer,* a division of *The Hierarchy of the Blessed Angels;* Taubman, *Bellum Anglicum;* Valmarana, *Demonomachiae;* Valvasone, *L'Angeleida;* Verallo, *La Guerra degli Angeli;* and Vondel, *Lucifer.* The influence of this theme penetrated such poems as the *Apollyonists* of Phineas Fletcher, and may be found in the *Strage degli Innocenti* of Marini.

God's Creation of the world, or the work of the Six Days, proved the central and dominating subject in Acevedo, *Creacion del Mundo;* Cornazono, *Creazione del Mondo;* Du Bartas, *La Semaine* (later known as *The First Week*); Lope de Vega, *Creacion del Mundo y Primera Culpa del Hombre;* Murtola, *Creazione del Mondo* (battle in heaven, Canto I); Passero, *L'Essamerone;* Tasso, *La Sette Giornate del Mondo Creato;* and Zanchius, *The Works of the Six Days.* A legion of poems, exemplified by Cowley's *Davidëis* and Joseph Beaumont's *Psyche,* described at varying length the work of creation. With this universally beloved subject, numerous writers also opened their treatises on History, Geography, and Cosmology.

The third major theme, that of the temptation and fall of man, proved slightly more popular in purely literary works than did the three remaining subjects. It held among others the principal interest of Andreini, *L'Adamo;* Du Bartas, *Eden, The Imposture, The Furies;* Gazaeus, *Lacrymae Adami;* Grotius, *Adamus Exsul;* Lancetta, *La Scena Tragica d'Adamo ed Eva;* Loredano, *Life of Adam;* Luis de Camoens, *Da Creação et Compolicão do Homen,* cantos tres; Malipiero, *L'Eva;* Masenius, *Sarcotis;* Serafino della Salandra, *Adamo Caduto;* Soranzo, *Dell' Adamo;* Vondel, *Adam in Ballingschap;* and Zieglerus, *Protoplastus.* With the group may be joined the major work in Ramsay's *Poemata Sacra,* a poem which concluded by stressing with optimism the redemption of man through Christ. Among a multitude of variant treatments are Goodman, *The Fall of Man,* and Joseph Fletcher, *The History of the Perfect, Cursed, Blessed Man.* During the Sixteenth and early Seventeenth Centuries, few historical treatises and religious poems failed to make some reference to the Fall.

The subsequent events of Biblical history, often those which open with the fourth chapter of Genesis, proved with poet and dramatist the least inviting of the four major topics. However, Du Bartas devoted by far the greater part of his *Second Week* to paraphrases of these events. As much may be said of Valmarana in the *Demonomachiae,* and to them Peyton gave the second and final book of *The Glass of Time.* Such poems as Cowley's *Davidëis* fall within this fourth group; and to a lesser degree, those comparable to Dryden's *Absalom and Achitophel.* Historians and geographers, whose widely read works often did not lack some literary merit, delighted in retelling the variegated experiences of Cain and Abel, and of Noah and his descendants.

As I have mentioned, works which belonged to the hexameral tradition normally included more than one, and on occasion employed each of the four related subjects. Others gave to a second theme minor but important emphasis. Acevedo, although primarily interested in the Creation, and following closely the *First Week* of Du Bartas, described in some detail the rebellion and battle in heaven. In Canto I, he pictured the unfallen Lucifer as the most beautiful of angels. Satan succumbed to pride, and plotted to equal God. To his aid came an assistant properly named Discord, who spewed out such black poisonous hatred that she won over hosts of angels. Acevedo described Lucifer in detail, comparing him to a maddened bull. The rebel army, in keeping with that of *Paradise Lost*, Book I, marched with a banner.

Clad in adamantine arms, the angel Michael led the loyal troops of God. A trumpet sounded the combat, and the hosts joined battle. Darts and arrows filled the sky; shields and helmets rang; arms were broken. The terrific struggle continued without bringing advantage to either force. Michael then met Lucifer in single combat, and driving his sword upon the Apostate's helm, overthrew him with one blow. The evil angels immediately fled, and tumbled with confusion into the abyss. Falling, they were transformed into hideous monsters.

An unusual circumstance lends further interest to Acevedo's *Creation*. Thibaut, who showed clearly its heavy indebtedness to the dominant *Divine Weeks* of Du Bartas, pointed out that in composing an extended section of the poem, Acevedo utilized his immediate source in reversed order. Specifically, he first drew upon lines beginning with verse 1066. Next, he borrowed from lines close to verse 900. The Spanish poet then moved to verse 550, later to 450, until such successive steps brought him near the opening. We shall note later that not infrequently the sequence or order of Milton's descriptions will prove the reverse of comparable passages found both in Du Bartas and other authors.

Within that group which emphasized chiefly the temptation and fall of man, writers normally described only in passing the rebellion and fall of Satan. As Andrieni and Grotius illustrate, they also provided an optimistic finale by promising the fallen Adam a Messiah and a future home in heaven. Grotius and Vondel pictured Adam and Eve as quarreling bitterly, and Adam as contemplating suicide. Vondel caused him to hope for death, and brought Eve to comfort and console him. The Eve of Andrieni voiced a further conception later employed by Milton, the idea that man does not live when he must exist in constant fear. This group, particularly where the literary form was dramatic, not only tended to mention in passing Satan's rebellion, but largely ignored the creation of the world and the events of Biblical history. By largely confining action to development of one major subject, treatments of the Fall achieved greater coherence. In so doing, however, they sacrificed the scope and comprehension which made possible a maximum of power. A virtuoso's intuitive desire for the latter may have persuaded Milton to abandon the long contemplated dramatic form.

In view of the distinguished criticism which has found *Paradise Lost* essentially didactic, I mention with Thibaut that within the hexameral tradition, didactic works gave the central and major place to the Creation. This Du Bartas did in the *First Week;* it is precisely what Milton avoided doing in *Paradise Lost.* The conventional epic treatment concentrated attention largely upon one character, Satan or Adam. Where the first was chosen, the fall of the angels received major emphasis; where the second, the seduction of man. Milton skilfully obtained the advantages of both methods by first giving Satan the central place, and secondly, by subsequently assigning it to Adam. Since man held the central position in the closing books of the epic, his fortunes and prospects received the greater structural emphasis.

As I have suggested, and as further chapters may show, the hexameral literature stands as the most important single source of *Paradise Lost*. From the varied books which made up this powerful and universally respected tradition, Milton drew consciously or unconsciously the great majority of the ideas, themes, and episodes which gave substance to his epic. We are obligated, I believe, to accept with few reservations the conclusion of Thibaut:

> Le réel mérite de Milton, c'est d'avoir dépassé merveilleusement tous ceux dont il s'est inspiré. . . . Lorsqu'il composa son *Paradis Perdu*, Milton était aveugle . . . il vit des idées, des images splendides qu'il construit. Il ne voit plus les choses de l'extérieur, rien ne distrait ses sens des visions de son âme, et, comme Beethoven sourd entendait les plus prestigieux accords, Milton voit, mieux que personne, les lumineuses divinités de son imagination. Ces figures qu'il avait contemplées autrefois dans sa jeunesse, chez Du Bartas; ces personnages de drames italiens, qui avaient fait surgir, dans son esprit, des couleurs et des lignes, il les revoit du fond de ses méditations; mais eux, qui avaient jadis des contours vagues, ont pris, avec le temps et l'obscurité, des contrastes lumineux et une grandeur épique.
>
> Les images sont restées bien reconnaissables, tout en devenant plus nettes; elles se modèlent selon l'esprit qui les perçoit; par élimination des détails, les traits s'accentuent et le relief devient saisissant; toutes les données se fusionnent et s'harmonisent; une vie nouvelle leur est insufflée, une synthèse inconnue les pénètre et les unit;

de ce chaos merveilleux, émerge une oeuvre finie et simple, un chef-d'oeuvre.

It would, however, be inexact to confine *Paradise Lost* within the hexameral tradition. This tradition supplied the heart and nerves of Milton's greatest work, but in shaping the epic he drew also upon religious literature in general, upon the classics, and upon a far ranging knowledge of philosophy, geography, and history.

Prior to concluding this limited introduction, I mention that in harmony with classical precept, Milton did not open *Paradise Lost* at the chronological beginning of its action. As a result, we often realize inadequately the precision with which his narrative moved from inception to completion. To make obvious this march of Milton's story, I normally discuss its major divisions and episodes according to their absolute chronological order, opening with the Exaltation of Christ and the consequent rebellion of Satan. Exactly how many days, or units of time, the action required, the poet failed to state specifically. On the basis, however, of the days or units implicitly or explicitly enumerated by him, the number stands as thirty-one. For many of the days, no episodes are described; others veritably overflow with activity. As an aid to subsequent discussion of the epic, I outline in their chronological order key events described in *Paradise Lost*. The figure given to the left indicates the day or days among the thirty-one during which these events took place.

(1)   Exaltation of Christ; Satan deserted at midnight.

(2-4)   Battle in heaven.

(5-13)   Satan and his host dropped into chaos and hell.

(14-22)   Satan and his angels lay stunned on the fiery lake.

(18)   God began the six days of Creation.

(23)   Sixth day of Creation:

Creation of Adam and Eve; their marriage.

Council in hell; Satan came to Paradise.
Second Exaltation of Christ, and revelation
of the Incarnation; first justification of God.

Satan attempted, unsuccessfully, to seduce the
sleeping Eve.

(24)   Raphael warned Adam of his enemy, and described such past events as the rebellion in
heaven and the creation of the world.

(30)   The temptation and fall; coming of Sin, Death,
inclement weather, discord, and strife.

(31)   Michael expelled Adam and Eve from Paradise,
having first revealed future events and promised Adam the Messiah.

Necessary departures excluded, Part I will follow this
chronological order, taking up in turn the rebellion and
battle in heaven, the Creation, Raphael-Adam dialogues,
the council in hell, Garden in Eden, the temptation and
fall of man, and the Michael-Adam dialogue which concluded the epic. Within the last of these seven divisions, I
include the justification of God set forth in Book III and
occasional subsequent passages. A further partial variation
occurs in the chapter devoted to the Raphael-Adam dialogues, two of which fall chronologically later than the
council in hell. In the first of the chapters following, I
trace from their Scriptural origins various ideas and episodes ultimately employed by Milton, and include speci-
mens of purely verbal borrowing. This I do in part as an
exemplar of the many sections of *Paradise Lost* which have
a similar history. No attempt is made to give the numerous
analogues collected, and I normally avoid repetition of
those easily available in Todd's variorum. An appre-

ciable group of the latter has from time to time been 'discovered' and re-discussed by contemporary writers. Todd's edition of the epic will also provide endless illustration of Milton's apparent assimilation of word and phrase from a wide variety of books.

Part II will be found less unified in its approach than Part I. I first discuss the immediate sources of the dialogue on astronomy. I may add that these sources have been accepted by the bibliographers of the Modern Language Association of America, and *The Year's Work in English Studies*, of Great Britain. A second chapter presents examples of Milton's use of structural patterns similar to those employed within works well-known to him. The subsequent chapters, XI and XII, review the pre-epic stages of *Paradise Lost*, and discuss the time and order in which Milton may have composed the several books of his poem. Not infrequently, the analyses presented in Part II are suggestive and exploratory, and for this reason make no pretense at certainty. A concluding chapter will take up various conceptions influential in current Miltonic criticism, and relate to this criticism the somewhat different interpretations which have developed during this survey of *Paradise Lost*.

I may again stress the point that the principal purpose of this volume is to make better known the tradition which gave heart and blood to Milton's epic. The better known the tradition, the greater our opportunity to understand the poet and his work. Truly to revere Milton is not to praise a character born in part of imagination, but to honor the man as he was, and as he desired to be.

PART I

Chapter II

THE BATTLE IN HEAVEN

TO the fateful rebellion of Satan, and the resulting battle in heaven, Milton devoted one-eighth of *Paradise Lost*. By placing such emphasis upon the revolt of the angels, he sacrificed the support of contemporary Protestant theology. He gained however that of many respected Fathers of the Church, and, what perhaps proved more important, a theme with distinct dramatic possibilities. This theme also possessed an enrichment brought by centuries of writers, together with the prestige and emotional values which only long use can provide a literary tradition.

The conventional literary treatment of Satan's rebellion and fall represented an evolutionary process conveniently divided into four stages. Throughout the first stage, commentators and theologians discovered allusions to the rebellion and battle in a wide variety of Biblical passages, all of which modern scholarship has found unconnected with either. A second stage brought together these passages, and in some measure unified them. Imagination then augmented further the primarily religious content, and as a final step added from classical and contemporary literature a wealth of decorative incident and verbal embroidery. The two later stages of development did not necessarily exclude the earlier, with the result that Scripture continued to provide forced interpretations long after the battle in heaven had become an established literary theme. In the development of the story which Milton set forth, each of the several stages had played an important part.

Among the varied Biblical passages which contributed to the narrative of *Paradise Lost*, only one described di-

21

rectly a celestial battle between the host of Satan and the angels loyal to God. This is Revelation 12. 4, 7-9. In his account of the battle waged in heaven, John identified the rival leaders, suggested the relative size of the contending armies, and announced the outcome of the struggle. Michael commanded the good angels; Satan the evil, who numbered a third of the spirits. The result was the expulsion of the latter:

[And behold a great red dragon] His tail drew the third part of the stars of heaven. And there was war in heaven: Michael and his angels fought against the dragon; and the dragon fought and his angels. And prevailed not; neither was their place found any more in heaven. And the great dragon was cast out, that old serpent, called the Devil and Satan, which deceiveth the whole world. He was cast out into the earth, and his angels were cast out with him.

As early theologians generally interpreted this section of Revelation, it unequivocally named Michael as the victorious commander of the army of God. Some few commentators, however, so altered the punctuation that the verses described Michael and Satan as having waged an indecisive conflict: 'Michael and his angels fought against the dragon, and the dragon fought and his angels: and [both] prevailed not.' Influenced by the many passages which directly or by implication made Christ the enemy and conqueror of Satan, these commentators asserted that the Son was the true victor over the rebellious Satan. According to this belief, Christ entered the drawn battle, and single-handed drove from heaven the warring forces of evil.

On occasion, the triumphant, embattled Son rode as the Cherubim envisioned by Ezekiel 10. 8-14. A further description, and one reflected in Milton's *Christian Doctrine*, drew heavily upon the vision of Isaiah 63. 1-4. Here the Prophet depicted Christ as glorious in apparel, and as coming in the greatness of his strength. By virtue of a strained interpretation of several basic words, the third of Isaiah's four verses yielded a description of Christ vanquishing the rebels single-handed: 'I have trodden the wine press [evil angels] alone. And of the people [angels of God] there were none with me. For I will tread them in mine anger, and trample them in my fury.' Perhaps more influential was the equally strained interpretation which caused Paul to say in 2 Thessalonians 2. 8: 'The Lord shall consume [Satan] with the spirit of his mouth, and shall destroy [him] with the brightness of his coming.'

For long centuries conventional Christendom placed hell within the bowels of the earth. There were, however, many theologians who disputed such a conclusion. As they interpreted the words, the 'outer darkness' of Matthew 8. 12; the impassable 'great gulf' of Luke 16. 26 which blocked the way from hell to heaven; and the 'bottomless pit' of Revelation 9. 1, all pointed unmistakably to a hell located without, and not within the earth. This conception received additional support from the belief that prior to creation of the physical universe, God cast the rebel Satan into hell. This Deity could not have done, said the argument, if hell were placed within the earth. Earth then did not exist.

The belief that Satan fell from heaven before God built the universe rested primarily upon a second idea, one which maintained that the angels had existed long before the world. Job 38. 6-7 had asked concerning the physical universe: 'Who laid the cornerstone thereof, when the morning stars sang together, and all the sons of God shouted for joy?' That the sons of God, known as the angels, raised their voices at the beginning of Creation, appeared some proof of their prior existence. Theologians found further evidence in Ezekiel 28. 14-17, actually nothing more than a castigation of the King of Tyre. Regarded as a description of Satan, the passage implied he had lived long in heaven before revolting from God. If this angel had lived prior to creation of the world, so ran the argument, other angels must have done likewise. As interpreted by centuries of commentators, Ezekiel had said of Satan:

> Thou art the anointed cherub that covereth; and I have set thee so. Thou wast upon the holy mountain of God; thou hast walked up and down in the midst of the stones of fire. Thou wast perfect in thy ways from the day that thou wast created, till iniquity was found in thee. By the multitude of thy merchandise they have filled the midst of thee with violence, and thou hast sinned. Therefore I will cast thee as profane out of the mountain of God; and I will destroy thee, O covering cherub, from the midst of the stones of fire. Thine heart was lifted up because of thy beauty, thou hast corrupted thy wisdom by reason of thy brightness: I will cast thee to the ground.

From these verses, commentators drew additional and perhaps more important conclusions. Before his fall, Satan had been a wise and beautiful angel, and had served his Lord with perfection for an indeterminate period of time. During this period, reasoned various exegetes, he enjoyed the special favor of God, and stood as the most important angel in heaven. The last conclusion seemed the more unescapable because Job 40. 19 had declared that Behemoth, known then as Satan, served as 'chief of the ways of God.' Isaiah 14. 12-15 contributed both the name Lucifer and the idea that Satan ruled the northern region of heaven. The embattled prophet had sought to censure the misguided King of Babylon, but to the imaginative commentator he spoke also of the Devil:

> How art thou fallen from heaven, O Lucifer, son of the morning! How art thou cut down to the ground, which didst weaken the nations! For thou hast said in thine heart, I will ascend into heaven, I will exalt my throne above the stars of God; I will sit also upon the mount of the congregation, in the sides of the north. I will ascend above the heights of the clouds; I will be like the Most High. Yet thou shalt be brought down to hell, to the sides of the pit.

In keeping with Ezekiel, the prophet Isaiah set forth an apparent reason for the downfall of the character whom he castigated. To Ezekiel, the fundamental flaw was personal vanity; to Isaiah, it constituted what may be termed reckless political ambition. Neither account suggested, however, the immediate cause which had loosed the reins to headstrong vanity and ambition. As a result, commentators found in these passages no hint of the specific event which metamorphosed a faithful servant of God into a vengeful and rebellious traitor. Many theologians rested content with the general explanation that pride, vanity, or ambition, had led Satan into evil. Other exegetes, much fewer in number, found the immediate cause in God's exaltation of Incarnate Christ. More precisely, the immediate efficient cause was God's exaltation of the Son when he proclaimed to the spirits Christ's future incarnation:

In the authoritative *Summa Theologica* I, 57, 5, Thomas Aquinas wrote that the 'mystery of the Incarnation' had been 'revealed . . . to the angels.' This belief was widespread in Christendom, and as its use by Saint Thomas

implies, brought with it no taint of heresy. With the revelation which announced the future Incarnation came God's
exaltation of Christ, supported by the divine command
that the angels should bow down before him. This tortured interpretation, theologians built upon two passages
from the epistles of Paul, Philippians 2. 5-10, and Hebrews
1. 2, 5-6:

> Let this mind be in you, which was also in Christ
> Jesus; who, being in the form of God, thought it not
> robbery to be equal with God. But made himself of
> no reputation, and took upon him the form of a servant,
> and was made in the likeness of men. And, being found
> in fashion as a man, he humbled himself, and became
> obedient unto death, even the death of the cross. Where-
> fore God also hath highly exalted him, and given him
> a name which is above every name; that at the name
> of Jesus every knee should bow, of things in heaven,
> and things in earth, and things under the earth.

> [God] hath in these last days spoken unto us by his
> Son, whom he hath appointed heir of all things. . . .
> For unto which of the angels said he at any time, Thou
> art my Son, this day have I begotten thee? And again,
> I will be to him a Father, and he shall be to me a Son?
> And again, when he bringeth in the first-begotten into
> the world, he said, And let all the angels of God worship
> him.

As I previously have implied, a majority of theologians
did not favor the interpretation that Satan revolted because
of Christ's Incarnation. John Calvin found the assumption
illogical and objectionable; and attacked it vigorously:
'Curious sophists have feigned,' he declared, 'that Satan
burned with envy when he foresaw the Son of God was
to be clothed in human flesh, but the speculation is friv-
olous. Since the Son of God was made man in order to

restore us—then already lost—from our miserable overthrow, how could that be foreseen which would never
have happened unless man had sinned.'

Two incidental details remain. Job had written in his
first chapter that 'there was a day when the sons of God
came to present themselves before the Lord.' By an interpretation not overly strained, this verse could imply
that at some stated period the angels assembled before God.
The second detail concerns the warriors who battled in
heaven. Revelation named only Michael and Satan, the
leaders of the two opposing hosts. Nothing daunted,
however, religious writers expanded the meagre list by
adding Gabriel and Raphael from canonical books, and
Uriel from the non-canonical 2 Esdras 4. 1 ff. Since the
three spirits had proved faithful to God, they logically
could be included among the host led by Michael. Canonical, together with non-canonical books in their several
versions, also provided a multitude of names suitable for
use as adherents of Satan. We meet among Milton's group
Belial, Moloch, Ramiel, Adramelech, Asmadai, Nisroch,
Ariel, and Arioch, all of whom patristic and later religious
writers had identified either as minor devils, or as heathen
gods. These gods, so one legend ran, had fought under
Satan, and fallen with him into hell. Subsequently, they
came to earth, and took the form of heathen idols.

When religious writers brought together the themes
thus far discussed, the resulting combination paralleled
closely the essential foundations of Milton's battle in
heaven. Arranged in the sequence of *Paradise Lost*, the several ideas and episodes included these essential elements of
the poet's narrative:

A. God created the angels prior to his building the
   physical universe.

B. The angels assembled before God upon a stated day.

C. God, within whom was Christ, announced to the spirits the Exaltation of the Son, and commanded that they bow before him.

D. Satan, or Lucifer, held a kingdom in the north of heaven, where he ruled one-third of heaven. Prior to his rebellion and fall, he not only was the most beautiful of angels and the favored spirit of God, but apparently ranked in heaven next to Deity.

E. Satan resented deeply the degradation which he imagined must result from the Exaltation of Christ, and rebelled against Father and Son.

F. He led his followers against Michael and the faithful angels, seeking to dethrone God and rule over heaven. Michael's army included the good angels named in Scripture; that of Satan, various characters widely known either as devils or as gods of the heathen.

G. After an inconclusive conflict between Michael and Satan, Christ vanquished single-handed the rebel host. As a just retribution, he cast them into a hell located beyond the earth, and within a region far removed from heaven.

Such parallels are indeed striking. They are however less so than a much larger number of correspondences, the majority of which belong to the ultimate stages of the tradition. During these stages, imagination expanded and gave literary expression to the often forced interpretations of Scripture. It added from classical and contemporary literature a variety of incident and much verbal embroidery. Comparison and summary will best show the close relationship between Milton's battle in heaven and the culminating steps of the general tradition. It obviously will be necessary to include and discuss some elements representative of the two initial stages.

Following 'the opinion of many ancient fathers,' among
whom he could have named Ambrose, Basil, Gregory
Nazianzen, Isidore, Jerome, and Origen, Milton set the
creation of the angels aeons before God had created the
physical world. Subsequent theologians, and particularly
the Latin Fathers, generally rejected this belief. Nevertheless, they did not condemn it as heretical. Thomas
Aquinas considered it less probable than the interpretation
that 'angels were created at the same time as corporeal
creatures,' but declared the conception 'is not to be deemed
erroneous; especially on account of the opinion of Gregory
Nazianzen, "whose authority in Christian doctrine is of
such weight that no one has ever raised objection to his
teaching," . . . as Jerome says.' The French poet Du
Bartas, whose influential *Divine Weeks and Works* passed
the two hundredth edition when Milton was yet a lad,
found it unimportant whether God created the angels
prior to, or during his creation of the world. The conception had, however, proved attractive to poets quite as
important as Du Bartas. Caedmon, or the pseudo-Caedmon,
had employed it during the Seventh Century, Spenser in
the late Sixteenth; and in Milton's own era, Odorico Valmarana and Justus van den Vondel. Each of these writers
utilized the theme in connection with, and preceding
description of the conflict in heaven.

The shortest treatment, and that in some major details
closest to *Paradise Lost*, Spenser provided in *An Hymn
of Heavenly Love*. The body of this poem opened much
as did Milton's more extended description. Spenser also
depicted the angels as gathered about God's throne, and
as singing hymns both day and night. He next passed to
the rebellion of Lucifer, identified as the brightest of
angels. I quote stanzas four, eight, ten, and twelve:

Before this world's great frame, in which all things
Are now contained, found any being place,
Ere flitting time could wag his eyas wings
About that mighty bound, which doth embrace
The rolling spheres, and parts their hours by space,
That high eternal Power, which now doth move
In all these things, moved in itself by love.

Yet being pregnant still with powerful grace,
And full of fruitful love, that loves to get
Things like himself, and to enlarge his race,
His second brood, though not in power so great,
Yet full of beauty, next he did beget,
An infinite increase of angels bright,
All glistring glorious in their Maker's light.

There they in their trinal triplicities
About him wait, and on his will depend,
Either with nimble wings to cut the skies,
When he them on his messages doth send,
Or on his own dread presence to attend,
Where they behold the glory of his light,
And carol hymns of love both day and night.

But pride, impatient of long resting peace,
Did puff them up with greedy bold ambition,
That they 'gan cast their state how to increase
Above the fortune of their first condition,
And sit in God's own seat without commission:
The brightest angel, even the Child of Light,
Drew millions more against their God to fight.

In citing the following comparable passages from Book
V of *Paradise Lost*, I conclude Milton's description of
Satan with a closely related fragment from Book IV. This
fragment represented Satan as the speaker:

As yet this world was not, and chaos wild
Reigned where these heavens now roll,
  where earth now rests,
Upon her center poised; . . . on such [a] day,
As heaven's great year brings forth, the empyreal
Host of angels, by imperial summons called,
Innumerable before the Almighty's throne
Forthwith from all the ends of heaven appeared . . .
In orbs of circuit inexpressible they stood,
Orb within orb. . . .
  That day, as other solemn days, they spent
In song and dance about the sacred Hill. . . .
[At night] they slept . . . save those who, in their
Course, melodious hymns about the sovran
Throne, alternate all night long. . . .
  Satan—so call him now . . . of the first,
If not the first archangel, great in power,
In favor, and preëminence . . . resolved
With all his legions to dislodge, and leave
Unworshiped, unobeyed, the Throne supreme. . . .
All obeyed the wonted signal, and superior voice
Of their great Potentate; for great indeed
His name, and high was his degree in heaven.
  [God] created what I was in that
Bright eminence. . . . Lifted up so high, I
[Di]sdained subjection, and thought one step
Higher would set me highest.

The most interesting feature of the Spenser-Milton parallel is the common sequence of events which began prior to creation of the world. Both poets described the angels assembling before the throne, and as singing songs by day and night. The rebellion of Satan followed. Beyond the common sequence, and the highly similar openings, the parallel probably has little significance. The details employed were too distinctly commonplace. The description of Satan, or Lucifer, as the brightest and most important angel descended directly from the forced interpretation of Isaiah and Ezekiel previously discussed. Following Augustine, Abelard named Satan as the prince who ruled over many angels, and added that he was the most illustrious among the spirits. Quoting Gregory the Great, Thomas Aquinas wrote that Satan 'was set over all the host of angels, surpassed them in brightness, and was by comparison the most illustrious among them.' The Lucifer of Vondel was 'the chief and most illustrious of the angels;' that of Taubman 'beautiful far beyond the rest of the angels, and the chief of the spirits.' Heywood eulogized him as the leader who possessed 'the three stupendous qualities of the most holy Trinity . . . Greatness, Wisdom next, then Pulchritude.' Above Michael, above Raphael, above Gabriel, 'was Lucifer instated, honored, exalted, and much celebrated.' The Satan of Marini had been 'the fairest and first-born smile of heaven.'

According to Milton's narrative, God convoked the angels that he might proclaim a divine decree. Under this decree, drawn largely from the forced interpretation of Philippians 2. 5-10 and Hebrews 1. 2, 5-6, God announced the Exaltation of Christ, named him as vicegerent, and commanded all knees in heaven to bow before him. The great Lucifer, who heretofore had stood next to God, resented this sudden and drastic change, and:

> Fraught with envy against the Son of God, that day
> Honored by his great Father, and proclaimed
> Messiah, King Anointed, could not bear
> Through pride, that sight, and thought himself
>   impaired.

As early as the Middle English *Christ and Satan*, medieval poetry had pictured Satan as revolting because he envied the Messiah. The proud angel openly challenged Christ,

'wuldres leoman, bearn helendes,' and set himself up as the
rival, not of God, but of the Son. During Milton's era, the
belief that the Exaltation (and Incarnation) occasioned
Satan's rebellion enjoyed appreciable literary prestige.
Taubman and Vondel touched upon the conception;
Francis Beaumont, Jacob Boehme, Thomas Heywood,
and Odorico Valmarana made serious use of it. Indeed,
Valmarana strikingly emphasized the theme by subtitling
his lengthy *Demonomachiae*, a poem more extended than
the *Iliad*, *The Battle of the Angels over the Incarnation
of Christ*. As Milton was to do three decades later, Valmarana agreed with Heywood that God 'did not reveal
his blessed Son's Incarnation, but with a strict commandment that they [the angels] should with all creatures God
and Man obey. Hence grew the great dissention that befell
betwixt Lucifer and the Prince Michael.'

Having determined to rebel, the Satan of *Paradise Lost*
entrusted all preliminary steps to an unnamed subordinate.
This subordinate called together his lieutenants, and to each:

> Tells the suggested cause, and casts between
> Ambiguous words and jealousies, to sound
> Or taint integrity.

The device of employing a subordinate to assist the villain
was of course a commonplace of tragedy. However, Acevedo previously had used in his *Creation* a subordinate to
Satan whom he appropriately named Discord. In a work
published during the year 1655, *The War of the Angels*,
Taubman gave to Lucifer a subordinate left unnamed and
unidentified. This assistant possessed unusual skill in dis-
simulation, and so effectively ensnared the angels that they
obeyed whatever he commanded them. Other similarities,
often faint and obscure, but nevertheless suggestive, occur
in the *Macbeth* of Shakespeare. These are best discussed
in a subsequent chapter.

Following the Exaltation of Christ, the first overt act of Milton's Satan was to lead one-third of the angels to his kingdom in the north of heaven. In so doing he paralleled exactly the action of the Lucifer of Valmarana's *Battle of the Angels over the Incarnation of Christ*. Excluding details which make up the first two days of the celestial conflict, Milton then followed closely a narrative pattern previously utilized in *The Victory of Christ*. This work, entitled in Latin *De Victoria Verbi Dei*, had for its author Rupertus Tuitiensis, a Roman Catholic abbot of the Twelfth Century. We have now largely forgotten Rupert, but both the Sixteenth and Seventeenth Centuries knew and respected his many theological discourses.

As the story runs in *Paradise Lost*, the rebellious Satan marched by night to his kingdom in the north. Having arrived at his palace, he assembled his legions, and denounced the newly exalted Christ. Faithful Abdiel immediately rebuked the Apostate, and declared his enmity against the Son wholly without foundation. This angel, who has imperfect counterparts in the Fama of Valvasone, and the Gabriel and Raphael of Vondel, then paraphrased John 1. 1-3 by stating that Christ not only stood higher than all angels, but was in fact their Creator. The last point Satan challenged on two grounds, the first, that Abdiel knew nothing of his creation or creator; the second, that the angels were self-begotten. Preferable to a summary, however, is Milton's own account:

> At length into the limits of the north
> They came, and Satan to his royal seat,
> High on a hill . . . affecting all equality
> With God . . . and with calumnious art
> Of counterfeited truth thus held their ears:
> 'Thrones, Dominations, Princedoms, Virtues. . . .
> Will ye submit your necks, and choose to bend

The supple knee? Ye will not, if I trust
To know ye right, or if ye know yourselves
Natives and sons of heaven possessed before
By none, and, if not equal all, yet free. . . .'
    Thus far his bold discourse without control
Had audience, when, among the Seraphim,
Abdiel, than whom none with more zeal adored
The Deity, and divine commands obeyed,
Stood up, and in a flame of zeal severe
The current of his fury thus opposed:
'O argument blasphemous, false, and proud. . . .
Thyself, though great and glorious, dost thou count
Or all angelic nature joined in one,
Equal to him, begotten Son, by whom,
As by his Word, the mighty Father made
All things, even thee, and all the spirits of Heaven
By him created in their bright degrees. . . .'
    The Apostate . . . more haughty, thus replied:
'That we were formed, then, say'st thou? and the work
Of secondary hands, by task transferred
From Father to his Son? Strange point and new!
Doctrine which we would know whence learned!
    Who saw
When this creation was? Remember'st thou
Thy making, while the Maker gave thee being?
We know no time when we were not as now;
Know none before us, self-begot, self-raised
By our own quickening power when fatal course
Had circled his full orb, the birth mature
Of this our native heaven, ethereal sons.
Our puissance is our own.'

Rupert is indeed close to these sections of *Paradise Lost*.
Having written that Satan rebelled against Christ, the
abbot declared he 'had no just cause for enmity against the
Son (*Dei Verbum*).' Rupert next related that Satan argued
with a group of angels, and by deceit 'persuaded some

that they accept him as God.' In partial recapitulation, the
Catholic theologian wrote that Satan convinced himself he
should be God. Because of this, he had the ability to per-
suade the angels both to trust completely in his great wisdom, and to accept without question his assertion, 'I am
God.' Nevertheless, Rupert argued, Satan spoke falsely.
Christ ruled over all, and Scripture had stated, 'In the beginning was the Word, and the Word was with God, and
the Word was God. The same was in the beginning with
God. All things were made through him; and without
him was not anything made that hath been made.'

Satan believed, continued Rupert, that 'no one had
knowledge of his own creation and founding, and therefore could not dispute his assertion that he [Satan] was
self-begotten.' He flatly declared, 'I am not a creation of
God, I was made by no one; I am self-made. Certainly,
none of the spirits or angels saw or heard when God
made him.' Having so spoken, Satan puffed up his heart,
and raged against God.

From their closely related dialogues, one held between
Rupert and Satan, the other between Milton's Abdiel and
Satan, the two writers turned with little delay to the battle
fought in heaven. In each instance, Michael led the angelic
army; and failed to achieve victory. Where Milton spread
the combat over three days, Rupert used no temporal
divisions. The decisive action however was precisely the
same. With Milton, this action began with the entrance
of Christ, coming as the cherubim envisioned by Ezekiel
10. 9 ff. In the battle which followed, the Son conquered
Satan by terrifying him and his host with fire and thunder-
bolt:

> Full soon among them he arrived, in his right hand
> Grasping ten thousand thunders, which he sent
> Before him, such as in their souls infixed

Plagues. They, astonished, all resistance lost,
All courage; down their idle weapons dropt . . .
From the fourfold-visaged four . . . every eye
Glared lightning, and shot forth pernicious fire
Among the accursed, that withered all their strength,
And of their wonted vigor left them drained,
Exhausted, spiritless, afflicted, fallen.

Rupert, who had argued at length that Ezekiel's vision was in fact a vision of the triumphant Christ, opened his similar description with a rhetorical question. What arms, he asked, were employed in the celestial battle? These arms, he replied, were not physical or material. Rather, they consisted of flaming fire brought by the Son. This ardent fire is unbearable to those hateful to Christ, concerning whom it is written in the Psalms, 'Terrible are you, and who can resist thee.' Continuing, Rupert declared, 'Truly, you are terrible, Lord, and no one can resist you. . . . And Satan feared nothing so much as the thunderbolts of the Word. . . . The evil angels fell prostrate in great terror. . . . When Christ rose up, these angels trembled with fear, and were purged with terror.' After having stated that Satan passed into the eternal fire prepared for him and his angels, Rupert twice described the Son as driving Satan from heaven by his thunder and flashing lightning. The defeated apostate then fell into the vast chaos.

The celestial battle having ended, both poet and abbot declared that discord ceased in heaven, and the faithful angels sang songs of praise to the triumphant Christ. In the words which Milton attributed to Raphael:

I have revealed . . . the discord which befell,
And war in heaven . . . and the deep fall
Of those too high aspiring who rebelled. . . .
Nine days they fell; confounded chaos roared,
And felt tenfold confusion in their fall
Through his wild anarchy; so huge a rout

Incumbered him with ruin. Hell at last,
Yawning, received them whole, and on them closed—
Hell, their fit habitation, fraught with fire
Unquenchable, the house of woe and pain. . . .
Sole victor, from the expulsion of his foes
Messiah his triumphal chariot turned.
To meet him all his saints, who silent stood
Eye-witnesses of his almighty acts,
With jubilee advanced; and, as they went,
Shaded with branching palm, each order bright
Sung triumph, and him sung victorious King.

Five centuries before *Paradise Lost*, Rupert had written
that Christ's victory over the Devil and his angels excluded
discord, and brought concord into heaven. Following a
repetition of this idea, he said that with the ejection of
Satan, serene peace returned to heaven, and the holy angels
began to utter song. Heaven echoed with the praise and
jubilation of angels honoring the triumphant Son. In a
fourth extended description, the spirits of heaven again
sang with exultation because the Word had conquered
Satan.

Having been cast from heaven, Milton's rebel angels fell
nine days before reaching hell. Precisely why Milton selected a period of nine days is not clear. His description
in Book I of the fallen angels lying nine days on the Biblical
lake of hell suggests poetic preference for a word combination, and that such a preference dictated his choice.
However, the defeated Satan of *Piers the Plowman* and
of George Turberville previously had fallen nine days in
passing from heaven to hell. The striking picture of Satan
plunging into chaos, employed by Rupert and Milton,
also had appealed to Valmarana. With picturesque phraseology, the Italian poet depicted the conquered Lucifer as
plummeting down through chaos and profound night.

As the story runs in *Paradise Lost*, the battle in heaven occupied three days; the events which led to it, one day. We can only conjecture why Milton devoted three units of time to the battle, and four to the complete episode. Whatever may have been the cause of its use, this division stands as a partial compromise between two important medieval beliefs. As Reginald Scot observed in 1584, one group of schoolmen held that Satan stood four 'instants,' or periods of time, and a larger group maintained that 'he fell the third instant.' The latter group supported its belief by the contention that 'it stood with God's justice to give them three warnings.' If Milton were half as well read as our evidence suggests, he knew of these beliefs. More to the point is the fact that his Satan was thrice warned: first, by God himself (V, 611 ff.); secondly, by the faithful Abdiel (V, 877); and thirdly, by the archangel Michael (VI, 262 ff.).

The ultimate basis for the first day of the battle proper was patently the conflicts of classical and neo-classical literature. Milton skillfully intertwined the stirring combats of individual heroes, mass fighting, and the courageous exploits of lesser figures. To assume, however, that Milton deliberately and consciously interfused classical and religious themes would be to forget that Christian humanism had long since consummated such a union. Some decades before *Paradise Lost*, Valmarana, Taubman, and other writers had followed the classical pattern in their description of the battle in heaven. In harmony with Valmarana, Vondel, and others, Milton made Gabriel, Raphael, and Uriel associates of Michael. He likewise followed predecessors in the field by adding to these warriors various fictitional angels whose names closed with the Hebrew *ale*, usually written *el*. Abdiel, servant of God, and Zophiel, spy of God, were thus coined

by Milton. The subordinates of Satan he apparently chose
at random from the large list of heathen gods and idols
regarded by patristic writers as originally members of
Satan's band. Such word combinations as 'Adramelech and
Asmadai, Ariel and Arioch,' indicate that the basis of selection was primarily poetic.

Having exhausted the dramatic possibilities of ancient
or classical warfare, Milton turned on the second day of
battle to the major military contribution of modern times
—the invention of gunpowder and firearms. Among other
poets, Ariosto, Drayton, and Spenser had attributed this
invention to the powers of hell. A further writer, Erasmo
di Valvasone, approached even closer to Milton, and in
his *Battle of the Angels* described Satan as inventing cannon
for use against Michael and his army. As we recall, the
good angels of *Paradise Lost* countered by hurling whole
mountains upon 'the cursed engines triple row.' Milton
may have borrowed here from Hesiod's *Theogony*, where
warriors flung rocks as missiles. A closer analogue comes
from the *Decay* of Du Bartas, a section of the *Divine
Weeks*. In the combat which the attacking force pressed
with revolutionary weapons, the defenders responded by
hurling 'mountains upon the engines new.' With heaven
torn asunder, and threatened with devastation, Milton
closed the second day. On the third and final day of conflict, Christ cast Satan into hell.

As Newton, Todd, Osgood, and numerous other scholars
have noted, the phraseology of Milton's description of
the battle includes echoes from a multitude of writers,
scriptural, classical, and modern. We meet with slight alteration the expression 'while he may be found,' of Isaiah
55. 6; 'our own right hand shall teach thee terrible things,'
from Psalm 45. 4; and the 'show thyself approved unto
God,' of 2 Timothy 2. 15. Milton's 'reluctant flames' reflect

The Battle in Heaven

the *Aeneid*, V, 682; the 'lighted from his gorgeous throne,' the *Iliad*, III, 29; and 'whence in perpetual fight they needs must last,' Hesiod's *Theogeny*, V, 635. Illustrations of apparent absorption from contemporary literature are 'knee-tribute' and 'supple knee,' based upon Shakespeare's *2 Richard*, I, iv; the 'sun-bright chariot' of Sylvester's Du Bartas, I, i; and 'the matin trumpet sung' of Tasso's *Jerusalem Delivered*, XI, 19. To these examples, many others may be added. The military maneuvers of Satan's host preparatory to the surprise artillery attack follow those described in current military treatises, and, according to Mr. Holly Hanford, probably came from Robert Ward's *Animadversions of War*, London, 1639.

Milton's description of the battle in heaven has conserved for posterity a vital literary tradition of the early Seventeenth and preceding Centuries. This powerful literary genre took its rise from the integrated contributions of unnumbered writers. Beginning as unrelated interpretations of scattered passages of Scripture, the tradition next achieved form through their partial unification. Imagination expanded further the religious elements, and as a culminating stage borrowed liberally from classical and European literature. Both the early theologians and subsequent lay writers frequently failed to agree on the time, the place, and the immediate efficient cause of the rebellion in heaven. Nevertheless, they held almost universally that there had been a time, a place, a cause, and a battle. As a result of strengthened Biblical exegesis, the interpretations which occasioned and then supported the battles were gradually rejected. The vitality of the tradition, once the product of theology, became during the Sixteenth Century a vitality which flowed from the use and acceptance of a literary form.

We cannot determine with accuracy the relative degree

to which Milton drew upon each of the four stages discussed. On the whole, the two latter steps proved the more important. Without entering upon the difficult question of the immediate sources utilized, we may say that Milton could have developed the battle from a relatively few works, all of which belong to the latter classifications. Rupert's *Victory of Christ* provides an excellent partial foundation. This work set the basic conflict between Christ and Satan, included the essential themes of the Abdiel-Satan controversy, described Michael as superseded by the triumphant Son, and concluded with both the episodes and many of the phrases found in the third day of Milton's conflict.

If we add to this framework such details and minor conceptions as appear in Spenser, Valmarana, Valvasone, and Taubman, together with the tradition of the three warnings and the three or four periods of various schoolmen, we have before us the major elements of Satan's rebellion. The conceptions, incidents, and episodes which make up the whole were never unique, and often were relatively commonplace. Milton's creative contribution in depicting the celestial battle consisted primarily of judicious selection and effective combination. This contribution he made greater by the magic which lives in a noble poetic style.

CHAPTER III

THE CREATION

FEW divisions of *Paradise Lost* suffer greater handicap than Milton's story of the Creation. The restless wheel of time has concealed the theological basis of the battle in heaven, so that Satan's rebellion now is read and enjoyed as imaginative literature. Such fortune has not befallen the tale of Creation. To the educated reader, the story inevitably recalls the verses of Genesis upon which it ultimately rests, and brings forcefully to mind their incompatibility with substantiated findings of modern science. Book VII of the epic thus becomes a gracious repetition of antiquated and outmoded ideas. Less obvious forces also are active. For some decades our world has emphasized creativeness less, and control more. On occasion, it has reversed completely Milton's inspired belief, that to create is greater than to destroy. Quite naturally, we do not stress the fecundity and creativeness of God as did the Seventeenth and preceding Centuries.

The prominence then given to God's creative fecundity may ultimately have developed from Plato or the neo-Platonic writers of the early Christian era. Other influences perhaps descended from such pre-Socratic Greeks as Anaximander, who apparently maintained that an unlimited creative power worked actively within the cosmos. Whatever the ultimate sources, medieval Christian philosophers proclaimed zealously the infinite creative power of Deity. Among other Aristotelian and related heresies, Stephen Tempier in 1277 condemned the proposition that God, the Prime Cause, could not create a plurality of worlds. By this condemnation the Bishop of Paris

43

did not seek to support the doctrine that other worlds actually exist. He sought rather to protect from limitation the creative power of God. Within the more radical philosophers, belief in the infinite potency and creativeness of God surged so vigorously, that they asserted flatly the existence of an infinite cosmos and of a plurality of worlds. Cardinal Cusanus, Giordano Bruno, and Thomas Campanella felt and set forth the claims of this conception. The idea grew into a commonplace with the close of the Seventeenth Century, and even more than the telescope, expanded the cosmological imagination of man. There lived however many writers, Milton included, who rejoiced in God's creative energy, but questioned sharply the doctrine of a plurality of worlds.

Understanding and appreciation face the additional handicap of a desultory acquaintance with the hexamera. For sixteen centuries prior to *Paradise Lost,* countless Christians had reveled in descriptions of the Six Days of Creation. This genre, Chapter I has noted, emerged as early as Philo, who circa 40 A.D. composed *The Creation of the World (De Opificio Mundi).* By the end of the Fourth Century, when Basil completed his hexameron, the genre had become well established. Contemporary and subsequent use by Ambrose and Gregory the Great ensured its prestige. During the Sixteenth Century, Tasso and Du Bartas wrote extended poems upon the Creation, and few histories and geographies of this and succeeding eras failed to devote long sections to the Six Days. The unnumbered men who followed the hexameral tradition rarely attempted innovation, with the result that a line of writers which extended beyond Milton, continued to repeat in the Seventeenth Century a number of the precise words that Ephraem had employed in the Fourth. As Mr. Frank E. Robbins observed three decades ago: 'The

hexamera tended to conform to certain types established
by a few pioneers. Subsequent authors not only followed
the general outlines that had been laid down by the greater
writers, and reproduced their topics, but even copied their
phraseology. Imitation is commoner in this branch of
literature than in almost any other, and the majority of
hexamera are consequently lacking in originality.'

Among the mass of hexameral writers, and in contrast
with various religious philosophers, the appreciation of
God's creative acts rested primarily upon a basis more
substantial than delight in his rich fecundity. Stated somewhat differently, these writers did not regard creation of
the universe as principally an expression of God's infinite
power. In harmony with the first chapters of Genesis,
they declared that God conceived and built the world as
a home and an empire for man. It then became the function of man to obey and glorify his Maker. Doing this, he
would in time move to heaven itself, and spend eternity
with the Ruler of all.

As events fell out, many early Fathers found incomplete
this explanation of the creation of man. The revolt of Satan,
they argued, had emptied one-third of heaven. Working
from such verses as Matthew 22. 30 and Luke 20. 36,
patristic exegetes voiced the belief that to a greater or
lesser degree, God created man to fill the celestial rooms
left vacant by the fallen angels. The unconventional Origen
went so far as to declare that man's creation constituted an
indirect punishment of the apostates. This variant conception Milton gave to the angered Satan of Book IX,
causing him to say of God:

> He, to be avenged, . . .
> Determined to advance into our room
> A creature formed of earth, and him endow,

Exalted from so base original,
With heavenly spoils, our spoils. What he decreed
He effected: Man he made, and for him built
Magnificent this world, and earth his seat,
Him Lord pronounced, and, O indignity!
Subjected to his service angel-wings.

A more common belief held that man, or the elect, would wholly or in part repair the damage done heaven by the rebellious Lucifer. Among the Fathers of the Church, its roll of direct and indirect supporters held such names as Anselm, Augustine, Catharinus, Gregory Nazianzen, and Peter Lombard. Among poets, this roll included Caedmon or the pseudo-Caedmon, Spenser, Tasso, and Jordan, author of the *Cornish Creation*. Spenser set forth the conception in the poem previously discussed, *An Hymn of Heavenly Love*, stanzas 15-16:

But that Eternal Fount of love and grace,
Still flowing forth his goodness unto all,
Now seeing left a waste and empty place
In his wide palace, through those angels' fall,
Cast to supply the same, and to enstall
A new unknowen colony therein,
Whose root from earth's base groundwork should begin.

Therefore of clay, base, vile, and next to nought,
Yet formed by wondrous skill, and by his might,
According to an heavenly pattern wrought,
Which he had fashioned in his wise foresight,
He man did make, and breathed a living sprite
Into his face most beautiful and fair,
Endued with wisdom's riches, heavenly, rare.

In *Paradise Lost*, and immediately after Satan's ejection from heaven, God announced to the triumphant Son:

At last our envious foe hath failed, who thought
All like himself rebellious . . . and into fraud

Drew many whom their place knows here no more.
Yet far the greater part have kept, I see,
Their station; heaven, yet populous, retains
Number sufficient to possess her realms. . . .
But, lest his heart exalt him in the harm
Already done, to have dispeopled heaven—
My damage fondly deemed—I can repair
That detriment, if such it be to lose
Self-lost, and in a moment will create
Another world; out of one man a race
Of men innumerable, there to dwell.

According to Divine plan, this new creation would live
upon earth:

> till, by degrees of merit raised,
> They open to themselves at length the way
> Up hither, under long obedience tried,
> And earth be changed to heaven, and heaven to earth:
> One kingdom, joy and union without end.

In the five last verses, Milton reiterated an idea which
had achieved distinct prominence by the Twelfth Century.
Under this conception of the Divine plan, man first was
placed upon the earth, from which, in the not uncommon
belief advanced by Bonaventure, Hugo of St. Victor, and
Peter Lombard, he would rise by humble obedience to the
realm of God. The belief that man would rise to heaven,
Bishop Tostatus carried somewhat further, or made more
specific. Man, obedient and unfallen, 'could attain spiritual
beatification through the divine vision,' and 'by degrees
could ascend to good.'

By way of completing this theological prelude to the
Creation, Milton restated a complex of propositions, most
of which custom had associated with descriptions of the
creating God. The principal function of the related prop-

ositions was to prove that the Maker acted freely in building this world. Having authorized the Son to create the universe, the God of *Paradise Lost* therefore announced:

> Boundless the deep, because I am who fill
> Infinitude; nor vacuous the space,
> Though I, uncircumscribed, myself retire,
> And put not forth my goodness, which is free
> To act or not. Necessity and Chance
> Approach not me, and what I will is Fate.

Religious writers had long delighted in stressing these conceptions of Deity, particularly the ideas that God is uncircumscribed, unlimited, and infinite; and that it is he who is omnipresent and fills all space. Damascene reiterated the point that God is uncircumscribed; Heywood declared in part that 'Himself without place, God instated all things;' and Wolleb-Ross wrote that 'God is neither circumscribed, nor defined by place; nor included within, nor excluded without it.' To More, the wide and endless stretch of chaos lay 'ever equal with the Deity,' and God existed everywhere, unbounded and infinite. Equally attractive to Christians of all creeds and ages were the related ideas, one stated, the other implied in Milton's passage, that God's goodness is free or not affected by necessity, and that he created the world because of his goodness. The apparently heterodox final line, 'and what I will is Fate,' likewise repeated a commonplace. As Thomas Aquinas had noted four centuries prior to *Paradise Lost*, 'The Divine power or will can be called fate, as being the cause of fate.'

In harmony with the customary interpretation of the opening verses of John, Milton described Christ, or the Word of God, as the immediate creator of the universe. First, he pictured the Son coming forth with his angels:

> Meanwhile the Son
> On his great expedition now appeared,
> Girt with omnipotence, with radiance crowned . . .
> About his chariot numberless were poured
> Cherub and Seraph, Potentates and Thrones,
> And Virtues, winged Spirits, and chariots winged
> From the armory of God, where stand of old
> Myriads, between two brazen mountains lodged
> Against a solemn day . . . Then stayed the
> Fervid wheels.

The setting is not the same, but the influential *Divine Weeks* of Du Bartas provided Milton with some precedent for such a description of Christ:

> The certain date of that Great Day is printed . . .
> Then, then, good Lord, shall thy dear Son descend,
> Though yet he seem in feeble flesh yspend,
> In complete glory, from the glistering sky:
> Millions of angels shall about him fly;
> Mercy and Justice, marching cheek by jowl,
> Shall his divine triumphant chariot roll,
> Whose wheels shall shine with lightning round about,
> And beams of glory each-where blazing out.

Paradise Lost next set forth the striking episode wherein Christ rode far into chaos, and taking the golden compasses of God, marked out the boundary of the terrestrial universe. Ultimately, Milton's conception rested upon two verses of Scripture. Proverbs 8. 27, to use again the King James Version, said definitely: 'He set a compass upon the face of the deep.' The supporting verse, Job 26. 10, stated: 'He hath described a boundary upon the face of the waters, unto the confines of light and darkness.' Originally unconnected with the Mosaic account of the Creation, the two passages became in time associated with it. Literary description of God's bounding the universe with compasses appeared as early as Dante's *Divine Comedy*, and in seventeenth-century England the picture of the divine hand circumscribing the cosmos was a well-known printer's ornament. Partially supporting this figure stood the Platonic idea of God, or the Son, as the architect of the universe, a conception alluded to by Milton in Book VIII. Both the figure and the idea previously had been joined by Godfrey Goodman in *The Fall of Man*, an extended treatise first published during 1616, and later republished in 1618 and 1629. The conservative Anglican divine, then a chaplain of the Queen, and later Bishop of Gloucester, emphasized especially the conception of Deity as the creating architect. 'In the beginning,' he wrote, 'God did square and proportion the heavens for the earth, using his rule, level, and compass: the earth as the center, the heavens for the circumference.' In employing the figure of the Son turning golden compasses, together with the supporting conception of Christ as an architect, Milton made use of widely known and generally accepted beliefs.

From this point the English poet largely employed the sequence and the ideas found in the Mosaic account of the Six Days of Creation. This is not to say that Milton followed closely the first chapters of Genesis. Rather, he took for his model conventional expansions of these chapters. Where Genesis had said, 'And the Spirit of God moved upon the face of the waters,' Milton wrote:

> On the watery calm
> His brooding wings the Spirit of God outspread,
> And vital virtue infused, and vital warmth,
> Throughout the fluid mass.

In the invocation which opens Book I, Milton similarly described this fecundating activity of the Holy Spirit:

Thou from the first wast present, and, with mighty
Wings outspread, dove-like sat'st brooding
On the vast abyss, and mad'st it pregnant.

The effective comparison of the Holy Spirit to a dove
had the support of Matthew 3. 16: 'The Spirit of God descending like a dove.' Equally important was the belief discussed by Hugo of Saint Victor in his frequently echoed
De Sacramentis; according to which 'the Holy Spirit re-
served for himself . . . the form of a dove.' Perhaps
more to the point, two decades prior to *Paradise Lost,* the
English poet Joseph Beaumont had employed the dove as
symbolic of the fecundating spirit of Creation:

Forth flew the Eternal Dove, and tenderly
Over the flood's blind tumult hovering,
Did secret seeds of vital warmth supply
By the sweet virtue of his sovereign wing:
Much like the loving hen, whose brooding care
Doth hatch her eggs, and them for life prepare.

We cannot say who first described the Spirit of God as
a brooding fowl. Scholars generally have credited the conception to Basil, but in using the figure, Basil stated emphatically: 'I do not give you my idea, but the idea of the
man of Syria (*Dicam tibi non meam, sed viri Syria sentent-
iam*).' The man of Syria, canonized St. Ephraem, described
the Spirit of God as the Holy Spirit. The Spirit 'incubated
the waters,' and 'inspired prolific virtue (*virtutem pro-
lificam inderet*).' In partial repetition, Ephraem declared:
'The Holy Spirit fomented the waters with vital heat
(*vitali calore*), and quickened them to production by infused warmth (*infuso ardore*). In this fashion he made
them fecund. We have,' concluded the Saint, 'an example
of this process in the hen, incubating her eggs.' Among
later followers of this interpretation, Abelard and Diodati

compared the fecundating Spirit to a bird hatching her eggs; Du Bartas, to a brooding hen. Mercer likened it to both a hen and an eagle, with his later choice apparently based upon a patristic gloss of Deuteronomy 32. 11: 'As an eagle that stirreth up her nest. . . . He spread abroad his wings.' Of special interest is the appearance in *Paradise Lost* of important key words which Ephraem had used thirteen centuries before Milton's era.

So numerous were literary and theological expansions of the first chapters of Genesis, that countless analogies could be presented for Milton's version of the Days of Creation. However, such procedure is as unnecessary as it would be cumbersome, for as Mr. Robbins has observed, most of the descriptions display a maximum of imitation, and a minimum of originality. With occasional supplements, I shall use but one book, Josuah Sylvester's translation of the encyclopedic *Divine Weeks* of Du Bartas. The work of the celebrated Frenchman is little known today, but during Milton's boyhood reigned unchallenged as the most widely read poem of all Europe. So frequently was it republished, that from a period of approximately fifty years, we have preserved more than two hundred and thirty editions, thirty-eight of which are English translations. Critics and writers of all creeds and nations read and praised this lengthy and relatively costly work.

The most striking of the Du Bartas-Milton similarities begin with their description of the third day of Creation. We may note, however, that at the opening of Book VII, Milton invoked Urania, goddess of the stars and heavens. In his conventional petition for aid, he asked to be 'up led' by her. Du Bartas used much the same pattern, calling upon the 'glorious guide of heaven's star-glistering motion.' He prayed that she should 'lift up my soul.' Among numerous details frequently unrelated to *Paradise Lost*, he included the holy rest which God had enjoyed prior to Creation, and advanced the belief that before Deity built this world, 'he built a hell' for the ungodly. Subsequently, he described as without beginning, without center, and without end the chaos from which came the universe. Having declared no void or vacuum existed, the French poet repeated the belief that God set the bounds of the physical world, but exempted his own essence from limitation. Next followed the picture of Christ and his accompanying angels which I previously quoted. In presenting either these, or comparable ideas, Milton employed precisely the same sequence as Du Bartas had used.

One phrase of the introduction to Book VII definitely implies Milton's awareness of Du Bartas. Subsequent to his invocation of Urania, he described himself as 'standing on earth, not rapt above the pole.' In the opening lines of the *Columns*, Du Bartas had sought 'my dear Urania's grace,' and had prayed for guidance 'through heaven's glistring palaces.' Exactly contrary to Milton, he hoped that his spirit might be *rapt above the pole*:

> If ever, Lord, the purest of my soul
> In sacred rage were rapt above the pole. . . .

Paradise Lost gave but little space to the first and second days of Creation. In fact, Milton confined himself largely to the few essential details mentioned in Genesis. His most noteworthy addition was an ancient patristic belief concerning the unbodied light that God first created, and on the fourth day placed within the globes of heaven. Since sun and stars were not made until this day, early commentators considered it necessary to provide for the light some preliminary function. As Milton's lines suggest, this function was to turn in a circle round the emerging earth:

> 'Let there be light,' said God, and forthwith, light . . .
> Sprung from the deep, and from her native east
> To journey through the aery gloom began,
> Sphered in a radiant cloud—for yet the sun
> Was not; she in a cloudy tabernacle
> Sojourned the while.

Du Bartas employed these ideas in a sequence precisely the reverse of Milton's, placing God's fiat at the conclusion of his comparable version:

> He spread a shining cloud . . .
> Upon the deep (yet all with waters blinded),
> Which flying round about, gave light . . .
> As now the sun, circling about this ball
> (The light's bright chariot), doth enlighten all.
> No sooner said he, 'Be there light,' but lo,
> The formless lump to perfect form 'gan grow.

Milton's treatment of the third day differed noticeably from that accorded the two days preceding. For the first time, he expanded markedly the brief verses in Genesis. In its outline, his description consisted of an introduction, a close paraphrase of Genesis 1.9, a highly expanded repetition of this verse, and a paraphrase of Genesis 1. 10-11, followed by a second amplification. Genesis 1. 12, the last of the four verses devoted to the work of the third day, Milton completely ignored. As the quoted lines will indicate, the first half of his description pictured the mountains and the plains rising high above the waters:

> Immediately the mountains huge appear
> Emergent, and their broad bare backs upheave
> Into the clouds; their tops ascend the sky.
> So high as heaved the tumid hills, so low
> Down sunk a hollow bottom broad and deep,
> Capacious bed of waters. Thither they

Hasted with glad precipitance, uprolled,
As drops on dust conglobing; from the dry
Part rise in crystal wall, or ridge direct
For haste: such flight the great command impressed
On the swift floods. As armies at the call
Of trumpet—for of armies thou hast heard—
Troop to their standard, so the watery throng,
Wave rolling after wave, where way they found:
If steep, with torrent rapture; if through plain,
Soft-ebbing; nor withstood them rock or hill.
But they, or underground, or circuit wide,
With serpent error wandering, found their way,
And on the washy ooze deep channels wore.

In his account of the third day of Creation, Du Bartas
paused to describe at length the rushing of water into
seas both deep and vast. He called the mountains heaven-
approaching rocks, and spoke of their broad backs. From
their tops the water leaped down, hasting its course. Unrelated parts excluded, the French poet then wrote, 'For
the dry earth, having these waters first, from rocky mountains, pours forth fountains.' God then commanded Neptune to marshal forth his floods. Further similarities, both
in mood and in detail, become apparent in related fragments drawn from the remainder of the Du Bartian account:

[Side caption] By an apt comparison, he showeth
How the water withdrew from off the earth.
As when the muffled heavens have wept amain,
And foaming streams assembling on the plain . . .
Even so the sea, to itself, itself betook . . .
Her waters, that from every side did run . . .
On every side, when one perceives his
Fellow to be gone; . . . he him accompanies;
After, another and another hies. . . .
And through the steep and stony hills

It gushes. [And the] large river, lord of
The plain, doth in some gulf discharge.
It pleased him to convey deep underground
Some arms of such a sea. . . . With winding
Turns [the water] mazeth to and fro;
On the smooth table crawling like a worm.
The deluge . . . in hollow sponges sinks,
And its ample arms in straiter channel shrinks.

We note with passing interest that both Du Bartas and
Milton introduced similies at much the same place in their
related descriptions. The French poet used the figure of
streams assembling on the plain; the English bard, that of
armies assembling before their flag.

The second half of the third day Milton devoted to the
creation of grass, herb, and tree. He again displayed his
consummate ability to give life to a list or catalog of
detail. I begin with the highly expanded repetition of
Genesis 1. 11:

He scarce had said, when the bare earth, till then
Desert and bare, unsightly, unadorned,
Brought forth the tender grass, whose verdure clad
Her universal face with pleasant green;
Then herbs of every leaf, that sudden flowered,
Opening their various colors, and made gay
Her bosom, smelling sweet; and, these scarce blown,
Forth flourished thick the clustering vine, forth crept
The smelling gourd, up stood the corny reed
Imbattled in her field; add the humble shrub,
And bush with frizzled hair implicit. Last
Rose, as in dance, the stately trees, and spread
Their branches hung with copious fruit, or gemmed
Their blossoms. With high woods the hills were
    crowned,
With tufts the valleys and each fountain-side,
With borders long the rivers.

By what may be curious coincidence, the description of Du Bartas presented virtually the same details in precisely the same sequence. However, the beginning of one sequence is the end of the other. Should we open with the last Du Bartian correspondence, we meet a picture of the dead earth reviving, and 'enriching shortly with his springing crop, the ground with green.' Continuing backward through the third day of Du Bartas, we find other pertinent descriptions, the first of which carried the caption: 'Of divers herbs and plants, and of their excellent virtues:'

Precious perfumes, fruits, plenty, pleasant
Flowers . . . the flax, which flowers at once . . .
In them the painter I admire, who
In more colors doth the fields attire . . .
There the amorous vine coiled in a thousand sorts . . .
Here the fine pepper, as in clusters hung;
There cinnamon and other spices sprung.

Early editors of *Paradise Lost* found extremely troublesome Milton's phrase, 'the smelling gourd.' Gourds do not smell, protested learned Richard Bentley, and declared the reading should be 'the swelling gourd.' We have however a pungently smelling gourd in the East Indian pepper of Du Bartas, who interestingly enough, gave to it the same relative place which Milton did later.

The *Divine Weeks* described sugar cane as 'the Hesperian plant, the precious reed,' and in other verses both spoke of corn as a reed, and likened 'fields of corn' to 'fields of combat.' Preceding a section descriptive of shrubs, Du Bartas reviewed with delight the fruit of various trees—the dainty apricot, the velvet peach, the scent-sweet apple, and damson black and white. His opening lines, as later did the closing verses of Milton, told of the 'trees growing in mountains and valleys:'

The lofty pine . . . evergreen box . . .
The airy mountains mantle round about.
The mastfull oak, the useful ash, the holm,
Coat-changing cork, white maple, shady elm,
Through hill and plain ranged their plumed ranks.
The winding rivers bordered all their banks
With slice-sea alders, and green osiers small,
With trembling poplars, and with willows pale.

Had Milton's description of the fourth day followed the
pattern or method used in the third, it would have named
the known planets and the great constellations of the
heavens. Under such a plan, the poet could transport his
reader through the realm of space, and paint a picture of
rare sublimity. Here was opportunity for the wonders
disclosed by the telescope, and for its story of unseen stars
and planets swimming in the void. But Milton rejected
such possibilities. He chose rather to continue within the
early hexameral tradition, and include cosmological beliefs
antiquated long before his century. In his disconcertingly
antiquated version, God formed the sun, moon, and stars,
and having set them in heaven, placed within them the
light created the first day. Of this light, the major part
fell to the sun, whose beams when reflected augmented the
much smaller portion allotted each star and planet. The
basic conception, according to which the clouded light
created the first day, became on the fourth the light that
gleams in sun and star, appeared in the *Divine Weeks* as
an alternative explanation.

Having first paraphrased and next supplemented the
Mosaic account, Milton then added a further description
of the newly created bodies of heaven. As had the two
which preceded it, this version confined itself to the sun,
the moon, and the stars which glimmered in heaven:

First in his east the glorious lamp was seen,
Regent of day, and all the horizon round

Invested with bright rays, jocund to run
His longitude through heaven's high-road; the grey
Dawn; and the Pleiades before him danced,
Shedding sweet influence. Less bright the moon,
But opposite in levelled west, was set,
His mirror, with full face borrowing her light
From him; for other light she needed none
In that aspect, and still that distance keeps
Till night; then in the east her turn she shines,
Revolved on heaven's great axle, and her reign
With thousand lesser lights dividual holds,
With thousand thousand stars, that then appeared
Spangling the hemisphere.

The French poet found attractive much the same characterization of the sun:

Day's glorious eye, even as a mighty king,
About his country stately progressing . . .
About the world thou ridest aye,
Which only lives by virtue of thy ray . . .
Thou radiant coachman, running endless course . . .
Life of the world, lamp of this universe.

Where Milton wrote of the grey dawn, Du Bartas had
written of a veil of morning clouds which hid the sun.
We meet again the Pleiades, and a section devoted to 'the
force and influence of celestial bodies upon the terrestrial.'
Du Bartas told of the moon in that 'aspect' where 'her face
is full,' and described her as a glass which reflected the
sun. Earlier in his account of the fourth day of Creation,
the French poet discoursed at length upon the bright stars
which 'richly spangled . . . the world's wide curtain.'

In delineating the Creation, Milton thus far has utilized
two methods: one of addition; the other, of division. His
account of both the first and second days enlarged Genesis
by adding supplementary detail concerning light, the

firmament, and the supposed celestial waters. The third day, Milton introduced the method of division, breaking the waters which covered the earth into floods, waves, torrents, slow moving streams, and rivers flowing underground. The subsequently created grass, herb, and fruit tree of Genesis blossomed forth into a variety of herbs, vines, and shrubs, and included shade and wood trees with those bearing fruit. On the fourth day, the poet returned to the method originally employed. His introductory paraphrase of Genesis described the stars, or lights of heaven, and later the sun and moon, or the two great lights. The next section again described sun, moon, and stars, with each of the three conceived as a unit. The concluding section retained these three units unaltered and undivided. No planets, either primary or secondary, were named, and but one star cluster, the Pleiades of the poets. Where Milton expanded Genesis by the method of division, rather than by that of addition or repetition, his version normally stood closest to the *Divine Weeks* of Du Bartas.

On the fifth day, as later on the sixth, Milton again utilized the method of division. First appeared the customary paraphrase of Genesis; and next, a somewhat detailed list of fish, fowl, and the great whales:

> Forthwith the sounds and seas, each creek and bay,
> With fry innumerable swarm, and shoals
> Of fish that, with their fins and shining scales,
> Glide under the green wave in sculls that oft
> Bank the mid-sea. Part, single or with mate,
> Graze the sea-weed, their pasture, and through groves
> Of coral stray, or, sporting with quick glance,
> Show to the sun their waved coats dropt with gold,
> Or, in their pearly shells at ease, attend
> Moist nutriment, or under rocks their food
> In jointed armor watch; on smooth the seal

And bended dolphins play. Part, huge of bulk,
Wallowing unwieldy, enormous in their gait,
Tempest the ocean. There Leviathan,
Hugest of living creatures, on the deep
Stretched like a promontory, sleeps or swims,
And seems a moving land, and at his gills
Draws in, and at his trunk spouts out, a sea.

Du Bartas likewise spoke generally of the many fry and
schools of fish inhabiting the water, using in addition such
expected descriptive terms as pearl and shining. By allusion to the Damon and Pythias legend, and to that of
Theseus, he expressed the idea that some fish swam with
mates, while others swam alone. A preceding section depicted 'the fishes feeding:'

One, like a pirate, only lives off prizes . . .
Another round about the rocks doth roam,
Nibbling on weeds; another, hating thieving,
Eats nought at all, on liquor only living.

The Du Bartian scene included both the polyp, or coral,
and the lobster, 'prone to theft and guile,' which 'floated
fearless' about the water. The dolphin of 'nimble motion'
appeared frequently, and also the great whale. To the last,
the French poet accorded scores of lines, scattered over
some eleven pages:

As a great carrack, cumbered and oppressed
With her self's burden, wends now east and west,
Starboard and Larbord, . . . and, as a large
And mighty limbed steed: . . . the huge whale
Hath not so nimble motions . . . Sailors,
On the Indian shore have sometimes noted some,
Whose bodies covered two broad acres room.
Methinks I see the wandring ile again,
Ortygian Delos, floating on the main. . . .

[When] these fell monsters cross, me seems
Some tempest all the seas doth toss. . . .
[There] moves the monstrous whirl-about,
Which in the sea, another sea doth spout.

The wallowing ship and 'mighty limbed steed' of Du
Bartas suggest at once Milton's 'wallowing unwieldy' and
'enormous in their gait.' The 'wandring ile' and 'moving
land' are one and the same. The whale upon the Indian
shore whose body encompassed two acres, is a whale that
'stretched like a promontory.' Other similarities scarcely
require comment.

From the fish and the great whales, Milton turned to the
birds which brood in tree and fen. Having set forth his
customary general description, he wrote of the eagle, the
stork, and the crane. Then came the songbirds and the
waterfowl, exemplified by the nightingale and the swan.
This catalog closed with what may be called the ground
birds, represented by cock and peacock. The extended
cyclopedic list of Du Bartas necessarily included both
these several classes and scores of specific birds unmentioned in *Paradise Lost*, with the result that duplication
may be wholly coincidence. Be that as it may, Milton's
verses on the crane, and on cock and peacock, merit comparison with those of his French predecessor. The English
poet wrote:

Part more wise . . . ranged in figure, wedge their way,
Intelligent of seasons, and set forth
Their aerie caravan, high over seas
Flying, and over lands, with mutual wing
Easing their flight. So steers the prudent crane
Her annual voyage. . . . Others on ground
Walked firm: the crested cock, whose clarion sounds
The silent hours, and the other, whose gay train

Adorns him, colored with the florid hue
Of rainbows and starry eyes.

Where Milton described with a word the prudence of
the crane, Du Bartas emphasized this trait by illustration.
In addition, the French poet linked quite closely the
unrelated cock and peacock:

> I hear the crane, if I mistake not, cry;
> Who in the clouds forming the forked Y . . .
> Forsake frost-firmed Strymon, and in autumn . . .
> [Seek] in southern climates for a milder winter.
> Afront each band a forward captain flies,
> Whose pointed bill cuts passage through the skies;
> Two skilful sergeants keep the ranks aright.
> One keeps the watch, and ever careful most . . .
> Another doth as much, a third, a fourth,
> Until, by turns, the night be turned forth. . . .
> There, the fair peacock beautifully brave,
> Proud, portly strutting, walking stately grave;
> Wheeling his starry train, in pomp displays
> His glorious eyes to Phoebus' golden rays.
> Close by his side stands the courageous cock,
> Crest-people's king, the peasant's trusty clock,
> True morning watch.

During the sixth day of Creation, God brought forth the
animals, the insects, and man. Subsequent to his usual
paraphrase of Genesis, Milton described animals in general,
and listed individually a group of nine. With one exception,
these and many other creatures are found in the comprehensive catalog of Du Bartas. Both writers described the
lion as rampant, placed together the ounce, leopard, and
tiger, and used the words 'branching head' in picturing
the deer. The English poet wrote that the 'elephant up-
heaved his vastness;' the French writer emphasized his

'towered back.' Each included the 'fleeced' sheep. Among the insects, Milton mentioned specifically only the ant and bee, closing with the serpent, 'subtlest beast of all the field.' The two men also inserted political sermons within their descriptions, Milton selecting the ant as his text:

> First crept the parsimonious emmet, provident
> Of future, in small room large heart enclosed—
> Pattern of just equality perhaps
> Hereafter—joined in her popular tribes
> Of commonalty. Swarming next appeared
> The female bee . . . The rest are numberless . . .
> Needless to thee repeated.

In discussing the ant, Du Bartas used the contrast so effectively employed by Milton—that of the small body and great heart. More suggestive of close relationship is a fact which easily escapes notice. Without exception, Milton provided extremely fragmentary lists of the particular creations of God. Only once did he consciously state or suggest that his catalog was incomplete. This unique admission he made regarding the insects. As we shall observe, Du Bartas similarly qualified his relatively extended survey:

> [The emmet] Mermecides [is] so small,
> That with her wings a bee can hide it all.
> Admire we then the all-wise omnipotence,
> Which doth within so narrow space dispense
> . . . so stout and valiant heart.
> For where's the state beneath the firmament,
> That doth excel the bees for government? . . .
> Sees here no city, that in rights and laws,
> For equity, near to their justice draws. . . .
> And all the rabbles of other insects,
> Endless to rehearse.

There remained for the hexameral writer the most important act of the six day's work, the breathing of life into man. More than a magnificent finale, the creation of man gave meaning and value to all that God previously had built. God made the world for man, and in his hands placed dominion over all things. For such favor man must and could only be grateful. He could only adore and praise his Creator. In the lines of Milton:

There wanted yet the master-work, the end
Of all yet done—a creature who, not prone
And brute as other creatures, but endued
With sanctity of reason, might erect
His stature, and, upright with front serene
Govern the rest, self-knowing, and from thence
Magnanimous to correspond with heaven;
But grateful to acknowledge whence his good
Descends. Thither with heart, and voice, and eyes
Directed in devotion, to adore
And worship God supreme, who made him chief
Of all his works.

We cannot question the sincerity underlying these words. Nevertheless, they gave utterance to beliefs incalculably greater than Milton's personal ideas. The voice is that of a tradition, of a pattern of thought, powerful, ancient, and respected. This tradition the representative Du Bartas set forth with less virtuosity, but with equal conviction:

Now of all creatures which his Word did make,
Man was the last that living breath did take. . . .
All the admirable creatures made beforn,
Which heaven, and earth, and ocean do adorn,
Are but essays, compared in every part,
To this divinest masterpiece of art. . . .

Yet not his face down to the earthward bending—
Like beasts that but regard their belly; ending
Forever all—but toward the azure skies'
Bright golden lamps lifting his lovely eyes. . . .
   Also thou plantest the intellectual power,
In the highest stage of all this stately bower,
That thence it might, as from a citadel,
Command the members, that too oft rebel
Against his rule.

The French poet subsequently wrote of man's eyes, 'full of infinite admiration,' of his voice, by which 'we warble to the King of Kings,' and of his heart.

In apparent disregard of their title, the early *hexamera* normally included description of the seventh day—the Sabbath upon which God rested, and contemplated his work. Later writers naturally and perhaps inevitably subscribed to this practice. As a result, Milton included in his account of the Sabbath much that was conventional, and re-enacted the familiar scenes wherein hosts of assembled angels praised the creating God. Despite these commonplaces, his version of the final day must stand as the most Miltonic of the seven. Indeed, it constitutes the one part of the Creation which is both largely and truly original.

In the conclusion of Chapter II, I suggested that the major outlines of the battle in heaven, or approximately two-thirds of Books V and VI, might be reconstructed from a limited number of works. The present discussion has said as much of Milton's story of the Creation. There remains the further step of bringing together these narrative units. Taken in combination, the two units have a common basis in the initial half of *An Hymn of Heavenly Love*, this basis beginning and ending with stanzas four

and sixteen. We recall easily the first, middle, and last
lines found in this section of Spenser's poem:

> Before this world's great frame, in which all things
> Are now contained, found any being place.

> The brightest angel, even the Child of Light,
> Drew millions more against their God to fight.

> [God] seeing left a waste and empty place
> In his wide palace, through those angels' fall,
> Cast to supply the same, and to enstall
> A new unknowen colony within.

> He man did make, and breathed a living sprite
> Into his face most beautiful and fair,
> Endued with wisdom's riches, heavenly, rare.

With the addition of Rupert's *Victory of Christ* and
Du Bartas' *Divine Weeks*, there has emerged a structure
whose major outlines and many of its important details
are precisely those utilized by Milton. With generally
less vital incidents from Valmarana, Valvasone, and related writers, together with commonplaces from patristic,
classical, and neo-classical literature, our eclectic structure
would stand complete.

To Book VII, and its story of the Creation, we then
may add Book VIII, not however as a sequel, but rather as
an integral part. Milton conceived, wrote, and first published the two books as one, the original Book VII. This
he did with good reason. As the following chapter may
suggest, the conventional story of God's creating the world
frequently included the basic themes presented so effectively in Book VIII.

CHAPTER IV

THE RAPHAEL-ADAM DIALOGUES

SO skilfully did Milton employ angelic ambassadors, that we sense only dimly the degree to which they guide and relate the story of *Paradise Lost*. We meet at one time a dialogue, at another a revelation, and in the third instance, a vision. Taken together, these variants of the method account for approximately one-half of the entire epic. Their most concentrated employment began with the latter half of Book V, shortly after God had commanded Raphael that he talk with Adam in Paradise. This visit opened with a dialogue, continued through Books VI and VII as successive revelations by the angel, and concluded in Book VIII with two further exchanges between Raphael and Adam. In discussing the three dialogues, I shall turn from that presented in Book V to the second and final dialogue of Book VIII, taking up last the preceding discourse on astronomy.

The purpose of Raphael's visit to Adam was both to warn him against Satan, and to provide him with essential knowledge. In assigning to Raphael, and subsequently to Michael, both the function of instructing Adam, and of conveying to him the decrees of God, Milton followed a widely respected and well-established tradition. Thomas Heywood wrote in representative lines that God employed angels to deliver messages to men, and that such archangels as Raphael and Michael 'are ambassadors, great matters to declare.' In the *Adamus Exsul* of Grotius, an angel informed Adam regarding cosmology and the wonders of the universe, of angelic life in heaven, and of man's conduct on earth. The earlier Cedrenus, following I Enoch, Syncellus, and probably other sources, said that the archangel Uriel instructed Adam concerning a variety of topics, including the Incarnation, the Flood, and the heavens. According to the Ethiopian text of I Enoch, the angel Raphael showed Enoch the tree of knowledge, and informed him of his parents' sin in eating its fruit; Gabriel had charge of Paradise; and Michael disclosed to Enoch 'all the secrets of the ends of heaven.' In the *Demonomachiae* of Valmarana, Michael related to the recently fallen Adam much the same history which in *Paradise Lost*, XI-XII, either is revealed by this angel or envisioned in his presence. The Michael of Andreini prophesied to Eve in the closing scenes of *L'Adamo*. Andrew Willet joined Pererius in questioning the belief, but repeated with him that 'some think . . . Adam and the woman were not ignorant of the fall of the angels, as Catharinus upon this place [Genesis 1. 28].' 'Because Adam yet lacked experience,' wrote Campanella, 'all learning was poured into him. '

But Adam and his angelic guest did not turn immediately to serious conversation. There came first, as a brief prelude, the hospitable reception of Raphael and his entertainment at dinner. As the scene opened, Adam called to his wife:

> Haste hither, Eve, and worth thy sight, behold
> Eastward among those trees what glorious Shape
> Comes this way moving; . . . Some great behest
>   from Heaven
> To us perhaps he brings, and will voutsafe
> This day to be our guest. But go with speed,
> And what thy stores contain bring forth, and pour
> Abundance fit to honor and receive our heavenly
> Stranger . . . She turns, on hospitable thoughts intent

> What choice to choose for delicacy best. . . .
> She gathers, tribute large, and on the board
> Heaps with unsparing hand. . . . So down they sat
> And to their viands fell. . . . Meanwhile at table
> Eve ministered naked, and their flowing cups
> With pleasant liquors crowned.

A modern reader may find incongruity, perhaps impropriety in Milton's scene. Nevertheless, Augustine, Du Bartas, and many intervening writers maintained that Scripture 'testifies angels have appeared to men as could not only be seen, but also touched.' The poet Vondel painted a related picture in the second act of the drama *Adam*. The spirit of Milton's passage also is that of numerous descriptions of Abraham's entertainment of the three angels. In keeping with such descriptions, his account 'presents a beautiful picture of domestic government,' and is both a 'commendation of' and a 'lesson in hospitality.' That the angelic guests of Abraham had for the time actual bodies and ate actual food, was among others the belief of Calvin, of the Roman Bishop Tostatus, and of the Anglican divine Andrew Willet. 'These angels,' said Willet with Calvin, 'as they were endued with true bodies for the time, so they did verily eat, as they did walk and speak, and do other actions of the body.' Further similarities between Genesis 18 and Milton's scene are found in the failure of Sarah and Eve to eat with the guests, and their overhearing the messages delivered by the angels, Sarah in her tent, and Eve, 'where she sat retired in sight.'

As Milton doubtless had planned, the eating together of Raphael and Adam provided an opportunity to present a somewhat complicated chain of argument, one more conveniently discussed in reverse order. The dual objective of this chain, if we may trust the poet's concluding statement, was first to point out to the then unfallen and immortal Adam his glorious prospects, and secondly to emphasize the necessity of obedience to God, if these prospects were to be realized. Speaking first of the food they had shared, Raphael declared to Adam:

> Wonder not then, what God for you saw good
> If I refuse not, but convert, as you,
> To proper substance. Time may come when men
> With angels may participate, and find
> No inconvenient diet, nor too light fare;
> And from these corporal nutriments, perhaps,
> Your bodies may at last turn all to spirit,
> Improved by tract of time, and winged ascend
> Ethereal, as we, or may at choice
> Here or in heavenly paradises dwell,
> If ye be found obedient.

Milton's emphasis upon the necessity of obedience to God, the major objective of his entire argument, stands as a peak of orthodoxy. As I have indicated in the preceding chapter, it was a traditional belief that man, unfallen and immortal, would gradually ascend or improve in status. To those who accepted this belief, there could be little of the heterodox in the related conception that the hypothetical unfallen Adam would have required food during his gradual ascent. In any event, Milton spoke quite as Augustine and Peter Lombard had spoken before him:

> Before Adam had sinned, his body had been created immortal in such a way that by assimilating nourishing food, it could be free from misery and death. The body of man therefore was formed incorruptible and immortal, insofar as man preserved his incorruptibility by observing the mandates of God. These mandates included one of particular importance: Adam must eat from only approved trees, and abstain from the for-

bidden tree of knowledge. By eating as God commanded, Adam would conserve the gift of immortality,
until, having multiplied his progeny, he came to the
period of life which the Maker desired. At this time, and
in accordance with his wish, he ate from the tree of life.
From this tree proceeded such perfect immortality that
he no longer required sustaining physical food.

In these words [commented Peter Lombard], Augustine patently holds that the body of the first man had
within it immortality. His body would have been preserved by the sustaining power of food until the time
of its translation into a better. He then would eat of the
tree of life, and make all immortal, so that his body
could not die. If Adam had stood fast, he would have
received from the tree of life complete immortality.

Milton's argument that Adam's body may in time turn
all to spirit rests on the conception that man, unfallen and
immortal, differed from angels in degree but not in kind.
Stated somewhat differently, both man and angel had
bodies similar in their basic substance, but different in the
extent to which this substance was refined. Supporting
this conception was the doctrine that in the beginning
God had created one first matter, and by giving to it
different forms and degrees of refinement, had produced
all things, including angels.

In setting forth this doctrine Milton moved beyond the
Aristotelian theory that the four elements of earth, air,
fire, and water, had developed from one prime matter. He
also passed the related belief that the primordial chaos,
to quote from the representative Mercator, 'comprehended
all the forms of things, substances, and qualities,' and had
'within its essence, the seed of all qualities and forms.'
Milton's thought was not that the various seed of many
things, each destined to develop according to its kind, had

existed from the beginning. His belief was that matter itself could be so modified by Deity that it gradually, and by degrees, would change to spirit.

The poet's doctrine of an evolving prime matter recently has been regarded as heretical, and as stamping him as a materialist. Precisely why we should consider materialistic a conception which, as Henry More logically demonstrated, ultimately resolved all things into spirit, and thus made the world of spirit the final end of all things, stands as yet undemonstrated. Be this as it may, it is doubtful if Milton believed heterodox either the doctrine, or the several ideas he associated with it. These inter-related conceptions had not been so considered by Origen, by Bonaventure, and by the author of a tractate assigned by Bonaventure and his age to Augustine. According to Origen:

> Physical bodily being . . . admits of diversity and variety of change, so that it is capable of undergoing all possible transformations, as, *e.g.*, the conversion of wood into fire. . . . Whatever we take as food, is converted into the substance of our body. . . . This universal matter possesses such properties as to enable it to be sufficient for all the bodies in the world which God willed to exist. . . . As we have remarked above, therefore, that material substance of the world, possessing a nature admitting of all possible transformations, is, when brought down to beings of a lower order, moulded into the crasser and more solid. When it becomes the servant of more perfect and more blessed beings, it shines in the splendor of celestial bodies, and adorns either the angels of God or the sons of the resurrection with the clothing of a spiritual body.

In discussing the question, 'Is the material from which are composed the bodies of angels, the same as the material of physical bodies?', Bonaventure turned to *The Wonders of the Sacred Scripture*, attributed by him to Augustine. In this book, he wrote, 'we see by the authority of Augustine, that "from the unformed matter which the omnipotent God first founded from nothing, he separated many species of all visible and invisible things; that is, of the sensible and insensible, the intellectual, and the comprehending." What does this mean?' In the subsequent conclusion, Bonaventure at least left the question an open one:

> According to various considerations, we may rightly say that angels and physical bodies are composed of the same substance. Profound indeed, and noble, as metaphysics, are those beliefs which judge all things to be the same. . . . Conceded, therefore, are the reasons which prove that in essence matter is the same in spiritual and corporeal being, as Augustine manifestly intimates in *The Wonders of the Sacred Scripture*, a book which may be considered the highest metaphysics.

It was not, however, the doctrine of one first matter that the Adam of *Paradise Lost* found most compelling. As Milton necessarily had planned, he responded instead to Raphael's concluding declaration that if man would rise to heaven, he must be obedient. Properly assisted by Adam's inquiry, Raphael then described the rebellion and battle in heaven, and related to man the difficulties he might face in rendering obedience to God. Further requests led successively to the story of Creation, and the dialogue on astronomy. The final Raphael-Adam dialogue, comprising the last two-thirds of Book VIII, returned to themes based primarily upon the second chapter of Genesis. The specific roots of Milton's narrative were verses 7-8, 15-25: the creation of man and his coming to Paradise; the subsequent creation of Eve, and her marriage to

Adam. Verses 9-14, a description of the Garden in Eden, Milton utilized in Book IV.

In charmingly intimate verse, Adam first informed Raphael of the feelings and experiences which came to him immediately following his creation. In full accord with Genesis, Milton described man as created outside the Garden:

> As new-waked from soundest sleep,
> Soft on the flowery herb I found me laid,
> In balmy sweat, which with his beams the sun
> Soon dried. . . . About me round I saw hill
> Dale, and shady woods, and sunny plains,
> And liquid lapse of murmuring streams. . . .
> Myself I then perused, and limb by limb
> Surveyed, and sometimes went, and sometimes ran
> With supple joints, as lively vigor led.

The conventional Du Bartas, writing in part under the caption, 'Adam admires the world in general,' previously had used comparable descriptions:

> In brief, it was a pleasant exercise,
> A labor liked, a pain much like the guise
> Of cunning dancers; who although they skip,
> Run, caper, vault, traverse, and turn and trip
> From morn till even; at night again full merry,
> Renew their dance, of dancing never weary. . . .
> Adam did admire the mansion rich and fair;
> The shady locks of forests. . . . Eden's earth
> Was then so fertile fat.

Pausing to rest upon a shaded bank, Adam soon fell asleep. In his dream, and in actuality, God brought him to the mountain of Paradise, the Garden in Eden. Awakening there, he soon discovered that 'what I saw of earth before, scarce pleasant seemed.' The Adam of Du Bartas likewise had found the world extremely beautiful—before he had seen the Garden:

> But when he once had entered Paradise,
> The remnant world he justly did despise.

Milton's Adam next glimpsed and talked with God, who shortly commanded that he taste not the fruit of the tree of knowledge:

>   He who was my guide
> Up hither from among the trees appeared,
> Presence divine. Rejoicing, but with awe,
> In adoration at his feet I fell submiss.
> He reared me, and, 'Whom thou sought'st I am,'
> Said mildly, 'Author of all this thou seest
> Above, or round about thee, or beneath.
> This Paradise I give thee; count it thine
> To till and keep, and of the fruit to eat.
> Of every tree that in the Garden grows
> Eat freely with glad heart; fear here no dearth.
> But of the tree whose operation brings
> Knowledge of Good and Ill, which I have set,
> The pledge of thy obedience and thy faith,
> Amid the garden by the Tree of Life—
> Remember what I warn thee—shun to taste,
> And shun the bitter consequence.'

Du Bartas recorded that 'man did converse in pleasant Paradise with heaven's great Architect, and happy there his body saw.' In the first discourse which followed Adam's creation, again as with Milton, the God described by Du Bartas commanded man to abstain from the tree of knowledge:

> 'Adam,' quoth he, 'the beauties manyfold
> That in this Eden thou dost here behold,
> Are all thine, only; enter, sacred race,

Come, take possession of this wealthy place . . .
I only ask one tree, whose fruit I will
For sacrament shall stand of Good and Ill.
Take all the rest, I bid thee; but I vow
By the unnamed name whereto all knees do bow,
And by the keen darts of my kindled ire,
More fiercely burning than consuming fire,
That on the Fruit of Knowledge if thou feed . . .
[You lose] the happy state thou hold'st of me.'

With this episode Milton completed development of
Genesis 2. 15-17. Had he continued to follow the sequence imposed by Scripture, he next would have expanded
verses eighteen to twenty: 'And the Lord God said, It is
not good that man should be alone; I will make him an
helpmeet for him. And out of the ground the Lord formed
every beast of the field, and every fowl of the air, and
brought them unto Adam to see what he would call them;
and whatsoever Adam called every living creature, that
was the name thereof. And Adam gave names to all cattle,
and to the fowl of the air, and to every beast of the field;
but for Adam there was not found a helpmeet for him.'
But Milton again departed from the order of Genesis.
He developed first the twentieth verse, and omitted entirely the preceding account of God's creating fowl and
beast. To the animals named by man, he added the fish,
unmentioned in Genesis 2. In a variation of perhaps greater
significance, Milton pictured the creatures coming before
Adam much as subjects would pay fealty to a feudal lord.
The speaker once more is Deity:

'Not only these fair bounds, but all the earth
To thee and to thy race I give; as lords
Possess it, and all things that therein live,
Or live in sea or air, beast, fish, and fowl.
In sign whereof, each bird and beast behold

After their kinds; I bring them to receive
From thee their names, and pay thee fealty
With low subjection. Understand the same
Of fish within their watery residence. . . .'
As thus he spake, each bird and beast behold
Approaching two and two, these cowering low
With blandishment; each bird stooped on his wing.

The *Divine Weeks* of Du Bartas first developed Genesis
2. 20, and took up subsequently verse eighteen. It omitted
reference to the second creation of beast and fowl, and
preserved the tradition which included the fish with them.
The picture of the naming of the creatures again is that
of a feudal lord and his subjects. In these lines, the author
addressed himself to Adam:

For, so soon as ever he had framed thee,
Into thy hands he put this monarchy;
Made all the creatures know thee for their lord,
And come before thee of their own accord;
And gave thee power, as master, to impose
Fit senseful names unto the host that rows
In watery regions; and the wandring herds
Of forest people; and the painted birds.

Continuing his dialogue with God, Milton's Adam lamented his loneness. He pointed out to the Father that
the animals 'rejoice each with their kind, lion with lioness,'
and that God fitly had combined them in pairs. In these
and related lines, Milton implied that Deity had served
the beast more generously than he had served man. This
argument, implicit in *Paradise Lost*, Du Bartas stated explicitly:

God, therefore, not to seem less liberal
To man, than else to every animal,
For perfect pattern of a holy love,
To Adam's half another half he gave.

But Adam's concern for a fitting mate proved unnecessary, because the Father had planned to give him a help-meet. In the words of Genesis, God then 'caused a deep sleep to fall upon Adam, and he slept; and he took one of his ribs, and closed up the flesh instead thereof. And the rib, which the Lord God had taken from man, made he a woman, and brought her unto the man.' In his version of these lines, Milton both added the detail that God closed Adam's eyes, and stressed the episode of Deity fashioning Eve from the extracted rib. As we might expect, he also conceived of the extraction in terms of contemporary surgery. These additions to Genesis proved equally attractive to Du Bartas:

> Even as a surgeon, minding off to cut
> Some cureless limb, before in ure he put
> His violent engines on the vitious member,
> Bringeth his patient to a senseless slumber . . .
> So God . . . sealed up his sparkling eyes . . .
> In brief, so numbed his soul's and body's sense
> That without pain opening his side, from thence
> He took a rib, which rarely he refined,
> And thereof made the Mother of mankind;
> Graving so lively on the living bone
> All Adam's beauties, that but hardly one
> Could have the lover from his love descried,
> Or known the bridegroom from his gentle bride.

In subsequent verses, Du Bartas surveyed the beauties of the newly created Eve. Not only had she 'a more smiling eye' than Adam, but:

> A smoother chin, a cheek of purer dye,
> A fainter voice, a more inticing face,
> A deeper tress, a more delighting grace,
> And in her bosom, more than lily white,
> Two swelling mounts of ivory, panting light.

No sooner Adam's ravished eyes did glance
On the rare beauties of his new-come half,
But in his heart he 'gan . . . calling her,
His love, his stay, his reed, his weal, his wife,
His other self, his help, him to refresh;
Bone of his bone, flesh of his very flesh.

Milton's Adam found equal pleasure, and equal amorous
delight, in the Eve whom God created for him:

The rib he formed and fashioned with his hands;
Under his forming hands a creature grew,
Man-like, but different sex, so lovely fair
That what seemed fair in all the world seemed now
Mean, or in her summed up, in her contained,
And in her looks, which from that time infused
Sweetness into my heart unfelt before,
And into all things from her air inspired
The spirit of love and amorous delight.
She disappeared, and left me dark; I waked. . . .
When, out of hope, behold her not far off,
Such as I saw her in my dream . . . I now see
Bone of my bone, flesh of my flesh, my self
Before me.

The traditional nature of Milton's description may
further be emphasized by turning to the *Psyche* of Joseph
Beaumont, sometime fellow of St. Peter's College, Cambridge. In this poem, published at London in 1648, Beaumont devoted more than a score of stanzas to Eve's many
excellencies. The Adam of Beaumont, in keeping with the
Adam of Milton, had envisioned Eve in a dream prior to
her coming before him. I begin with Beaumont's description of God creating Eve from the rib of Adam:

The bone he handled with such breeding art
That it dissolved into many more,
And yielded all materials for each part

Of an accomplished body; what before
Was nothing but a rib, is now alone
Blood, flesh, skin, entrails, sinews, muscles, bone.

And that the work might answer its sweet shop,
In which was formed no creature else but this,
The willing Garden's beauties he did crop
This Paradise of Paradise to dress:
All sweets and delicacies flowed thither,
And in one Eve were moulded up together.

Upon these precious cushionets did lie
Ten thousand beauties, and as many smiles,
Chaste blandishments, and genuine courtesy,
Harmless temptations, and honest guiles:
For heaven, though up betimes the maid to deck,
Ne'er made Aurora's cheeks so fair and sleek.

Her blessed bosom moderately rose,
With two soft mounts of lilies, whose fair top
Two cherry branches for their station chose,
And there their living crimson lifted up;
The milky countenance of the hills confessed
What kind of springs within had made their nest.

She walked; by that mild importunity
To break the chains of sleep which bound her spouse.
But he wakes more by powerful sympathy
Which on the sudden in his bosom glows:
At first he thought his dream had still possessed him,
And with a fairer apparition blessed him.

But by his wise and most discerning eyes,
Examining the graceful object, he
Pries into all the truth, and smiling cries:
This nothing but my other self can be;
From me she sprung, a woman from a man,
And is but Adam in reflection.

In Book IV of *Paradise Lost*, Adam brought Eve to the bower in Eden. She there decked her bridal bed, and heavenly choirs sung the hymenean. The two side by side were laid, nor turned, wrote Milton, 'Adam from his fair spouse, nor Eve the rites mysterious of connubial love refused.' In Book VIII of the epic, after the Creator had brought Eve to Adam, Milton partially repeated this scene. Adam again led Eve, blushing like the morn, to the nuptial bower. The choir of nature sang, and from the amorous bird of night came a hymenean which 'bid haste the evening star' to 'light the bridal lamp.' Such repetition may seem gratuitous, if indeed it does not suggest imperfect organization. However, the tradition which Milton thus far had followed in Book VIII demanded the epithalamium and marriage. At precisely this place, the representative Du Bartas included a section on the 'epithalamie or wedding song' of Adam and Eve, and in this section described their marriage.

Having completed his delightful picture of the espoused Adam and Eve, Milton wrote with equal charm upon the influence which feminine beauty exerts over masculine reason. He then turned to his major theme, one which Du Bartas had characterized as 'The commodities of marriage.' Milton, however, departed noticeably from Du Bartian thought, and, indeed, from concepts of love previously announced in Book IV. His major purpose was to relegate sex to a distinctly minor rôle, and to emphasize the importance in marriage of social and spiritual values. Human love, Milton declared through Raphael, should not descend to that of the animal. Guided by reason, it should ascend to heavenly love. We note with passing interest that Gregory the Great and Bonaventure had described one function of Raphael as warning mankind

against concupiscence; and that Milton's Raphael did not
neglect this duty:

> [Eve is] fair, no doubt, and worthy well
> Thy cherishing, thy honoring, and thy love;
> Not thy subjection. . . . Of that skill the more thou
> Knowest, the more she will acknowledge thee her
> Head, and to realities yield all her shows—
> Made so adorn for thy delight the more. . . .
> But if the sense of touch, whereby mankind
> Is propagated, seem such dear delight
> Beyond all other, think the same voutsafed
> To cattle and each beast; which would not be
> To them made common and divulged, if aught
> Therein enjoyed were worthy to subdue
> The soul of man, or passion in him move.
> What higher in her society thou findest
> Attractive, human, rational, love still;
> In loving thou dost well; in passion not,
> Wherein true love consists not. Love refines
> The thoughts, and heart enlarges—hath his seat
> In Reason, and is judicious; is the scale
> By which to heavenly love thou may'st ascend,
> Not sunk in carnal pleasure; for which cause ·
> Among the beasts no mate for thee was found.

With an eye upon the tragic first marriage, we easily
may read into Milton's lines echoes from his life with
Mary Powell. Bitter personal experience perhaps lent
vigor to poetic expression, but the ideas themselves are those
normally found in Christian discourses on marital relations.
Man, Calvin had said, should keep his affections in harmony with reason, should live modestly with his wife, and
cultivate 'mutual society.' Man and woman, wrote Willet,
are not one flesh 'only in respect to copulation, for so brute
beasts, but in respect of their bodies and minds.' David

Pareus viewed the divine end of holy wedlock as 'the mutual assistance of man and woman, not only for the generation of children, a thing also found among brutes . . . but chiefly because it called forth a truly benevolent life and a precious intimate society.' To Mercer, man and woman should be one less in the body and more in the union of their minds; Bonaventure stressed the necessity of spiritual union and intellectual love, and Goodman that of 'kind offices and mutual helps.'

By way of emphasizing Raphael's counsel, Milton caused Adam to repeat its major points:

> Neither her outside formed so fair, nor aught
> In procreation, common to all kinds . . .
> So much delights me as those graceful acts,
> Those thousand decencies, that daily flow
> From all her words and actions, mixed with love
> And sweet compliance, which declare unfeigned
> Union of mind, or in us both one soul.

Included within or at times suggested by Milton's lines are a number of themes sacred to the general tradition to which these verses belonged: the high place accorded intellect or reason (God's image in man); the beliefs that man was the ruler of woman and should not be directed or controlled by her; that he should rule her gently, cherish and protect her; and that woman was not the servant but the helper, comforting companion, and inspiring associate of man.

The poet's stressed reference to heavenly love suggests a work which I have mentioned repeatedly, the *Hymn* of Edmund Spenser. Milton definitely implied that heavenly love is the best and highest; and, if I read his lines aright, held firmly that grosser loves should be renounced. Spenser's *Hymn of Heavenly Love* went somewhat further than Milton, but a partial parallelism seems unquestionable:

> All other loves, with which the world doth blind
> Weak fancies, and stir up affections base,
> Thou must renounce, and utterly displace.

This parallelism has special interest because it suggests Milton's use of Spenser's *Hymn* both at the climactic point of Book VIII, and at the chronological opening of *Paradise Lost*, V, 577.

Remaining details include the unexpected explanation by Raphael that Adam's mate had not come from the animals lest he submerge himself in carnal pleasures. Precisely why the angel should introduce the idea of mixing species is not wholly clear. However, both Du Bartas and Andrew Willet followed their discussion of human cohabitation with explicit references to 'unnatural conjunctions.' More important is Adam's often criticized inquiry regarding the love of the angels. Among other theologians, Bonaventure and Thomas Aquinas discussed the question, with the latter considering it at great length. We also find the theme in Beaumont's *Psyche*, where, as in *Paradise Lost*, it followed immediately extended description of the love of Adam and Eve. Indeed, Beaumont's angel devoted the initial lines of one stanza to the love of man, and the four final lines to the love of his fellow spirits. To make more clear the context, I add two verses from a preceding stanza:

> Adam beholds himself more sweet in Eve,
> In him she reads herself more high and grave. . . .
> In this condition did they live and love,
> And each with other interchange their heart,
> Fairly transcribing our [the angelic] sweet life above,
> Where every angel's eye his soul doth dart
> Into his fellow's breast, that all may be
> In common blest by one felicity.

Beaumont's conception that angelic love called for an intermingling of one spirit with another represents basically the
conception set forth by Milton's blushing Raphael:

> Let it suffice thee that thou knowest
> Us happy, and without love no happiness.
> Whatever pure thou in the body enjoyest—
> And pure thou wert created—we enjoy
> In eminence, and obstacle find none
> Of membrane, joint, or limb, exclusive bars.
> Easier than air with air, if Spirits embrace,
> Total they mix, union of pure with pure
> Desiring, nor restrained conveyance need
> As flesh to mix with flesh, or soul with soul.

Among the three Raphael-Adam dialogues, only one
has consistently attracted the modern reader. This discourse is the famous dialogue on astronomy, wherein
'Adam inquires concerning celestial motions; is doubtfully
answered, and exhorted to search rather things more
worthy of knowledge.' Many facets of interest appear in
this extended discussion: the problem of its immediate
sources, its relationship to men and organizations active
in England, together with its place in an international controversy which shortly before had reached its height.
Equally vital questions concern the historical background
of the dialogue, its purpose and meaning, and the light
which it throws upon Milton. The first three of the six
points will be taken up in a subsequent chapter; I shall
consider here only the group last named.

The dialogue on astronomy contains no reference to the
conceptions most generally advocated by mid-seventeenth
century astronomers, the now forgotten geo-heliocentric
theory and the fourth system of the world. With perhaps
a satiric allusion to the complexities of the Ptolemaic hypothesis, it confines discussion to a triumvirate of cosmological

doctrines Through the mouth of Adam, Milton first presented the ancient theory of the daily axial rotation of the earth. This theory, one with widespread acceptance during Milton's day, fixed the rotating earth in the center of the cosmos. As the poet's magnificent verses tell us, this theory drew strong support from two axiomatic propositions, the first being that God and nature do nothing the more difficult way, and the second, that the ethereal globes of heaven are more noble than the gross earth. Well might Adam ask of Raphael why the immeasurable heavens should hasten about our sphere:

When I behold this goodly frame, this world,
Of heaven and earth consisting, and compute
Their magnitudes—this earth, a spot, a grain,
An atom, with the firmament compared,
And all her numbered stars that seem to roll
Spaces incomprehensible (for such
Their distance argues, and their swift return
Diurnal) merely to officiate light
Round this opacous earth, this punctual spot,
One day and night, in all their vast survey
Useless besides—reasoning, I oft admire
How nature, wise and frugal, could commit
Such disproportions, with superfluous hand
So many nobler bodies to create,
Greater so manifold, to this one use—
For aught appears—and on their orbs impose
Such restless revolution day by day
Repeated, while the sedentary earth,
That better might with far less compass move,
Served by more noble than herself, attains
Her end without least motion, and receives,
As tribute, such a sumless journey brought
Of incorporeal speed, her warmth and light:
Speed, to describe whose swiftness number fails.

In his partial denial of the validity of Adam's two arguments, Raphael advanced double the number. Paraphrasing Genesis 1. 14, he declared that God set before man his book of the heavens:

Wherein to read his wondrous works, and learn
His seasons, hours, or days, or months, or years;
This to attain, whether heaven move or earth,
Imports not.

We well may differ with Milton's contention that the only justifiable ends of astronomy are to raise wonder at God's work, and to develop a serviceable calendar. We cannot, however, dispute his definite implication that such a calendar can be built upon either a fixed or a rotating earth. To mention a commonplace, our accurate Gregorian calendar once rested upon the assumption of a central and unmoved earth. Milton stood here upon solid ground.

Raphael's next argument can best be described as ridicule. He first pictured Deity as including cosmological information among the divine secrets hidden from man. To be sure, he continued, God did leave the heavens to the disputes of astronomers:

Perhaps to move
His laughter at their quaint opinions wide
Hereafter, when they come to model heaven,
And calculate the stars; how they will wield
The mighty frame; how build, unbuild, contrive
To save appearances; how gird the sphere
With centric and eccentric scribbled o'er,
Cycle and epicycle, orb in orb.

Having demonstrated by dialectic that the theory of the earth's axial rotation is unnecessary to man, and that astronomical inquiry is both foolish and unavailing, the angel then answered directly the two propositions urged by Adam. Responding first to the second argument, he asserted that it failed to apply, for the noble heavens did not serve the lowly earth. They were rather the servants of man. As for the immeasurable space necessarily traversed by a revolving cosmos, declared Raphael, let this bespeak:

> The Maker's high magnificence, who built
> So spacious, and his line stretched out so far,
> That man may know he dwells not in his own—
> An edifice too large for him to fill—
> Lodged in a small partition, and the rest
> Ordained for uses to his Lord best known.
> The swiftness of those circles attribute,
> Though numberless, to his omnipotence.

However, said Raphael, his purpose was not to disprove the motion of the earth. Rather, he sought to demolish the arguments advanced by Adam in support of the theory. As a conclusion to the section, Raphael then reiterated the point that astronomical inquiry and investigation are useless and foredoomed to failure:

> God, to remove his ways from human sense,
> Placed heaven from earth so far, that earthly sight,
> If it presume, might err in things too high,
> And no advantage gain.

Subsequent to this reiteration of obscurantism, Milton attempted to describe the heliocentric hypothesis. He drew, however, upon a source many years out of date, for he thought in terms of the triple motion of the earth postulated by Copernicus in 1543. Kepler, in 1618, Galileo, in 1632, and all subsequent advocates of the hypothesis either ignored or specifically rejected the erroneously conceived third movement. Milton also set forth the notion that the earth's triple motion explained the progressive, retrograde, and stationary movements of the planets postulated by Ptolemaic astronomy. Actually, these imaginary movements are explained by one motion, the annual or orbital revolution of the earth about the sun. From discussion of the Copernican hypothesis, Raphael returned to that of the earth's axial rotation, and thence to the speculative doctrine that the moon is an inhabited world. Then followed a limited sketch of the Brunoian and Cartesian idea of other and inhabited solar systems. A further return to the earth's axial rotation concluded the poet's description of cosmological beliefs.

But the end was not yet. There remained the final indoctrination and its acceptance by Adam. In sum, Raphael urged man that he rest content with the revelations of Scripture, and not meddle with secrets proper to God:

> Solicit not thy thoughts with matters hid:
> Leave them to God above; him serve and fear . . .
> Joy thou in what he gives to thee, this Paradise
> And thy fair Eve; heaven is for thee too high
> To know what passes there. Be lowly wise;
> Think only what concerns thee and thy being;
> Dream not of other worlds, what creatures there
> Live, in what state, condition, or degree:
> Contented that thus far hath been revealed
> Not of earth only, but of highest heaven.

Properly convinced, Adam repeated with variations the lesson in obscurantism taught by the divine interpreter:

> How fully hast thou satisfied me, pure
> Intelligence of heaven, angel serene;
> And, freed from intricacies, taught to live
> The easiest way, nor with perplexing thoughts
> To interrupt the sweet of life, from which

God hath bid dwell far off all anxious cares,
And not molest us, unless we ourselves
Seek them with wandering thoughts, and notions vain!
　But apt the mind or fancy is to rove
Unchecked; and of her roving is no end,
Till warned, or by experience taught, she learn
That not to know at large of things remote
From use, obscure and subtle, but to know
That which before us lies in daily life,
Is the prime wisdom: what is more is fume,
Or emptiness, or fond impertinence,
And renders us in things that most concern
Unpractised, unprepared, and still to seek.
Therefore from this high pitch let us descend
A lower flight, and speak of things at hand
Useful; whence, haply, mention may arise
Of something not unseasonable to ask,
By sufferance, and thy wonted favor, deigned.

In sharp contrast with his scathing denunciation of cosmological inquiry stand Milton's compelling descriptions of the theories discussed. So marked is this contrast, that countless readers have regarded it as a contradiction, and have thought of the poet as presenting sympathetically the claims of the conceptions set forth in outline. Sympathy provides, however, the least acceptable explanation for the beauty of Milton's lines. His was the grand style, and in this style he described the palace which rose in hell, the crafty Satan who plotted the downfall of man, as well as the hypnotic serpent which tempted the unsuspecting Eve.

The author of a text on logic, and well versed in the works of the schoolmen, Milton knew thoroughly the method and requirements of dialectic. One must delineate accurately and without bias the argument of his opponent. This the poet did. He then might challenge the theory or contention in a number of ways, one of which called into question its importance. A second possible method proved that trustworthy and precise information could not be obtained, and therefore no dependable or accurate propositions could be advanced. A third plan attacked directly the pertinence of assumptions employed in support of the argument. These three methods, particularly the final two, Milton employed effectively in the dialogue. Having turned or demolished the propositions advanced by the affirmative, he had won the contest. In renaissance dialectic, as in modern debate, the burden of proof rested heavily upon the affirmative advocate. Be that as it may, Milton himself provided our most accurate evaluation of his purpose in the summary which precedes Book VIII: 'Adam inquires concerning celestial motions, is doubtfully answered, and exhorted to search rather things more worthy of knowledge. Adam assents.'

In its placing of Revelation above the concepts of astronomers, together with its condemnation of cosmological speculation, Milton's dialogue is a mirror reflecting countless religious works. During the second quarter of the third century, Hippolytus included within his *Philosophumena* an attack upon numerous physical hypotheses. Here he castigated variant phases of the doctrine of innumerable worlds, and described belief in them as heresy. Both the *Divine Institutes* of Lactantius and the *Epitome* ascribed to him censured scientific inquiry and the doctrine of a plurality of universes. Eusebius satirized at length the 'vain conceits' of philosophers, including their ideas regarding the position and motion of the earth. A century later, and much in the manner of Eusebius, Theodoret pitted the conflicting views of scientific speculators one against the other, and emphasized the 'discord' among them.

The more philosophic Augustine proved almost equally un-
sympathetic, and Isidore of Seville placed in his book of
heresies the doctrine of a plurality of worlds.

At the opening of the Seventeenth Century, the traditional religious opposition to non-Biblical astronomy remained vigorous. Godfrey Goodman paused in his *Fall
of Man* to mention and reject the motion of the earth;
and Valmarana found opportunity in his *Demonomachia*
to censure the doctrine of other inhabited globes. In
1635, John Swan criticized at length both this hypothesis and the Copernican theory. During the same year,
Thomas Heywood twice interrupted his *Hierarchy of the
Blessed Angels* to inveigh against a multiplicity of inhabited
earths. Within the decade which brought forth *Paradise
Lost*, Robert Heath attacked as sophistry the conception
'that there are more worlds than one,' and fifty pages later
sought to prove 'the deepest scholars are the shallowest
asses.' Especially offensive to Heath was the great John
Kepler, whose 'lunacy transported him beyond his new
world in the moon, into the third heaven and fantastic
Empyreum of those giddy chymeras.'

We cannot doubt that a custom established by anti-
scientific religious writers appreciably influenced Milton's
comments in the dialogue on astronomy. These writers did
not, however, lead the poet to place his animadversions
within Book VIII of *Paradise Lost*. This book stood originally as a part of Book VII, and with it retold the two
Biblical stories of the Creation. To hold fast to the hexameral tradition was to include within description of the
Creation some discussion of cosmological theories. The
discussion, commonly adverse, might be given in a gloss
on one or more of three days, the first, the second, or the
fourth. By the Seventeenth Century, comment on at least

two days had become somewhat general. A lengthy poem or commentary easily absorbed repetition of extended attacks upon astronomy and astronomical inquiry. This Milton's relatively brief summary of the Creation could not do. With one of his flashes of genius, the poet consolidated the traditional discussions and presented them immediately following the seven days of Creation.

Hexameral literature began early to attack extra-Biblical ideas concerning the heavens. In discussing the first day of Creation, Ambrose censured the doctrine of a plurality of worlds. Under the second day, Basil did likewise. A third hexameron by Eustathius, close friend of Basil, criticized the rotation of the earth on the first day, and the doctrine of other worlds on the second. I may add in passing that Eustathius's reference to the earth's rotation is the first I have noticed among fourth-century hexamera.

Eleven centuries later, and again under the first day of Creation, Bishop Tostatus declared at some length that the earth does not move. During the following century, the Sixteenth, Calvin attacked the plurality doctrine in his exposition of this day. However, he commented during the fourth day upon astronomy in general, and in contrast with Milton, defended it against aspersion. 'Moses makes two great luminaries,' wrote Calvin, 'but astronomers prove by conclusive reasons that the star of Saturn, which on account of its great distance, appears the least of all, is greater than the moon. Here lies the difference: Moses wrote in a popular style things which, without instruction, all ordinary persons endued with common sense are able to understand; but astronomers investigate with great labor whatever the sagacity of the human mind can comprehend. Nevertheless, this study is not to be reprobated, nor this science condemned, because some frantic persons are wont boldly to reject whatever is unknown to them.'

In harmony with the commentary on Genesis of Bishop Tostatus, that of Benedict Pererius argued on the first day against the motion of the earth. The erudite and influential Jesuit brought into play both Aristotle and the many scattered passages of Scripture believed to prove the mobility of heaven and the immobility of earth. The *In Genesin* of the protestant theologian David Pareus struck vigorously at the plurality doctrine both in his discussion of the works of this day and in a subsequent section. As centuries of hexameral writers had done before him, he confined censure to the atomistic school of Leucippus, Democritus, Epicurus, and the later Lucretius.

This school Andrew Willet likewise attacked in discussing the opening verse of Genesis. In setting forth other views, he disagreed with the idea of one first matter, but preceded Milton in following the conventional belief that heaven and earth were 'first created in the matter, afterwards perfected in form, and lastly beautified with their ornaments.' While discussing the light which God created on the first day, Willet noted that various Fathers 'think it was a bright and lightsome cloud, which was carried about, and gave light to the world, as Beda, Lyranus, the Master of the Sentences [Peter Lombard], et cetera. Others, that it was a light without a subject, afterwards fastened to the body of the sun, as Basil, *Homily in Genesis*, VI, 5. Others, that it was an exceeding bright shining light . . . afterwards dispersed into diverse bodies of the sun, moon, and stars, so Gregory Nazianzen and Theodoret.' The Angelican theologian concluded that from such examples 'we see how variable and inconstant men's opinions are, when they search into curious matters, and inquire after hid things.'

In the hexameron which opened *Purchas his Pilgrimage*, this English geographer and divine continued the customary attack upon the motion of the earth and the doctrine of other worlds. To this he added a specific censure of Copernicus, and declared in his conclusion that the 'strange and fantastical or phrenetical opinions of heretics or philosophers, which have otherwise related of the mystery of the Creation than Moses, they need not confuting.' By far the most extended discussion of the early Seventeenth Century came from a man of some scientific distinction, Marin Mersenne, who devoted more than fifteen hundred folio columns to exposition of the early chapters of Genesis. Scores of pages analyzed and rejected a wide variety of extra-Biblical cosmological conceptions, both ancient and modern. Among other ideas and themes utilized by Milton in his modest hexameron, Mersenne also discussed the belief that the angels assisted Christ, or God, in the creation of the world.

Such a representative and encyclopedic hexameral poem as the *Divine Weeks and Works* might be expected to include discussion of cosmological doctrines. This it does, with the result that on the first day of Creation, Du Bartas described and attacked the Democritian conception of a plurality of worlds. On the fourth, he censured the theory of the earth's daily rotation and the original Copernican hypothesis of its triple motion. He derided those who sought to number the stars, and, again as Milton did later, associated the vast sweep of the star-filled heaven with 'the unniggard hand of Majesty.' In the *Little Bartas* he once more wrote of the axial rotation of the earth, and in keeping with Milton's introductory lines on the Creation, described the earth as self-balanced:

> And the heavy earth, propless though downward tending,

Self-counterpoised, 'mid soft air suspending.

By what may be curious coincidence, the fourth day of the *Divine Weeks* discussed in sequence the earth's axial rotation and the original Copernican theory of its triple motion. Du Bartas also fell into the error of assuming that this triple motion solved the 'appearances of the stars;' that is, the phenomenon of the apparent retrograde, progressive, and stationary motions of the planets. As I have mentioned, only the earth's annual or orbital movement is required to explain this phenomenon. Having presented various arguments against the motion of our globe, the French poet declared:

> Armed with these reasons, 'twere superfluous
> To assail the reasons of Copernicus;
> Who to solve better of the stars the appearance,
> Unto the earth a three-fold motion warrants;
> Making the sun the center of this all.

Milton's partially similar account included the Keplerian idea that a magnetic virtue reposing in the sun and planets enabled the latter to traverse their orbits. As with Du Bartas, the word 'stars' refers to planets:

> What if the sun
> Be center to the world, and other stars
> By his attractive virtue and their own
> Incited, dance about him various rounds?
> Their wandering course, now high, now low, then hid,
> Progressive, retrograde, or standing still,
> In six thou seest; and what if, seventh to these,
> The planet earth, so steadfast though she seem,
> Insensibly three different motions move?
> Which else to several spheres thou must ascribe,
> Moved contrary with thwart obliquities.

CHAPTER V

THE COUNCIL IN HELL

THE shifting panorama of Milton's epic now has disclosed the coming of evil into heaven, the overthrow of Satan, and the creation of man and his world. From the new-born earth, the scene shifted to hell, where Milton developed the second preliminary step to the origin of evil among mankind. To this essential step he devoted the whole of Books I and II, so constructing his narrative that its center and heart became the council in hell.

This magnificent segment of *Paradise Lost* is at once the least and the most original part of Milton's poem. We meet in prodigal abundance unusually powerful dramatization, sustained poetic virtuosity, and a host of living characters. In no other books are theme and episode so vitalized. However, it is equally true that no other section employed such a number of conventional ideas. Few practices achieved more popularity than describing the horrors of hell, or presenting a catalog of pagan deities. As the work of Beaumont, Crashaw-Marini, Phineas Fletcher, Tasso, Vondel, and other writers may suggest, it was wholly conventional to place in hell a city, a court, or a palace, and to describe Satan either as sitting upon a throne or as surrounded by subordinates. Equally traditional were the idea of a council or gathering in hell, allusion to the battle lost in heaven, utterance of defiance to God, the decision to wage a new or second war on Deity, and initiation of a plan for the seduction of mankind.

Subsequent to the traditional opening invocation, Milton summarized briefly the circumstances which had brought Satan and his band to the fiery lake of hell. In making this digest, however, the poet turned to a new and different explanation of Lucifer's rebellion. We now hear nothing of Christ's exaltation, and Satan's hatred of the Son. Instead, we meet the more commonplace explanation which various early Fathers had wrung from Isaiah's condemnation of Nebuchadnezzar. Milton repeated faithfully this forced interpretation, according to which the Apostate fell through pride and a resulting desire to equal the Most High:

> The infernal serpent; he it was whose . . . pride
> Had cast him out from heaven, with all his host
> Of rebel angels, by whose aid, aspiring
> To set himself in glory above his peers,
> He trusted to have equalled the Most High;
> If he opposed, and, with ambitious aim
> Against the throne and monarchy of God,
> Raised impious war in heaven and battle proud,
> With vain attempt.

Exactly why Milton abandoned Christ's exaltation as the stated cause of Satan's revolt probably must remain a mystery. Nevertheless, its appearance in Book I would seriously have interfered with its employment, under quite different circumstances, in the closely related Book III.

With the apparent support of Matthew 8. 12, Luke 16. 26, and Revelation 22. 14-15, together with the example of various theologians and poets, Milton placed hell within the realm of chaos and eternal night. Its internal characteristics included the furnace of fire from Matthew 13. 42, and the burning lake of fire and sulphur, or brimstone, of Revelation 20. 10. The celebrated line, 'yet from those flames no light, but rather darkness visible,' expressed a conception long favored by writers. Basil had described the fire of hell as one which burns, but gives no light;

Gregory the Great, as a fire which burns but gives no
light; Thomas Heywood, as one which gives 'no lustre at
all.' Equally standard was the belief that 'the fire of hell
. . . doth always burn, but neither wasteth itself, nor that
which it burneth.'

The related ideas that hell gave forth extreme cold,
and contained ice so freezing that it burned the damned,
were not uncommon among religious writers. Giles and
Phineas Fletcher had described hell as a place 'flaming
in icy fires,' where sinners 'shall fry in ice,' and 'snow
should burn as fire.' The author of the anonymous *Discourse of Devils* pictured the torture of evil spirits as
'exceedingly aggravated' because 'excesses of cold and heat,
drought and moisture are continually raging among them.'
'Neither,' he added, 'is there any light or lustre to be seen
within their courts.' Such classical elements as the rivers
of Hades had entered Christian literature as early as the
Book of Enoch, and became extremely popular with the
Renaissance. I Enoch, whose descriptions at times approached those of *Paradise Lost*, also had placed hell within
a chaos:

> And I proceeded to where things were chaotic. And
> I saw there something horrible: I saw neither a heaven
> above nor a firmly founded earth, but a place chaotic
> and horrible. . . . And from thence I went to another
> place . . . more horrible than the former, [and saw] a
> great fire there which burned and blazed. . . . This place
> is the prison of the angels, and here they will be im-
> prisoned forever.

To the classical, patristic, and contemporary sources drawn
upon by Milton, Miss Marjorie Nicolson recently has
added his personal recollections of the volcanic Phlegraean
Fields. Her analysis, developed independently of earlier

discussions, finds that Milton obtained from this region colorful detail for his description of hell.

In the *Summa Theologica*, Thomas Aquinas said with Peter Lombard, Bonaventure, and many additional theologians, that having once chosen evil, the Devil must remain confirmed and obstinate in it. In brief, Satan must continue rebellious, proud, and envious of God, or, in the words of Anselm, 'it is impossible for the Devil to be reconciled.' The Apollyon of Fletcher declared he. had a 'heart unbroke, which neither hell can daunt, nor heaven appease,' and the Lucifer of Vondel called upon his associates 'with irreconcilable hate and furious craft, the heavens to persecute and circumvent.' The Satan of Beaumont vowed he would never surrender to God:

'I yield not yet; defiance, heaven,' said he,
'And though I cannot reach thee with my fire
Or scepter; yet my brain shall able be
To grapple with thee, nor canst thou be higher
Than my brave spite: know, though below I dwell,
Heaven has no stouter hearts than live in hell.'

From this respected tradition sprang the defiant Satan of *Paradise Lost*. Half-stunned, and chained on the fiery lake of hell, his first utterance breathed an implacable hatred:

What though the field be lost?
All is not lost—the unconquerable will,
And study of revenge, immortal hate,
And courage never to submit or yield:
And what is else not to be overcome?
That glory never shall his wrath or might
Extort from me. . . . In foresight much advanced,
We may with more successful hope resolve
To wage by force or guile eternal war,
Irreconcilable to our grand Foe.

This declaration of unyielding enmity, Milton's Satan voiced to Beelzebub, 'his nearest mate.' Long regarded as a major devil in treatises on pagan gods and idols, Beelzebub necessarily assumed such a rôle in literature. Vondel went further in his *Lucifer*, and gave to this devil precisely the position which he later held in *Paradise Lost*—that of the chief associate and 'privy councillor' of Satan. As we first meet Beelzebub, however, he stands primarily as a foil for his master. Replying to Satan's defiant outburst, he suggested that better than struggle unequally against God, the spirits should serve contentedly 'as his thralls,' and 'do his errands in the mighty deep.' The response thus invited gave posterity the famous lines:

> Fallen cherub, to be weak is miserable,
> Doing or suffering; but of this be sure—
> To do aught good never will be our task,
> But ever to do ill our sole delight.

Throughout his dialogue with Beelzebub, Satan remained bound to the burning lake, his gigantic body extending 'long and large,' and in bulk as massive as Leviathan or the Titans who warred on Jove. Such a monster was the 'Dragon' of Phineas Fletcher, 'bound in adamantine chains,' with 'his tail whose folds were wont the stars to shed, now stretched at length.' Suddenly, and unexpectedly, God released Satan from his chains:

> Forthwith upright,
> He rears from off the pool his mighty stature . . .
> Then with expanded wings he steers his flight
> Aloft, incumbent on the dusky air,
> That felt unusual weight.

Among other precedents for his flying monster, Milton had the dragon of Spenser's *Faerie Queene*. This dragon also proved too heavy for the air, spread out his wings, and moved somewhat as a ship:

Himself up high he lifted from the ground,
And with strong flight did forcibly divide
The yielding air, which nigh too feeble found
Her flitting parts, and element unsound,
To bear so great a weight. He, cutting way
With his broad sails, about him soared round.

Moving to the shore of hell, Satan voiced the third of
his memorable utterances. Much as a stout-hearted Colum-
bus discovering an unknown continent, he saluted the
new-found world:

Hail, horrors! hail
Infernal World! and thou, profoundest hell,
Receive thy new possessor—one who brings
A mind not to be changed by place or time.
The mind is its own place, and in itself
Can make a heaven of hell, a hell of heaven . . .
To reign is worth ambition, though in hell:
Better to reign in hell than serve in heaven.

Satan's vigorous last line expressed the sentiment of
Valvasone's Lucifer, who, having lost heaven, sought to be
lord of another world, and found satisfaction in the thought
of ruling over earth. Somewhat closer to Milton's character stands the Devil of Anthony Stafford: 'For as much as
I was once an angel of light, it was the will of Wisdom
to confine me to darkness, and to create me Prince thereof;
that so I, who could not obey in heaven, might command
in hell. And believe me, sir, I had rather control within
my dark diocese, than to reinhabit coelum empyreum,
and there live in subjection under check.' To this powerful tradition likewise belonged the Ruler of darkness described by Phineas Fletcher:

Once a bright and glorious star . . .
To be in heaven the second he disdains:
So now the first in hell and flames he reigns.

Having introduced to the reader both Satan and Beelzebub, Milton turned to the rebel host, lying scattered on
the flaming sea 'thick as autumnal leaves that strow the
brooks in Vallambrosa.' Roused by their leader, the
broken warriors filed upon the plain, coming in numbers greater than the hungry Goths which deluged Europe.
At this place, the poet made effective use of a patristic
conception much in vogue during the Seventeenth Century, one that regarded Satan's angels as the gods and
idols later worshipped by the heathen world. The result
was the famous 'epic catalog' of Book I.

Miltonic scholarship has long described this enumeration of devils as an imitation of the list of ships and heroes
found in the *Iliad*, Book II, and the related catalog presented in the *Aeneid*, Book VII. A lover of the Classics
who knew and respected Homer and Virgil, the poet un-
doubtedly was influenced by their use of the device.
Nevertheless, we should not ignore other and perhaps
more significant forces. *Paradise Lost* is replete with lists
of various kinds, and as his *Commonplace Book* tells us,
Milton had early a passion for cataloging. He also knew,
among others, of the catalogs employed by Tasso in
Jerusalem Delivered, Book I, and by Spenser in the *Faerie
Queene*, II, x. Steeped in the religious literature current
during the Seventeenth Century, he had some acquaintance
with such enumerations of idols and heathen gods as were
set forth by Augustine, Cedrenus, Cowley, Heywood,
Ross, Scot, and Selden, to say nothing of the multitude of
works cited by this group. The practice of cataloging
heathen deities was unquestionably a commonplace.

To picture the pagan gods as an army of embattled warriors appears somewhat rare. Milton had however a substantial precedent in the English poem *Davidëis*, published
during the particular year when he probably worked upon

Book I. Cowley's enumeration suggests, but does not reach the magnitude achieved by Milton:

> Far through an inward scene an army lay,
> Which with full banners a fair fish display . . .
> Moloch, their bloody god, thrusts out his head;
> Grinning, through a black cloud . . . he still did eat
> New roasted babes, his dear delicious meat . . .
> Down went the calves with all their gold and cost . . .
> Like end Astarte's horned image found . . .
> The double Dagon neither nature saves.

Among the many lists of idols easily available to Milton, that closest to his catalog occurs in the popular *Pansebeia* of Alexander Ross. First published in London in 1653, this *View of all Religions* reached a second edition in 1655, and a fourth in 1664. An edition which included both English and Dutch texts reached a fifth impression in 1671; and in 1666, 1667, and 1669 there were published translations in French and German. Such popularity bespeaks both its influence and its conventionality. With minor exceptions, Ross discussed each pagan god or deity named by Milton within a single and relatively limited section, the second half of 'The Religions of Asia.' He also made it a practice to condemn the idols which he described.

We may note that shortly after Milton composed *Lycidas*, Ross had both preached and printed a sermon attacking the corruption of the English clergy. Some years later he published an annotated translation of Wolleb's *Christian Divinity*, a theological compendium from which Milton borrowed liberally in writing *The Christian Doctrine*. As a subsequent chapter will show, the poet turned to Ross when he composed the Raphael-Adam dialogue on astronomy.

My present purpose however is not to urge Milton's indebtedness to the catalog of the English divine. The point is rather that having assembled the host of Satan, Milton employed such a pattern as that found in the generally conventional *Pansebeia* of Alexander Ross, and enumerated and condemned the heathen gods and religions which surrounded and on occasion seduced the children of Israel. In comparing the two catalogs, I normally follow the sequences used by Milton. Occasional variations excluded, the sequences of *Paradise Lost* are precisely the reverse of comparable enumerations by Ross. I give first Milton's poetical description:

> First, Moloch, horrid king, besmeared with blood
> Of human sacrifice, and parents' tears;
> Though, for the noise of drums and timbrels loud,
> Their children's cries unheard that passed through
> Fire, to his grim idol. Him the Ammonite
> Worshipped . . . Next Chemos, the obscene dread of
> Moab's sons. . . . Peor his other name, when he
> Enticed Israel in Sittim, on their march from Nile,
> To do him wanton rites, which cost them woe;
> Yet thence his lustful orgies he enlarged
> Even to that hill of scandal.

[Ross] Moloch or Molech, from Malach, to reign, was a great idol among the Moabites and Ammonites . . . to whom the superstitious Gentiles and Jews also offered their sons and daughters to be burned. The Moabites worshipped Chemosh. Baal-Phegor or Peor, that is, the gaping or naked lord, so called from the naked posture in which he was worshipped. . . . Some take him for Priapus [son of Bacchus and Venus].

From the deities of the Moabites and Ammonites, Milton turned to the gods of the Babylonians, with a discussion of which Ross had opened section two of *Pansebeia*. The first description is again that of *Paradise Lost:*

With these came they who, from the bordering flood
Of old Euphrates to the brook that parts
Egypt from Syrian ground, had general names,
Of Baalim and Ashtaroth—Those male,
These feminine. . . . For those the race of
Israel oft forsook their Living Strength . . .
Bowing lowly down to bestial gods, for
Which their heads, as low bowed down.

[Ross] the ancient Babylonians . . . worshipped
divers gods, or idols rather; the two chief were Belus,
or Bel, or Baal, by whom they meant Jupiter; the other
was Astaroth . . . by whom Juno was understood. . . .
Divers ways they had in worshipping of their idols, sometimes by bowing the head, sometimes by bending the
knee, sometimes by bowing or prostrating the whole
body.

Having described in a second independent section of
Book I the principal gods of the Babylonians, the poet
returned in a third unified passage to a second group included by Ross in his account of the religions and idols
of the Syrians. The survey of Milton, in keeping with that
of Ross, alluded to Ezekiel 8. 14, and described briefly
the apostasy of King Ahaz. In the verse cited, the prophet
Ezekiel records that Jaazaniah 'brought me to the door of
the gate of the Lord's house, which was toward the north;
and, behold, there sat women weeping for Tammuz:'

                        With these in troop
Came Astoreth, whom the Phoenicians called
Astarte, queen of heaven, with crescent horns;
To whose bright image nightly by the moon
Sidonian virgins paid their vows and songs.

[Ross] The Phoenicians . . . worship Astarte in
the form of a sheep. . . . Astaroth or Astarte was goddess of the Sidonians; the word signifieth a flock of

sheep, or sheep fold, . . . and in the form of a sheep
they worshipped the moon.

> Thammuz came next behind,
> Whose annual wound in Lebanon allured
> The Syrian damsels to lament his fate
> In amorous ditties all a summer's day
> (While smooth Adonis from his native rock
> Ran purple to the sea—supposed with blood),
> Of Thammuz yearly wounded. The love tale
> Infected Sion's daughters with like heat,
> Whose wanton passions in the sacred porch
> Ezekiel saw.

[Ross] *Gods of the Syrians.* Thammuz, mentioned
[by] Ezekiel 8. 14, is by Jerome taken for Adonis. . . .
In the temple of Venus were celebrated the annual rites
of Adonis, . . . to whom they perform solemn obse-
quies. . . . This Adonis is that Thammuz, Ezekiel 8. 14,
as Saint Jerome thinks, for whom the women did mourn.

> Next came one who mourned in earnest . . .
> Dagon his name, sea-monster, upward man
> And downward fish; yet had his temple high
> Reared in Azotus . . . and Accaron and Gaza's
> Frontier bounds. . . . Him followed Rimmon . . .
> He also against the house of God was bold . . .
> Ahaz, his sottish conqueror, whom he drew
> God's altar to disparage, and displace
> With one of Syrian mode.

[Ross] Dagon, from dag, a fish, because from the
naval downward he was made in the form of a fish,
but upward like a man. This was a great idol among the
Philistines, and thought to be the same as Neptune or
Triton.

Gods of the Syrians. King Ahaz no sooner gave himself
to idolatry, but he presently shows his sacrilegious cove-

tousness in robbing the house of the Lord of its wealth, 2 Chronicles 28.

Following his description of the Phoenician, Philistine, and Syrian idols, Milton characterized the heathen deities which came from Egypt to infect Israel. Then marched the fictitious Belial—to be discussed last—and on his heels a trio from the many gods of ancient Greece:

> After these appeared
> A crew who under names of old renown—
> Osiris, Isis, Orus, and their train—
> With monstrous shapes and sorceries abused
> Fanatic Egypt and her priests to seek
> Their wandering gods disguised in brutish forms
> Rather than human. Nor did Israel 'scape
> The infection, when their borrowed gold composed
> The calf in Oreb.

[Ross] Egypt may be called the mother of all superstition and idolatry, worshipping the sun and moon under the names of Osiris and Isis. . . . They multiplied their gods so fast, that every beast, spring, river, tree, . . . had its own peculiar deity. . . . Their deified beasts . . . were fed by their priests in their temples with choice food; when any dieth, it is wrapped in clean linen and embalmed, and buried in a consecrated place with much lamentation. . . . The Egyptian god Osiris . . . after his death was honored under these shapes . . . dogs, oxen, and other beasts.

We may admire the madness of those men, who being made after the image of God, so subject and enslave themselves to dead images, to senseless blocks and stones. . . . They can part from their gold and silver, their jewels and ear-rings to make them a golden calf.

> The rest were long to tell;
> Though far renowned the Ionian gods—of Javan's

> Issue held gods, yet confessed, later than
> Heaven and earth, their boasted parents. . . .
> Jove usurping reigned . . . [and] Saturn old
> Fled over Adria to the Hesperian fields.

[Ross] The whole story of Jupiter . . . does testify
he was but a man; and if we look on his . . . impiety
against his father Saturn, whom he drove out of his
kingdom, and forced to hide himself in Italy; if, I say,
we consider these things, we must needs say, that he
was so far from being a god, that he scarce deserved
the name of a man.

In the epic catalog of *Paradise Lost* one deity had no
place of origin, and stood as a personification of vicious-
ness which expressed itself in lust, violence, injury and outrage, drunkenness and rape. This was the despicable Belial:

> Than whom a spirit more lewd
> Fell not from heaven, or more gross to love
> Vice for itself. To him no temple stood
> Or altar smoked; yet who more oft than he
> In temples and at altars.

Such an idol does not appear in Scripture, nor does he
represent any known god of Palestine, of Egypt, or of
Greece. He is more a representative of the sins which
Christians declared proceeded from idolatry; he is in effect
its evils personified. In *Pansebeia* Ross twice described
pagan gods who had 'neither temples, altars, nor images,'
and four paragraphs preceding attacked, and in effect personified idolatry. He gave to it no place of origin or activity; from it came all sin, and particularly 'carnal un-
cleanness.' Specifically, it occasioned 'murders, rapine . . .
intemperance . . . . adultery, fornication, and sodomy.'
The Belial of *Paradise Lost* is a character which combined
Ross's personification of idolatry and his gods who had

neither temple nor altar. I may add that in religious literature of the Seventeenth Century, Belial frequently personified the varied evils attributed to idolatry.

Although Milton was well acquainted with the heathen gods described in the catalog, he apparently obtained direct assistance from such a work as *Pansebeia*. In the poem on the Nativity he wrote briefly of a number of these deities, 'Peor and Baälim . . . moonèd Ashtaroth' and others. However, because he was familiar with these gods, and had written concerning them, it is not without significance that the combination of the nativity poem, 'Peor and Baälim,' became in the catalog, 'Baalim and Ashtaroth—those male, these feminine.' Similarly, 'moonèd Ashtaroth' became 'Astoreth, whom the Phoenicians called Astarte.' In *Pansebeia* the combination is Belus or Baal and Astaroth— Jupiter and Juno, by implication male and female. Likewise Astaroth of the Sidonians is Astarte of the Phoenicians. Milton's general thesis held that the pagan deities were fallen angels; Ross repeatedly described them as devils. The latter also declared that the gods of Greece were men; the poet so departed from his general thesis as to suggest they were not of spiritual origin. The reason which Ross gave for his statement that the Grecian gods were human beings, is that they conducted themselves as men. Particularly did he emphasize the family relationships of these gods, and pointed the finger of scorn both at the cruelty of Saturn, and the impiety of Jupiter, who drove his father from his kingdom, and forced him to hide in Italy. Many were the things which such a classicist as Milton could have said regarding the Grecian gods, but the one point he paused to stress was their family relationships.

For the necessary prelude to a digression on the nature of spiritual beings, we return to the first Raphael-Adam dialogue. During the initial stage of his conversation with

Adam, Raphael not only ate terrestrial food, but described
all angels as composed of basically the same substance as
man. Although not heretical, this belief was scarcely the
conventional one. The traditional conception was that
which Milton set forth in the epic catalog, where he described all spirits as non-corporeal:

> Spirits, when they please
> Can either sex assume, or both; so soft
> And uncompounded is their essence pure;
> Not tied or manacled with joint or limb,
> Nor founded on the brittle strength of bones,
> Like cumbrous flesh; but, in what shape they choose,
> Dilated or condensed, bright or obscure,
> Can execute their aery purposes,
> And works of love or enmity fulfill.

'The best theologians assert,' wrote Heywood in his
Hierarchy, that angels 'are substances intelligent, immortal,
incorporeal,' and 'void of all matter.' Spirits and devils,
asserted the author of the anonymous *Discourse on Devils*,
'as they are capable of increasing into distinct and separated
substances, so are they likewise again contracted.' The
nature of spirits, 'whether heavenly or hellish, being to
dilate or contract themselves into a narrow compass, as
they please, . . . in a moment they can be as big in circumference as an hundred worlds, or on a sudden reduce
themselves to the compass of an atom.' In the *Discovery of
Witchcraft*, Reginald Scot discussed the equally commonplace idea that spirits made or selected the bodies in which
they appeared.

When he described the wounded Satan as 'gnashing for
anguish,' Milton utilized a further current belief. As stated
by Scot in the *Discovery*, the belief held 'that the bodies
of spirits and devils can feel and be felt, do hurt, and be

hurt.' This middle-ground interpretation of the nature of spirits, the poet employed at various places in his epic. Perhaps the most outstanding instance occurs in Book V, where the joyous angels of heaven quaffed ruby nectar, and fed on mellifluous dews and pearly grain. Interpreted literally, the King James Version of Psalm 78. 24-25 supported adequately such a notion. Speaking of God's care of his people, the Psalmist wrote that the Father 'had rained down manna upon them to eat, and had given them of the corn of heaven. Man did eat of angels' food; he sent them meat to the full.' The Beelzebub of Vondel's *Lucifer* spoke of 'our . . . food celestial,' and Du Bartas depicted the angels as 'carousing nectar of eternity.'

Having completed his catalog of pagan idols, Milton brought the fallen angels before Satan. So far as my reading has progressed, such a gathering resulted immediately in a council. Without exception, the assembled group then decided to wage a second war on Deity by seducing mankind. This traditional pattern Milton utilized, but in doing so, made significant departures from custom. His first variation consisted in treating the gathering as no more than a preliminary meeting, one which suggested an attack upon man, but postponed development of a plan until a formal council could be called. Use of this procedure doubtless resulted from Milton's official experience as Latin Secretary. A second variation was the building of Pandemonium, the palatial edifice wherein the grand council should convene. By these two departures, together with others which were to follow, Milton heightened suspense in a time-worn story whose outcome every contemporary knew well in advance.

During the preliminary assemblage of his warriors, Satan appeared in a rôle both new and old. He remained the

proud and defiant leader, but for the first time displayed
the human qualities of pity and remorse:

> Their dread commander . . . above the rest
> In shape and gesture proudly eminent,
> Stood like a tower. His form had yet not lost
> All her original brightness, nor appeared
> Less than archangel ruined, and the excess
> Of glory obscured. . . . Darkened so, yet shon
> Above them all the Archangel; but his face
> Deep scars of thunder had intrenched, and care
> Sat on his faded cheek, but under brows
> Of dauntless courage, and considerate pride
> Waiting revenge. Cruel his eye, but cast
> Signs of remorse and passion, to behold
> The fellows of his crime, the followers rather—
> Far other once beheld in bliss—condemned
> Forever now to have their lot in pain. . . .
> Thrice he assayed, and thrice, in spite of scorn,
> Tears, such as angels weep, burst forth; at last
> Words interwove with sighs found out their way:
> 'O myriads of immortal spirits! O Powers
> Matchless, but with the Almighty! . . . Who
>   overcomes
> By force hath overcome but half his foe.
> Space may produce new worlds, whereof so rife
> There went a fame in heaven that he ere long
> Intended to create, and therein plant
> A generation whom his choice regard
> Should favor equal to the sons of heaven.
> Thither, if but to pry, shall be perhaps
> Our first eruption. . . . But these thoughts
> Full counsel must mature. Peace is despaired;
> For who can think submission? War, then, war
> Open or understood, must be resolved.'

More than a half-century prior to *Paradise Lost*,
Thomas Nash wrote that before their fall, the bodies of

the apostate spirits 'were bright and pure,' but 'after their transgression, they were obscured with a thick, fiery matter.' Quoting Gregory the Great, Thomas Aquinas stated that although Satan had 'lost beatitude, still he has retained a nature like to the angels.' In a further section of the *Summa Theologica*, the Saint wrote that 'the demons are darkened by privation of the light of grace,' and experience 'fear, sorrow, joy, and the like, insofar as they denote simple acts of the will. . . . The Devil is punished with the grief of sorrow.' Similar ideas prevailed during Milton's generation, when the author of the *Discourse of Devils* declared them 'capable of hunger, grief, passion, and vexation.' In keeping with Milton, Marini combined these ideas in describing the fallen but rebellious Satan:

> He calls to mind the old quarrel, and what spark
> Set the contending sons of heaven on fire . . .
> He tossed his troubled eyes, embers that glow . . .
> While new thoughts boiled in his enraged breast,
> His gloomy bosom's darkest character,
> Was in his shady forehead seen expressed.
> The forehead's shade and grief's expression there . . .
> Those stings of care that his strong heart oppressed,
> A desperate, 'Ah me,' drew from his deep breast . . .
> 'And yet whose force fear I? Have I so lost
> Myself? My strength too with my innocence? . . .
> Heaven saw us struggle once, as brave a fight,
> Earth now shall see, and tremble at the sight.'

As we have noted, the preliminary convocation of *Paradise Lost* reached the important decision that war, direct or indirect, must be waged. The precise nature of attack, however, should be determined only after ordered consultation. This consultation demanded a fitting edifice, and such a structure Mammon and Mulciber set out to

provide. The result was Pandemonium, 'high capital of
Satan and his peers.' Milton's description of the palace
shows evidence of indebtedness to Spenser, but this question is best discussed in a later chapter. The impressive
edifice completed, a trumpet assembled the angels, and the
weighty consultation began.

According to tradition, the infernal council opened
with Satan given the dominant position. Quite as traditionally, it closed with a plan to obtain revenge upon God by
seducing mankind. These twin traditions are admirably
exemplified by the *Lucifer* of Vondel. The indomitable
hero of the Dutch poet:

> In that dim, infernal consistory,
> High-seated 'mid his Councillors of State
> With bitter rage 'gainst God he thus began:
> 'Ye Powers, who for our righteous cause have borne
> With such fierce pride, this injury, 'tis time
> To be revengèd for our wrongs. . . . 'Tis my design
> Both Adam and his seed now to corrupt.'

In Milton's immortal lines:

> The great Seraphic Lords and Cherubim
> In close recess and secret conclave sat,
> A thousand demi-gods on golden seats
> Frequent and full. After short silence then,
> And summons read, the great consult began.
>   High on a throne of royal state, which far
> Outshon the wealth of Ormus and of Ind . . .
> Satan exalted sat. . . . And, by success untaught,
> His proud imaginations thus displayed. . . .
> 'For, since no deep within her gulf can hold
> Immortal vigor, though oppressed and fallen,
> I give not heaven for lost . . . There is a place—
> If ancient and prophetic fame in heaven

Err not—another world, the happy seat
Of some new race, called man, about this time
To be created like to us, though less
In power and excellence. . . . Though heaven be shut,
And heaven's high Arbitrator sit secure
In his own strength, this place may lie exposed . . .
Some advantageous act may be achieved
By sudden onset—either with hell-fire
To waste his whole creation, or possess
All as our own, and drive, as we are driven,
The puny habitants; or, if not drive,
Seduce them to our party. . . . This would surpass
Common revenge, and interrupt His joy
In our confusion, and our joy upraise.

A further example of the council in hell tradition may be had from Phineas Fletcher, who several decades prior to *Paradise Lost* painted a scene comparable to Milton's. In the opening canto of the *Apollyonists* we meet 'a full foul senate' gathered in hell's 'deep conclave.' As with Milton, appropriate silence preceded deliberations:

At the midst, but lowest (in hell's heraldry
The deepest is the highest room), in state
Sat lordly Lucifer. His fiery eye, much
Swollen with pride, but more with rage and hate,
As censor mustered all his company,
Who round about with awful silence sat. . . .

As the infernal council progressed, Milton made further contributions to its traditional treatment. For the first and most vital addition, he provided new power and veri-similitude by assigning to different characters diverse and conflicting rôles. His second variation made Beelzebub, not Satan, the sponsor of the plot which challenged God by seducing man. Apparently in deference to tradition, he stated with emphasis that the plot had been devised, and in part first proposed by Lucifer. Among the poet's four contrasting characters, the first to rise in council was Moloch:

> [Satan] ceased; and next him Moloch, sceptered king,
> Stood up—the strongest and the fiercest spirit
> That fought in heaven, now fiercer by despair.
> His trust was with the Eternal to be deemed
> Equal in strength, and rather than be less
> Cared not to be at all; with that care lost
> Went all his fear: of God, or hell, or worse . . .
> 'My sentence is for open war. Of wiles,
> More unexpert, I boast not; them let those
> Contrive who need, or when they need; not now.
> For, while they sit contriving, shall the rest—
> Millions that stand in arms, and longing wait
> The signal to ascend—sit lingering here,
> Heaven's fugitives, and for their dwelling-place
> Accept this dark opprobrious den of shame,
> The prison of his tyranny who reigns
> By our delay? No! let us . . . force resistless way
> Turning our tortures into horrid arms
> Against the Torturer. . . . What can be worse
> Than to dwell here, driven out from bliss, condemned
> In this abhorred deep to utter woe;
> Where pain of unextinguishable fire
> Must exercise us without hope of end.'

Among partial analogues of Milton's council, the closest I have met occurs in the previously cited first canto of Fletcher's *Apollyonists*. As the passage quoted may have shown, Fletcher's council opened with Lucifer seated in majesty and surrounded by his silent vassals. However, instead of a series of discourses, as with Milton, there followed one extended declamation. At the conclusion of this speech, rather than at the beginning of the council,

Lucifer requested that 'now you States of hell give your advice.' Despite these differences, important similarities exist, and we find Fletcher's Apostate setting forth themes assigned by Milton to Moloch and Belial. That the poet did assign themes to figures created in part for them, is suggested by the new characterizations of these devils which appeared in Book II. Moreover, Moloch here received credit for a rôle in the celestial battle which he did not play—that of the strongest and fiercest warrior of the conflict—and is described as having refused to be less than, or second to God. Such had been the rôle of Satan.

In Milton's infernal council, Moloch insistently demanded open war with God, and defended this war by emphasizing the sad condition of the fallen angels. Contributory to their lamentable state was the loss of bliss, an expression which to the Seventeenth Century meant a loss of heaven and God. These basic themes, Fletcher's character voiced with feeling and power:

> But me, oh never let me, spirits, forget
> That glorious day, when I your standard bore,
> And scorning in the second place to sit,
> With you assaulted heaven, his yoke foreswore.
> My dauntless heart yet longs to bleed and sweat
> In such a fray. The more I burn, the more I hate . . .
> Where are those spirits? Where that haughty race,
> That durst with me invade eternal light? . . .
> Dare we with heaven, and not with earth to fight? . . .
> But we fast pinioned with dark fiery chains
> Shall suffer every ill, but do no more,
> The guilty spirit here feels extremest pains,
> Yet fears worse than it feels, and . . . sore complains:
> Oceans of ills without an ebb or shore . . .
> And worst of all, God's absent presence gives
> A thousand living woes.

In the council of *Paradise Lost*, Belial next arose. Departing sharply from two previous rôles, he now appeared the crafty dissembler, whose 'tongue dropped manna,' and 'could make the worse appear the better reason.' His mould was that of the Belial of Vondel, who had no master in concealment, and 'varnished smooth his face with dissimulations's hue.' Regarded from a different point of view, Milton's Belial duplicated the Beelzebub of Book I, who there urged upon Satan a policy of appeasement. As such a cog in the narrative of Book II, he provided a dramatic contrast for the enraged and bellicose Moloch. His principal contentions were two: the first, that the punishment meted to the rebellious angels was just; and the second, that upon their good behaviour God 'in time may much remit his anger.' These themes, with the second stated ironically, also appear in Fletcher's extended discourse:

> This be our comfort, we did get and win
> The fires and tortures we are whelmed in . . .
> Shall we repent, good souls? or shall we 'plain? . . .
> Lay down our spite, wash out our sinful stain?
> May be he'll yield, forget, and use us well.

Milton's third character of the dialogue, the traditionally avaricious Mammon, quickly urged a further plan—the development of an empire within hell, and exploitation of its gems and gold. The assembled angels long applauded this project, but as tradition had predetermined, they soon determined to seek revenge by seducing mankind. Again in harmony with the dominant tradition, Milton next described Satan as setting forth to destroy Adam. With the council dissolved, the evil spirits scattered over and throughout hell, choosing such diversions as opportunity or interest might dictate. The poet's subsequent picture of the angels discussing theology, indulging in music, and investigating

THE COUNCIL IN HELL

natural phenomena had of course the support of accepted belief. As Wolleb and Ross remarked, they retained after the fall both 'natural and experimental knowledge.' According to Heywood, 'theologists affirm them pregnant in theology. In music they are skilled, expert in physics, in grammar, logic and arithmetic.' Milton likewise observed the tradition that each spirit in hell retained the hierarchial rank which he had possessed in heaven. Here, however, as elsewhere in *Paradise Lost*, the poet did not list in full the nine recognized orders of Angels, Archangels, Principalities, Powers, Virtues, Dominions, Thrones, Cherubim, and Seraphim.

If Satan may stand as Milton's greatest character, the monsters Sin and Death are surely his most striking. Brought together by the poet, the three characters could not but produce a situation of tremendous power. Of such power is the episode wherein the earth-bound Satan faced these monsters, and forced a passage through the gates of hell. God had commanded Sin and Death that they hold unceasing watch over the gates, but Sin first, and later Death, proved faithless to their trust. Yet Sin had the justification that she was the daughter of Satan, born like Minerva from the head of her father. The first of women, she was sired by her parent, and gave birth to Death. These related conceptions, in keeping with other ideas utilized by Milton, rested indirectly upon Scripture. With *lust* interpreted as representing Satan, James 1. 15 lent strong support to this belief: 'Then the lust, when it hath conceived, beareth sin; and the sin, when full-grown, bringeth forth death.' During the Middle Ages, if Lydgate's account may be taken as representative, Satan was regarded as having committed incest with his daughter. Other analogues by Peyton and Purchas characterized Sin as 'a foul misshapen monster,' and Death as 'the deformed issue of Sin.' Various English writers of the Seventeenth Century, including Joseph Beaumont and Phineas Fletcher, pictured one or both at the mouth of hell.

Milton patently had the support of tradition for the major outlines of his two monsters. In Fletcher, and to an incidental degree in Spenser, he had also a precedent for many vital details. The awe-inspiring Death, Miltonic creation that he largely is, has much in common with two figures described by Spenser's disciple. The first of Fletcher's characters is Black Despair, inseparable companion of Sin:

> The second in this rank was Black Despair,
> Bred in the dark womb of eternal Night,
> His looks nailed fast to Sin, long sooty hair.
> His body all was framed of earthly paste
> And heavy mold . . . Though 'kin to hell. . . .
> Two weapons sharp as death he ever bore . . .
> Which from far he deadly darts.

The second character, a warden at the gate of hell, bore the name of Sin, but was called Death:

> The porter to the infernal gate is Sin,
> A shapeless shape, a foul deformed thing,
> Nor nothing, nor a substance (as those thin
> And empty forms, which through the air fling
> Their wandring shapes) . . . It serves, yet reigns as
> King. It lives, yet's Death; it pleases full of pain:
> Monster! ah who, who can thy being fain?
> Thou shapeless shape, live Death.

Combined in a single character, these inseparable companions provide a warden at hell gate, a shapeless shape, and a thing comparable to shadowy forms which pass through the air. Bred in eternal night, its color appropriately is black. The character stands as a monster which darts forth deadly weapons, is comparable to a king, and may be likened to hell. Such a composite being provides a not inadequate precedent for Milton's Death, the subordinate guardian of hell:

> Before the gates there sat on either side
> A formidable shape . . . [Death] the other shape—
> If shape it might be called that shape had none,
> Distinguishable in member, joint or limb;
> Or substance might be called that shadow seemed,
> For each seemed either—black it stood as Night,
> Fierce as ten furies, terrible as hell,
> And shook a dreadful dart; what seemed his head
> The likeness of a kingly crown had on. . . .
> The monster moving onward came as fast
> With horrid strides. . . . 'He my inbred enemy
> Forth issued. . . . I fled, and cried out *Death!*'

A second composite character, built of Spenser's Error and Fletcher's Hamartia, closely resembles Milton's Sin, mother of Death and principal warden of hell gate. When first discovered by Spenser's Knight of the Red Cross, the monster Error lay within a darkened pit:

> Half like a serpent horribly displayed,
> But the other half did woman's shape retain . . .
> Her huge long tail her den all overspread,
> Yet was in knots and many boughts upwound,
> Pointed with mortal sting. Of her there bred
> A thousand young ones, which she daily fed . . .
> Soon as that uncouth light upon them shone,
> Into her mouth they crept, and sudden all were gone.

Milton's chief departure from Spenser described Sin's progeny as kenneled, not in her mouth, but in her womb:

> [Sin] seemed woman to the waist, and fair
> But ended foul in many a scaly fold,
> Voluminous and vast—a serpent armed
> With mortal sting. About her middle round

A cry of hell-hounds never-ceasing barked . . .
Yet, when they list, would creep, if aught disturbed
Their noise, into her womb and kennel there.

The more complete pattern occurs in Fletcher, whose
Purple Island described Hamartia as a creature physically
similar to Sin, and pictured her issuing from her father. He
wrote that the Dragon cohabited with the first woman,
and begat a monster. The employment of the word *Dragon*
in one narrative, and *Satan* in the other constitutes less a
difference than a further similarity, for Dragon had served
centuries as a synonym for the Devil. The antecedent of
his in the first line is Fletcher's dragon:

> The first that crept from his detested maw
> Was Hamartia, foul deformed wight . . .
> A woman seemed she in her upper part . . .
> The rest, though hid, in serpent's form arrayed,
> With iron scales, like to a plaited mail:
> Over her back a knotty tail displayed . . .
> The end was pointed with a double sting.
> Of that first woman her the Dragon got,
> The foulest bastard of so fair a mother.

In the *Apollyonists*, so frequently cited in this chapter,
Fletcher approached even nearer to basic conceptions
used by Milton. The shapeless shape known as Sin, but
called Death, Fletcher described both as the child of
Satan and the first woman, and as a birth so monstrous
that the mother thought to fly from it. The 'old serpent'
is of course the Devil:

> (It lives, yet's Death. . . . Thou shapeless shape)
> Of that first woman, and the old serpent bred,
> By lust and custom nurst, whom when her mother
> Saw so deformed, how fain would she have fled
> Her birth, and self.

Milton's Sin announced to Satan, her father and her
husband:

> (The other shape . . . that shape had none)
> Pregnant by thee, and now excessive grown . . .
> At last this odious offspring . . . tore through
> My entrails. . . . I fled, and cried out *Death!*

As she continued, Sin described her rape by Death, that
by this act became both son and husband. Being a woman,
the shapeless shape of Fletcher attempted no rapine. Nevertheless, she sought to destroy her parent 'and all her brood.'
In attempting this act, she was stopped by a third character,
who, like the Death of *Paradise Lost* was 'his mother's
sire, his children's brother.' Because Milton's creations
rise above all comparable figures, and contain so much
peculiarly his own, it is no derogation to add that Sin and
Death represent traditional concepts. Nor is this greatness
lessened by a willing use of precedents left to posterity by
Spenser and his disciple Phineas Fletcher.

Having made allies of his son and daughter-wife, Milton's Satan prepared for the final adventure of Book II.
Sin unbarred the massive gates of hell, bringing to view the
ceaseless tumult of chaos. 'She opened,' wrote the poet,
'but to shut excelled her power.' For a passing moment,
Satan then 'stood on the brink of hell,' and from this point
calmly surveyed the whirling elements. The 'brink' of hell
Beaumont previously had used in his *Psyche*, and, interestingly enough, had placed there two foul monsters,
'ghastly Death and poisnous Sin.' In the *Apollyonists*,
unnamed fiends opened 'hell's iron gates . . . framed with
wondrous art.' Later in this poem, the warden of hell
found he could open, but 'cannot shut' its gates. The chaos
which Satan scanned belonged to the classic tradition, but
the handling of detail savors of Du Bartas. Be that as it

may, we obtain from the *Divine Weeks* a substitutable parallel for Milton's scene. The French poet wrote in part:

> [That unordered world] was a most formless form,
> A confused heap, a chaos most deform,
> A gulf of gulfs, a body ill-compacked,
> An ugly medley, which all difference lacked;
> Where the elements lay jumbled all together,
> Where hot and cold were jarring each with either . . .
> The dank against the dry; the blunt with sharp . . .
> The hard with soft, the base against the high . . .
> Earth, air, and fire, were with the water mixed,
> Water, earth, air, within the fire were fixed.
> Fire was no fire, the water was no water,
> Air was no air, the earth no earthly matter . . .
> Where in confusion, reigned such debate.

The survey of chaos completed, Milton's Satan plunged fearlessly into the warring elements, and came at last to Night and such a Demogorgan as Spenser had described. Guided by the spirits who ruled the abyss, he soon saw before him:

> The empyreal heaven, extended wide
> In circuit, undetermined square or round,
> With opal towers and battlements adorned
> Of living sapphire, once his native seat,
> And fast by, hanging in a golden chain,
> This pendent world, in bigness as a star.

To depict the towers and battlements of heaven long had been sacred to Christian poets. Milton, Du Bartas, and other writers may not have believed in the literal truth of the picture, but certainly they found it effective. The golden chain stands as a creative development of the Homeric links which joined earth to heaven. Precisely what meaning Milton gave to it is impossible to determine.

Spenser once described a golden chain as the bond of virtues and noble minds, and later as a connection between heaven and hell which lent apparent aid to the overly ambitious. Various writers considered it symbolic of unity with God; others, as representing Divine Love. During the year 1640, William Hodson saw in it a constant support which came from the hand of Deity. This conception Hodson set forth in *The Divine Cosmographer*, and on the frontispiece linked earth to heaven by the traditional chain. Allan H. Gilbert adds that in the *Emblems* of Achilles Bucchius, Bologna, 1574, a chain supports the celestial globe. Of the sustained world, Bucchius wrote, 'Coelesti demissa manu.'

Chapter VI

THE GARDEN IN EDEN

THE stormy tumult of chaos behind him, Satan had completed the major part of his journey. There remained before him the double task of reaching the earth and entering Paradise. This adventure and its related episodes Milton described in Books III and IV, the first of which served two diverse objectives. The initial function was to open and partially develop Milton's explicit justification of God, particularly to harmonize effectively His eternal providence with man's approaching fall. This argument I shall discuss later, in connection with the final justification set forth in Book XII. The second of the two objectives proved structural rather than doctrinal. To be more specific, it provided the transition which brought Satan from the outskirts of chaos to the boundary of Eden.

In developing and adorning this transition, Milton wrote untrammeled by space restrictions. Although he made the introduction to Book III the longest found in the epic, it totalled but fifty-five lines. The subsequent justification of God had lost in effectiveness if extended beyond its three hundred and sixty verses. Moreover, relatively few lines were required to transport Satan to the opening which topped the outer shell, to carry the Apostate down through the universe, and to place him before the land of Eden. As a result, Milton could make Book III the shortest book among the original ten, and yet retain for expansion or embellishment more than two hundred verses. The added incident and decorative detail he built around two primary episodes, the journey of Satan across the world's outer

128

shell, and the Apostate's subsequent meeting with the angel Uriel.

As conceived by Milton, the outer shell of the mundane universe was a hollow spherical body both impenetrable and opaque. It enclosed the several planetary spheres which Ptolemaic astronomy placed about an unmoved and central earth, and protected both earth and its world from the storms of chaos. For the simple idea that a shell or covering surrounded the world, many analogues exist. Among the Hebrews it appeared as a curtain or solid firmament; and as reported by Eusebius and Diogenes Laertius, various ancient Greeks regarded the cosmos as bounded by a tunic, a membrane, or a crystal shell. Seneca wrote that Artemidorus described the sphere as a hollow globe formed by the flying up and accumulation of atoms. The medieval philosopher Richard of Middleton found it an enclosing surface, and, as Mr. Allan H. Gilbert noted some years ago, both Basil and Thomas Aquinas believed the world surrounded by an encircling substance. During the Seventeenth Century, the conception was referred to by Thomas Tymme, Johannes Johnstonus, and John Swan, the last of whom declared, 'The firmament is a vaulted roof,' comparable to 'a certain husk, shell, or box, inclusively containing all things without the heaven of heavens.'

Milton, however, went far beyond the idea of a shell which enclosed the universe. His 'firm opacous globe' is a world in itself, hollow to be sure, but nevertheless a world:

[God then looked down on Satan,] ready now
To stoop, with wearied wings and willing feet,
On the bare outside of this world, that seemed
Firm land embosomed without firmament. . . .
[Subsequently] upon the firm opacous globe

> Of this round world, whose first convex divides
> The luminous inferior orbs, enclosed
> From Chaos and the inroad of Darkness old,
> Satan alighted walks. A globe far off
> It seemed; now seems a boundless continent,
> Dark, waste, and wild, under the frown of Night.

In after times, said Milton, this shell-like world became a repository for 'all things vain,' a conception probably drawn in part from the *Orlando Furioso* of Ariosto. With their vanities came those who had loved them, together with 'embryos and idiots, eremites and friars.' To these and other figures, Milton added:

> All the unaccomplished works of Nature's hand,
> Abortive, monstrous, or unkindly mixed,
> Dissolved on earth, fleet hither, and in vain,
> Till final dissolution wander here.

Quite different, however, was that part of the outer shell which lay beneath the gates of heaven. At the foot of the retracting stairs which Milton's poetic imagination had fashioned from the ladder of Jacob:

> A bright sea flowed
> Of jasper or of liquid pearl, whereon
> Who after came from earth sailing arrived,
> Wafted by angels, or flew o'er the lake
> Rapt in a chariot drawn by fiery steeds.

From what source or sources Milton constructed this unique world remains a most difficult question. Mrs. Josephine Bennett recently suggested Plato's Vision of Er from Book X of the *Republic*. In this vision the soul of Er came with a great company to a plain lying between heaven and earth. Two holes pierced the plain, and in heaven, directly above these holes, were two additional openings. 'In the intermediate space,' wrote Plato, 'were judges seated, who commanded the just . . . to ascend on the right hand,' and, 'in like manner, the unjust were bidden by them to descend on the left.' The vision does provide a physical body situated between heaven and earth, with openings through which souls may ascend (and descend).

Much closer to Milton than Plato's analogue is the hitherto unnoted account which Origen preserved in his celebrated *Peri Archon*. Quite unfortunately, the learned Greek Father failed to name those who had advanced the idea:

> Above that sphere which they call fixed, they will have another sphere to exist, which they say—exactly as our heaven contains all things under it—comprehends by its immense size and indescribable extent the orbs of all the spheres within its more magnificent circumference, so that all things are within it. . . . They would have this earth of ours, which formerly was called *dry*, to have derived its appellation from the name of that earth-like world. . . .
>
> [When from men] all corruption has been cleansed and shaken off, and when the whole of the space occupied by this world (that universe in which the spheres of the planets are said to exist), has been left behind and beneath, then is reached the settled abode of the pious and the good situated above that sphere [of the universe] which is called fixed; as in a good land, in the land of the living, which will be inherited by the meek and gentle. To this land belongs that heaven which, with its more magnificent extent, surrounds and contains that land itself—that heaven which is truly and chiefly called heaven. . . .
>
> These [men from earth] after their apprehension and their chastisement for the offenses (which they have undergone by way of purgation), may, after having fulfilled and discharged every obligation, deserve a habi-

tation in that land [above the fixed sphere]. Those who have been obedient to the word of God, and henceforth by their obedience have shown themselves capable of wisdom, are said to deserve the kingdom of that heaven or those heavens [which lie above the good land]. . . . In this way, therefore, a kind of road seems to be opened up for the departure of the saints from that earth-like world to those heavens; so that they do not so much appear to abide in that land, as to inhabit it with a specific intention—to pass on to the inheritance of the kingdom of heaven, when they also have reached that degree of perfection.

Important differences separate the accounts of Milton and Origen. The world described by the Greek Father was both a good land, and one inhabited by meek and gentle spirits. That pictured by Milton proved for the most part exactly the opposite. Save for the region directly beneath heaven, turbulent storms swept its surface, and its inhabitants were either monstrous or spiritually unworthy. Despite these differences—perhaps less significant because diametrical opposites—the two descriptions include vital similarities. Each world is a populated hollow shell enclosing the physical universe, and specifically is said to encompass the spheres or orbs of universe. Both lie between heaven and earth, and contain elements suggestive of a purgatory. We find in each a picture of souls which passed through space in an upward journey.

I have emphasized the Origen analogue for several reasons. The Father's *Of the Origin of Things* not only was available to the Seventeenth Century, but had long been widely known. In this work Origen set forth the doctrine of one first matter, that idea which Milton's Raphael expounded to Adam in such detail. Thirdly, and perhaps of greatest importance, the analogue occurs in religious rather than in secular literature.

There remains one of Milton's most picturesque digressions, the account of the Paradise of Fools. The poet apparently had in mind the Limbo of the Fathers which various medieval schoolmen had placed nearer hell than heaven. His revised limbo, Milton prepared both for pilgrims and those who thought to reach heaven by belated entrance into a monastic order. Roaming over the outside shell until at last they come to 'heaven's ascent,' they no sooner lift their feet:

> When lo!
> A violent cross wind from either coast
> Blows them transverse, ten thousand leagues awry,
> Into the devious air. Then might ye see
> Cowls, hoods, and habits, with their wearers, tost
> And fluttered into rags; then reliques, beads,
> Indulgences, dispenses, pardons, bulls,
> The sport of winds: all these, upwhirled aloft,
> Fly o'er the backside of the world far off
> Into a Limbo large and broad, since called
> The Paradise of Fools; to few unknown
> Long after, now unpeopled and untrod.

Having completed his description of the outer shell, and subsequently that of the portal and stairs of heaven, Milton prepared for the final major episode of Satan's journey to earth and Eden. Dropping through the opening which pierced the outer shell, the Apostate:

> Down right into the world's first region throws
> His flight precipitant, and winds with ease
> Through the pure marble air his oblique way
> Amongst innumerable stars, that shon
> Stars distant, but nigh-hand seemed other worlds.
> Or other worlds they seemed, or happy isles,
> Like those Hesperian Gardens famed of old,
> Fortunate fields, and groves, and flowery vales;
> Thrice happy isles! But who dwelt happy there
> He stayed not to inquire.

Although the plot of *Paradise Lost* required that Satan cross the universe, Milton had ample precedent for describing a spirit in flight between heaven and earth. It was of course a recognized function of angels—the celestial messengers—to do just this. Among other writers, Tasso had pictured Michael winging his way earthward past sphere and planet, and both Beaumont and Masenius had shown Satan himself in rapid flight through the heavens. Somewhat more individual, at this particular place, was Milton's suggestion that spirits might inhabit the stars; but, in keeping with Raphael's admonition, 'Dream not of other worlds,' Satan did not pause for inquiry.

The goal of the Apostate proved to be the sun, and this, quite curiously, Milton described with a medley of conceptions old and new, scientific and non-scientific. His point that the sun's 'magnetic beam' may turn the globes of heaven, coupled with the praise showered upon it, has a Keplerian flavor. The conception of the sun as 'arch-chemic,' and the producer of gold, silver, and gems, reflects an idea which, as Mr. George W. Whiting recently observed, had appeared at least as early as Diodorus. According to the Sicilian historian, 'the stone called crystal is composed of pure water, congealed not by cold, but by the force of a continual heat.' Again, the 'heat of the sun gives to stones that color of gold which they have' and 'likewise makes carbuncles of divers sorts.' Closer to Milton's explicit description of the sun as a chemist stands that of Shakespeare, set forth in the drama *King John*:

> To solemnize this day, the glorious sun
> Stays in his course, and plays the alchemist;
> Turning, with splendor of his precious eye,
> The meager cloddy earth to glittering gold.

As Satan moved over the surface of the sun, he saw far in the distance a glorious angel. Lest he be discovered, and his search for man prove abortive, the cunning Apostate took quickly the disguise of a good spirit:

> And now a stripling cherub he appears,
> Not of the prime, yet such as in his face
> Youth smiled celestial, and to every limb
> Suitable grace diffused; so well he feigned.
> Under a coronet his flowing hair
> In curls on either cheek played; wings he wore
> Of many a colored plume sprinkled with gold;
> His habit fit for speed succinct; and held
> Before his decent steps a silver wand.

In placing an angel upon the sun, Milton consciously drew upon Revelation 19. 17: 'I saw an angel standing in the sun.' The second basic idea, according to which Satan disguised himself as a good spirit, rested ultimately upon 2 Corinthians 11: 14: 'For Satan himself is transformed into an angel of light.' Few beliefs had wider currency in Christendom than this, and among scores of writers the idea appeared in Beaumont, Du Bartas, Heywood, Peyton, and the Spanish Bishop Tostatus. Why Milton selected a young or stripling angel, I cannot say, but it is suggestive that two of his poetic idols, Tasso and Spenser, had used such a spirit. As translated by Fairfax some decades prior to *Paradise Lost*, Tasso said of Gabriel:

> Like to a man in show and shape he fared,
> But full of heavenly majesty and might;
> A stripling seemed he thrice five winters old,
> And radiant beams adorned his locks of gold.
> Of silver wings he took a shining pair. . . .

The slumbering Sir Guyon of Spenser had dreamed:

> Beside his head there sat a fair young man,
> Of wondrous beauty and of freshest years . . .

His snowy front, curled with golden hairs,
Like Phoebus' face adorned with sunny rays
Divinely shone, and two sharp-winged shears,
Decked with diverse plumes, like painted jays
Were fixed at his back, to cut his aery ways.

After having discovered the glorious angel to be Uriel,
the masquerading Satan humbly asked where he might find
man, Gods' latest creation:

'Uriel! for thou of those seven spirits that stand
In sight of God's high throne, gloriously bright . . . Tell
In which of all these shining orbs hath man
His fixèd seat—or fixèd seat hath none,
But all these shining orbs his choice to dwell—
That I may find him, and with secret gaze
Or open admiration him behold
On whom the great Creator hath bestowed
Worlds, and on whom hath all these graces
    poured. . . . '
So spake the false dissembler unperceived,
For neither man nor angel can discern
Hyprocisy—the only evil that walks
Invisible, except to God alone.

The characterization of Uriel as one of the seven angels
who stand before God's throne, 'and are his eyes,' finds
no support in Scripture. It was however quite old, and
during the early Christian era appeared in I Enoch. Among
the seven archangels who watched before the Lord, I
Enoch named Uriel as the first, and included him with the
four Presences of the Throne. Thomas Aquinas held in
the *Summa Theologica* that God alone, and neither man
nor angel, can so probe thought as to detect hypocrisy.
As Milton's Satan subsequently obtained from Uriel necessary information regarding the whereabouts of his pros-
pective victim, so the Satan of Beaumont's *Psyche* had

obtained this from Christ. Disguised as a good angel, Beaumont's character boldly entered heaven itself. But he could not long withstand the 'lightning' of Jesus's eyes, and at last 'his polished looks, his curled grove of hair,' and 'all the stolen things' of his disguise dropped away.

Petitioned so skilfully by Satan, Uriel directed him to earth, and the Garden in Eden. This he did in a new capacity, not as one of the seven watchers, but as Regent of the sun. The information given he twice prefaced, first with a homily on the proper appreciation of God's works. He then set forth briefly a second and different account of the creation of the universe:

> [Uriel,] Regent of the sun . . . to the fraudulent
> Impostor foul . . . answer thus returned:
> 'Fair angel, thy desire, which tends to know
> The works of God, thereby to glorify
> The great Workmaister, leads to no excess
> That reaches blame, but rather merits praise . . .
> I saw when at his word, the formless mass,
> This world's material mould, came to a heap:
> Confusion heard his voice, and wild Uproar
> Stood ruled, stood vast Infinitude confined;
> Till, at his second bidding, Darkness fled,
> Light shon, and order from disorder sprung.
> Swift to their several quarters hasted then
> The cumbrous elements: earth, flood, air, fire;
> And this ethereal quintéssence of heaven
> Flew upward, spirited with various forms,
> That rolled orbicular, and turned to stars
> Numberless, as thou seest, and how they move:
> Each had his place appointed, each his course;
> The rest in circuit walls this universe.'

The conception of Uriel as Regent of the sun perhaps developed from the meaning of his name: 'the light of

God,' or 'God is my light.' In the Twelfth Century, Bonaventure included Uriel with Michael, Gabriel, and Raphael as a major angel, and described him as 'the light, or the fire of God.' During the Seventeenth Century, Henry More named Uriel 'the fire of God, and angel of meridional sun: he that rules in the power of the meridian sun.' At approximately the time when Milton was at work upon *Paradise Lost,* the anonymous author of the *Discourse of Devils* made this angel ruler of the stars, the planets, and their influences. The related interpretation of Uriel as the spirit who revealed the secrets of astronomy had appeared in I Enoch, and passed from this book into the *Chronographia* of Syncellus and the *History* of Cedrenus.

Milton's shorter and largely secular account of the Creation contains much that is classical, including the Aristotelian doctrine of the quintessence. There existed however no apparent objection to employing such a mixed version; nor, indeed, of using it within a work which stressed the orthodox account provided by Genesis. The conventional Du Bartas had done precisely the latter thing. Minor exceptions excluded, the secondary and mixed version given in the *Divine Weeks* resembles closely that employed subsequently in *Paradise Lost.* The French writer, however, employed no character to present his description:

> When the Mouth Divine
> Opened, to each his proper place to assign:
> Fire flew to fire, water to water slid,
> Air clung to air, and earth with earth abid.
> Earth, as the lees, and heavy dross of all
> (After his kind), did to the bottom fall:
> Contrarywise, the light and nimble fire
> Did through the crannies of the old heap aspire
> Unto the top; and by his nature, light,

No less then hot, mounted in sparks upright. . . .
  I do deprive the heavens of element,
And mixture too; and think, the omnipotence
Of God did make them of a quintessence;
Since of the elements, two still erect
Their motion up; two ever down direct:
But the heaven's course, not wand'ring up nor down,
Continually turns only roundly round.

Having completed his variant account of the Creation, Uriel pointed out to Satan both the earth and the exact spot where he might find Paradise. Bowing low, Satan at once took his leave, and sped toward the Garden in Eden. In keeping with the Mercury of Virgil, and the Gabriel of Tasso, he alighted first upon a mountain, and hastened from there to his objective.

.   .   .   .   .

As we turn from Book III to Book IV of *Paradise Lost,* we meet a multiplicity of major themes and episodes, all developed with unusual effectiveness. Following the opening lamentation by Satan, Milton presented in turn portraits of the external and internal details of Paradise, descriptions of man's first parents, and homilies on marriage, obedience to God, and the relationship of husband and wife. Then came the first temptation of Eve, the successful patrol of the angel guard, and the ejection of Satan, three episodes which I shall discuss in the next chapter. Clustered about, and decorating basic elements of the narrative are such passages as Eve's dream regarding her creation, and the description of evening fading slowly into night. So far as proves feasible, discussion of theme and episode will follow the order of *Paradise Lost.*

In what may be termed one phase of the orthodox justification of Divine Providence, innumerable writers stressed the essentially Biblical conception that Satan was the first author and instigator of evil. This type of justification dwelt at length upon the Devil's venom against both God and man, the first of whom he hated because of the loss of heaven, and the creation of man to occupy his rooms. Man he hated because destined to take his place, and envied because of his happiness. On occasion it included the minor theme, discussed above, that Satan burned with revenge because God had created man to despite him. So appealing was this negative defense, doubtless in part because of its dramatic possibilities, that if anything it received in literature more space and emphasis than the positive. Milton suggested accurately this situation in the many passages of *Paradise Lost* devoted, first, to Satan's hatred of God and desire to obtain revenge upon Him through man; and secondly, to Satan's envy of man's present and future state.

A closely related belief held that the fallen angels, and necessarily Satan, always carried hell and its excruciating tortures within them. As Thomas Aquinas wrote, 'although the demons are not actually bound within the fire of hell while they are in this dark atmosphere, nevertheless their punishment is none the less.' Therefore, 'it is said in a gloss upon James 3. 6: "They carry the fire of hell with them wherever they go." ' In the words of Bonaventure, 'The devils, wheresoever they may be, are tortured by the tortures of hell.' 'The infinite source of their misery is in themselves,' said the anonymous *Discourse of Devils*, 'and is continually before them.' They 'can never enjoy any rest, being absent from the presence of God. . . . Go whither they will, they are in darkness, and the cause is within them, not without them.' Should any devil, continued the treatise, 'go to the utmost bounds of the earth, he cannot leave his perplexed and tormented mind behind him.'

A character regarded by Christendom as undergoing perpetual torture, as irrevocably confirmed in evil, and filled with hatred and envy of God and man, necessarily displayed envy, despair, and anger upon viewing either Paradise or the inhabitants for whom it had been created. The devil described by Phineas Fletcher envied Adam and Eve, and grew pregnant with pride and hate. As he moved swiftly toward the sacred Garden, the Antitheus of Masenius appeared cruel and menacing, and showed the pangs of jealous rage and despair. Such a Satan was the Devil of Du Bartas, as he prepared to tempt Eve:

> While Adam bathes in these felicities,
> Hell's Prince, sly parent of revolt and lies,
> Feels a pestiferous busy-swarming nest
> Of never-dying dragons in his breast,
> Sucking his blood, tearing upon his lungs,
> Pinching his entrails with ten thousand tongues,
> His cursed soul still most extremely racking;
> Too frank in giving torments, and in taking:
>   Above all, hate, pride, and envious spite,
> His hellish life do torture day and night. . . .
> For, the hate he bears to God, who hath him driven
> Justly forever from the glittering heaven,
> To dwell in darkness of a sulphury cloud—
> Though still his brethren's service be allowed—
> The proud desire to have in his subjection,
> Mankind enchained in gyves of sin's infection:
> And the envious heartbreak to see yet shine
> In Adam's face God's image all divine,
> Which he had lost; and that man might achieve
> The glorious bliss his pride did him deprive . . .
> Spur on his course, his rage redoubling still . . .
> Doth fire a hell of furies in his fell desire:
> His envious heart, self-swollen with sullen spite.

From this ancient tradition came the Satan who approached and entered Milton's Garden in Eden:

> Now first inflamed with rage, came down
> The tempter, ere the accuser of mankind,
> To wreak on innocent frail man his loss
> Of that first battle, and his flight to hell. . . .
> Begins his dire attempt; which, nigh the birth
> Now rolling, boils in his tumultuous breast,
> And like a devilish engine back recoils
> Upon himself. Horror and doubt distract
> His troubled thoughts, and from the bottom stir
> The hell within him; for within him hell
> He brings, and round about him, nor from hell
> One step, no more than from himself, can fly
> By change of place.
>   Now conscience wakes despair
> That slumbered; wakes the bitter memory
> Of what he was, what is, and what must be. . . .
> 'Me miserable! which way shall I fly
> Infinite wrath and infinite despair?
> Which way I fly is hell. . . . they little know . . .
> Under what torments inwardly I groan,
> While they adore me on the throne of hell. . . .'
> The Fiend saw undelighted all delight . . .
> Two of far nobler shape, erect and tall,
> God-like erect, with native honor clad
> In naked majesty, seemed lords of all,
> And worthy seemed; for in their looks divine
> The image of their glorious Maker shon. . . .
> When Satan still in gaze as first he stood,
> Scarce thus at length failed speech recovered sad:
> 'O hell! what do mine eyes with grief behold?'

For the same good reason that transport planes now fly the stratosphere, the early Christian Fathers placed Paradise high upon a mountain. The ever delightful

Garden, they believed, stood well above the winds that brought tumultuous storm, and swift extremes of heat and cold. This respected custom Milton followed in *Paradise Lost*. Indeed, as we shall note later, he went so far as to locate the Garden upon two radically different mountains, the first of which provided the setting for Satan's initial entry:

> So on he fares, and to the border comes
> Of Eden, where delicious Paradise,
> Now nearer, crowns with her enclosure green,
> As with a rural mound, the champain head
> Of a steep wilderness, whose hairy sides
> With thicket overgrown, grotesque and wild,
> Access denied. . . . so thick entwined,
> As one continued brake, the undergrowth
> Of shrubs and tangling bushes had perplexed
> All path of man or beast that passed that way. . . .
> Overhead upgrew insuperable height
> Of loftiest shade . . . Yet higher than their tops
> The verdurous wall of Paradise upsprung . . .
> And higher than that wall a circling row
> Of goodliest trees, loaden with fairest fruit,
> Blossoms and fruits at once of golden hue.

This mountain of Paradise differed noticeably from those common to religious literature. It had however an analogue in the stately mount which Spenser placed within his earthly Paradise, the Garden of Adonis:

> Right in the middest of that paradise
> There stood a stately mount, on whose round top
> A gloomy grove of myrtle trees did rise,
> Whose shady boughs sharp steel did never lop,
> Nor wicked beasts their tender buds did crop,
> But like a garland compassed the height.

Of the garden itself, Spenser said:

> It sited was in fruitful soil of old,
> And girt in with two walls on either side,
> The one of iron, the other of bright gold.

To emphasize properly the sweetness of Paradise, Milton compared its perfumes with the odours most famous in his day—the wind blown scents which came from Arabia:

> Now gentle gales . . . dispense
> Native perfumes, and whisper whence they stole
> Those balmy spoils. As, when to them who sail
> Beyond the Cape of Hope, and now are past
> Mozambic, off at sea northeast winds blow
> Sabean odours from the spicy shore
> Of Araby the Blest—with such delay well pleased
> They slack their course, and many a league
> Cheered with the grateful smell old Ocean smiles.

A similar heightening comparison previously had been made by Beaumont, who declared that 'every odour of Arabia's beds, would beg to borrow' from Paradise a 'richer sweetness.' The pleasing anecdote of mariners cheered by the perfumes of Arabia echoed a description found in the *History* of Diodorus of Sicily. This account by the Sicilian writer, discovered by Wakefield, cited by Todd, quoted by Allan H. Gilbert, and recently discussed anew by Mr. George W. Whiting, probably was Milton's ultimate, if not his immediate source. The idea that sailors paused to enjoy the exquisite perfume, the poet may well have added, for Diodorus made no mention of it. 'Arabia the Happy,' wrote the historian, is 'naturally perfumed all over; almost everything growing there, sending forth continually most excellent odours. Along the sea coasts grow balsam and cassia,' and 'in the heart of the country' are 'stately trees of frankincense and myrrh, palm trees, calamus, and cinnamon, and suchlike odoriferous plants.' Their fragrance 'is such that it even ravishes the senses with delight, as a thing divine and unutterable; it entertains them that sail along the coast at a great distance with its pleasures and delights. For in springtime the winds from off the land waft the air, perfumed with the sweet odours of myrrh and other odoriferous plants, to those parts of the sea which are next to them.'

Pleased by the perfumes of Paradise, Satan pushed his way to the bounding wall; and, with a single leap, entered the Garden. Doubtless with more than a hint from John 10. 1, but also as Du Bartas had done before him, Milton compared the invader to both a thief and a felon. In subsequent lines, the poet abruptly changed his rhetorical figure, and drawing upon the conventional belief that Satan might assume any shape he chose, wrote the famous lines:

> Thence up he flew, and on the Tree of Life,
> The middle tree and highest there that grew,
> Sat like a cormorant; yet not true life
> Thereby regained, but sat devising death.

From this high point of vantage, the Apostate looked out over Paradise, and through his eyes we see for the first time the physical details and the inhabitants of the Garden.

To the cultured of the present age, the Garden which Satan glimpsed has little or no importance. Until recent centuries, however, it possessed a living and vital interest to a majority of Christian mankind. Ambrose, Basil, Moses Bar Cepha, and Du Bartas, to mention a few more important writers, composed treatises upon the beauty spot of Eden. Poets writing both within and without the hexameral tradition gave it space, and commentaries on Genesis frequently devoted scores of pages to the subject. During the early Seventeenth Century, no atlas could be considered complete should it lack a map delineating the region and location of Paradise.

In his description of the celebrated Garden in Eden, Milton followed a practice used elsewhere in the epic, particularly in the latter two-thirds of Book VII. He first paraphrased either Scripture or a standard interpretation of the verses involved, and secondly developed a complementary (or supplementary) version generally more extended than the original. For his account of the Garden, Milton versified a conventional interpretation of Genesis 2. 8-14. In this instance, the relatively standard interpretation of Scripture which he followed had made to Genesis three additions, all interrelated. The first held that Paradise stood high upon a mountain; the second, that the river running southward through Eden passed into or underneath this mountain; and the third, that the subterranean stream rose within Paradise as a fountain, and in this fashion 'watered the garden.' Among a host of respected men, these additions to Genesis had the support of Basil, Ambrose, Isidore, Abelard, and Hugo of St. Victor.

Having satisfied the requirements of tradition, Milton stood free to add such a complement as he desired. Once again he apparently made good use of Spenser's Garden of Adonis, or, if not this, one or more accounts closely related to it. Milton's expression, 'under pendent shades,' sets forth much the idea of Spenser's 'in the thickest covert of that shade fashioned above.' Again, a 'bower' or 'happy rural seat' blessed with 'unpierced shade' falls within the same category as 'a pleasant arbor,' whose trees and vines joined so closely that 'neither Phoebus's beams could through them throng.' Milton described flowers 'which not nice art in . . . curious knots,' but nature 'poured forth.' Spenser wrote of an arbor 'not by art, but of the tree's own inclination made, . . . knitting their rank branches

. . . with wanton ivy twine entrailed.' In Eden were 'groves whose rich trees wept odourous gums and balm,' and in the Garden of Adonis stood a 'grove of myrtle trees,' whose 'fruitful sides sweet gum did drop,' and from the ground 'threw forth most dainty odours.' Other trees in both gardens hung low with fruit; birds sang in both, and there lived eternal or continual spring.

This is not to say that Milton's complementary description failed to include ideas first developed by religious writers. The belief that earth and the world were created during spring descended directly from them. To theologians he owed that phrase in his description of the Garden which posterity has treasured most: 'Flowers of all hue, and *without thorn the rose.*' Thirteen centuries before Milton, Basil and Ambrose advanced the idea in their treatises on Paradise. Among contemporary English poets, Robert Herrick employed it in *Noble Numbers* exactly two decades prior to publication of the epic:

> Before man's fall, the rose was born,
> St. Ambrose says, without a thorn.

Milton likewise followed the tradition which denied Paradise was located in Ethiopia, or under the equinoctial line. These closely related conclusions, if digression may be pardoned, came originally from a curious interpretation of Genesis 3. 24. After the fall of man, said the account of Moses, God 'placed at the east of the garden of Eden cherubims, and a flaming sword which turned every way, to keep the way of the tree of life.' The moving flaming sword which guarded the tree, various early commentators translated into the earth's torrid zone, a region then thought impenetrable to man. A further step then localized the Garden on the most famous peak under the equinoctial—the Ethiopian Mount Amara.

The conventional rejection of Amara, Milton made one part of a rhetorical device previously utilized by Peyton and a number of other poets—that of enhancing the splendor of Paradise by comparing its beauties with those of other celebrated gardens:

> Not that fair field of Enna . . . nor that sweet
> Grove of Daphne . . . might with this Paradise
> Of Eden strive; nor that Nyseian isle
> Girt with the river Triton, where old Cham . . .
> Hid Amalthea, and her florid son young Bacchus . . .
> Nor where Abassin kings their issue guard,
> Mount Amara, though this by some supposed
> True Paradise, under the Ethiope line
> By Nilus' head, enclosed with shining rock,
> A whole day's journey high, but wide remote
> From this Assyrian garden, where the Fiend
> Saw undelighted all delight.

The details of Mount Amara Milton apparently drew from the colorful descriptions of Purchas and Heylyn. In *Purchas His Pilgrimage* the first geographer wrote that Amara 'is situate . . . under the equinoctial line, where the sun may take his best view thereof.' Because of the great hill's 'lovely presence,' he stated, 'some taking [take] it for the place of our forefathers' Paradise.' In the widely read *Cosmography*, Heylyn joined Purchas to say of Amara 'that some have taken—but mistaken—it for the place of Paradise.' Continuing, Heylyn described the mountain as 'a day's journey high,' almost precisely the expression later used by Milton. 'The rock,' he continued, is 'cut so smooth and even . . . that no wall can be more evenly polished.' On the top, he said, 'the younger sons of the Emperor are continually enclosed, to avoid sedition. They enjoy there whatsoever is fit for delight, or princely education.' 'The mountain hath but one ascent up, which is impregnably fortified.' As Richardson pointed out some two centuries ago, and Todd noted in his variorum, Milton probably obtained from Diodorus of Sicily the story of Amalthea and Bacchus. Traditionally, the latter was the son of Semele.

Returning to the fiction which described Paradise through the Apostate's eyes, Milton pencilled his memorable picture of Adam and Eve:

> God-like erect, with native honor clad
> In naked majesty seemed lords of all:
> And worthy seemed; for in their looks divine
> The image of their glorious Maker shon,
> Truth, wisdom, sanctitude severe and pure . . .
> Not equal, as their sex not equal seemed;
> For contemplation he and valor formed;
> For softness she and sweet attractive grace.

In these and following lines, the poet set forth the traditional expansion of Genesis 1. 27, emphasizing the upright carriage, perfection, and virtue of mankind, particularly the majesty of Adam. He accepted here and elsewhere the convention which stressed the great beauty of Eve, and eulogized nakedness and the simplicity which it represented. His seeming delight in the human form some recent critics have interpreted as related to the ecstatic pleasure of a nudist, but such a conclusion has misjudged badly both the author and his age. Eve, wrote Milton, yielded to Adam:

> With coy submission, modest pride,
> And sweet, reluctant, amorous delay.
> Nor those mysterious parts were then concealed;
> Then was not guilty shame, dishonest shame
> Of nature's works, honor dishonorable,
> Sin-bred, how have ye troubled all mankind
> With shows instead, mere shows of seeming pure,
> And banished from man's life his happiest life,
> Simplicity and spotless innocence!

Artistic virtuosity makes unusual the words of Milton, but the ideas belong to the conventional pattern equally well reflected by Calvin in his commentary on Genesis. The theologian's discussion amplified Genesis 2. 25, 'And they were both naked, the man and his wife, and were not ashamed:'

> That the nakedness of man should be deemed indecorous and unsightly, while that of cattle has nothing disgraceful, seems little to agree with the dignity of human nature. We cannot behold a naked man without a sense of shame. . . . Moreover, every one is ashamed of his own nakedness, even though other witnesses may not be present. Where then is that dignity in which we excel? The cause of this sense of shame, to which we are now alluding, Moses will show in the next chapter. He now esteems it enough to say, that in our uncorrupted nature there was nothing but what was honorable. From this it follows that whatsoever is opprobrious in us, must be imputed to our own fault, since our parents had nothing in themselves which was unbecoming until they were defiled with sin.

Intimately related to this section of Book IV are those subsequent passages which detail so charmingly both the passing amours and the nuptials of Adam and Eve. Milton's obligation to Scripture necessitated some account of the first marriage, but equally potent was the popularity of the sacrament in hexameral poetry, in commentaries on Genesis, and in related books. As we might expect, these works praised Christian marriage, and in their discussion of the command, 'Increase and mulitply' of Genesis 1. 28, commented at varying length upon the relations of man and woman. Among Protestants it was, as with Calvin, not uncommon to defend somewhat vehemently the 'chaste use of the lawful and pure ordinance of God,' or with Willet, to speak emphatically against the 'popish inhibition of marriage.' Satan was held up as a foe of matrimony, in part because he desired both to increase license and to diminish population. To those who believed God created man in part to replenish the loss occasioned by the revolt of the fallen angels, it was a logical deduction that the Apostate would oppose vigorously the multiplication of humanity. The Christian union of man and woman, as the lines of the conservative Du Bartas suggest, commonly was regarded as serving three desirable ends, 'domestic sweets,' procreation, and the taming of lust:

> Source of all joys . . . O blessed bond!
> O happy marriage, . . . by thy dear favor,
> After our decease . . . we leave behind
> Our living images. . . . By thee, we quench
> The wild and wanton fires, that in our
> Soul the Paphian shot inspires.

This interpretation of marriage, together with the remaining themes clustered about it, Milton set forth as effectively and much more attractively than his predecessors and contemporaries. His opening lines will recall the general belief that Adam and Eve consummated marriage the first night following their creation. Equally widespread was the assumption that, *if* copulation had occurred in Paradise prior to man's fall, it would have been effected without lust. Under the heading, 'On Copulation in the State of Innocence, and at Present,' Bishop Tostatus said that in Paradise concupiscence did not rebel against reason; no venial appetite existed; reason ruled and guided copulation, and cohabitation was only for procreation and never because of concupiscence. Augustine held in the *City of God* that 'marriage, worthy of the happiness of Paradise, should have had desirable fruit without the shame of lust, had there been no sin.'

Night having fallen, Adam and Eve went to their inmost bower, where:

> Straight side by side were laid; nor turned, I ween
> Adam from his fair spouse, nor Eve the rites
> Mysterious of connubial love refused:
> Whatever hypocrites austerely talk
> Of purity, and place, and innocence,
> Defaming as impure what God declares
> Pure, and commands to some, leaves free to all.
> Our maker bids increase; who bids abstain
> But our Destroyer, foe to God and Man?
> Hail, wedded Love, mysterious law, true source
> Of human offspring, sole propriety
> In Paradise of all things common else!
> By thee adulterous lust was driven from men
> Among the bestial herds to range; by thee
> Founded in reason, loyal, just, and pure,
> Relations dear, and all the charities
> Of father, son, and brother, first were known. . . .
> Perpetual fountain of domestic sweets.

Subsequent to Satan's first glimpse of Adam and Eve, Milton's pencil drew a picture generally similar to that which Rubens had painted a few decades earlier. With poet and with artist, Satan looked down from a tree. Near at hand were Adam and Eve, and about them:

> All beasts of the earth, since wild, and of all chase
> In wood or wilderness, forest or den.
> Sporting the lion ramped . . . Others on the grass
> Couched, and, now filled with pasture, gazing sat,
> Or bedward ruminating.

Here the first man and woman ate the nectarine fruits 'which the compliant boughs yielded them,' scooped water 'from the brimming stream,' and enjoyed themselves as lovers may. Both directly and indirectly, they subsequently expressed their gratitude and adoration for God. In Milton's complete scene, but in the words of Samuel Purchas:

> We have beheld . . . our first parents, the lively images of the Creator and the creature; whom we have somewhat leisurely viewed in a naked majesty, delighting themselves in the enamelled walks of their delightful garden. The rivers . . . ran to present their best offices to their new lords. . . . The trees stooped to behold them, offering their shady mantle and variety of fruits, as their natural tribute, [while] they enjoyed all mutual comforts in the Creator, the creatures, and in themselves. A blessed pair, who enjoyed all they desired; [the] lords of all, and of more than all; content . . . in all they saw, to see their Maker's bounty, and . . . that infinite greatness and goodness which they could not but love, reverence, admire, and adore.

In full harmony with Calvin, Du Bartas, Mercer, Pererius, Willet, and other writers, Milton declared that man should labor, and not live idly, even in Paradise. The poet also described Adam as exemplifying the belief voiced by Willet, 'that being thus occupied in continual beholding of the goodly plants of Paradise, he might thereby be stirred up to acknowledge the goodness and bounty of the Creator.' The extended discourse to Eve on the subject of angels, stars, and celestial influences, suggests definitely the learned and contemplative Adam envisioned by Calvin, Campanella, Mercer, Pererius, and Tostatus.

All implicit and explicit homilies, important though they were, stand dwarfed beside the lesson which Adam had received from Raphael, and must in turn convey to Eve. This lesson was that of obedience to God, proof of which consisted in abstinence from the tree of knowledge. By repeatedly emphasizing this point, Milton supported a broad and popular tradition, one which held it not only necessary, but also proper, that Adam should obey his Creator. To do this, man was particularly obligated, for he had received but a single and easy commandment, which was chiefly a pledge or just lesson in obedience. To reject the one simple precept was obviously to be ungrateful, haughty, and indifferent toward God.

By taking the position that the Creator delivered the precept to Adam, and Adam, as master, transmitted the commandment to Eve, Milton made use of the opinion most common among theologians. To name its many advocates would be futile, and perhaps endless, but I may mention Ambrose, Augustine, Lancetta in his *Adam and Eve*, Mercer, Peter Lombard, Pererius, and Rupert. One group of writers, among them Andrew Willet, believed 'it more probable that God gave the charge to them both.' Still others, as Bishop Tostatus, did not decide with finality whether God issued the commandment to Adam and Eve singly, together, or to Adam alone. The second interpretation Milton perhaps accorded some recognition when he described Eve as having overheard Raphael's warning against the Apostate.

Throughout Adam's dialogue with Eve, Satan proved an interested spectator. He found especially important the injunction against eating the fruit of the tree of knowledge, and declared:

> Yet let me not forget what I have gained
> From their own mouths. All is not theirs, it seems;
> One fatal tree there stands, of Knowledge called,
> Forbidden them to taste . . . I will excite their minds
> With more desire to know, and to reject
> Envious commands.

In hexameral and related literatures, we rarely meet the idea which Milton stressed here. Lancetta described Satan as having overheard in concealment a conversation between Adam and Eve. His work, if Milton knew it, may have suggested the Apostate as an eavesdropper. The basic idea—that Satan heard Adam convey the precept to Eve— probably reached Milton through the *Paradise* of Moses Bar Cepha, a work both known and used in England, and available in three printings of Masius's Latin translation. In his somewhat extended discussion of this and closely related conceptions, the Syrian Bishop first considered the question: 'Did Satan hear God give to Adam the precept that he should not eat?' Seemingly in part for the reason that he questioned God's speaking in a voice audible to a third party, Bar Cepha himself found it doubtful 'that the Devil heard the mandate and law which God placed upon Adam.' He then recorded that various men 'believe Satan heard the mandate which was given to Adam (. . .*censent Satanam audivisse mandatum quod Adamo dabatur*).' This interpretation, of course, does not say what speaker Satan overheard. Having presented and discussed a divergent conclusion reached by 'Philoxenus, Theodorus Nestorianus, and others with them,' the Bishop turned to the precise conception utilized by Milton. 'Master Ephraem and others,' wrote Bar Cepha, 'said first that Adam was created outside Paradise; and, secondly, that he received from God in Paradise the mandate that he should not eat from the tree of knowledge.' Thirdly, after 'Eve had been formed from Adam's body, Adam instructed her concerning the precept in such a voice that could be heard; wherefore Satan heard perfectly (*exaudisse Satanum*) the words Adam spoke to his wife.' I may add that available editions of Ephraem include no work which discusses the conception.

Sharply contrasting with the rarity of this belief was the universal commonplaceness of the idea, previously mentioned, that Satan held for man a deadly and unrelenting envy. The major support of the idea, developed most completely in Book IX of the epic, proceeded from the apochryphal Wisdom of Solomon 2. 24: 'through envy of the Devil came death into the world.' So it fell out that when Purchas declared, 'Satan did see, disdain, and envy' Adam and Eve, he repeated what centuries of Christian writers had believed and stated before him. Upon viewing the happy lovers of Paradise, Milton's Devil turned aside 'for envy, yet with jealous leer malign, eyed them askance.' In a verse previously cited, Satan had exclaimed, 'O Hell! what do mine eyes with grief behold!' As the Apostate concluded, he added what appears a Miltonic contribution to the tradition—the idea that Satan pitied Adam and Eve, and was loath to seek revenge through them. This contribution, however, the poet ultimately qualified by questioning its sincerity.

By way of finale to the present chapter, I mention an interesting and perhaps significant fact previously touched on in passing. This is Milton's use of two different and distinct mountains as the location of Paradise. The first, comparable in many details with the mountain of Spenser's garden, he described as a thicket-covered and wooded hill; the second, he pictured as a rock of alabaster, rising high to the clouds. Moreover, the second mountain is in fact derived from the famous Mount Amara which Milton earlier had rejected as the seat of Paradise:

> The setting sun
> Slowly descended, and with right aspect
> Against the eastern gate of Paradise
> Levelled his evening rays. It was a rock
> Of alabaster, piled up to the clouds,

Conspicuous far, winding with one ascent
Accessible from earth, one entrance high;
The rest was craggy cliff, that overhung
Still as it rose, impossible to climb,
Betwixt these rocky pillars Gabriel sat,
Chief of the angelic guards.

With the exception of the words, 'one ascent,' which occur in Heylyn's account, this second hill of Paradise is precisely such a mountain as the Amara described by Samuel Purchas. 'The sun himself,' wrote the geographer, is 'so in love with the sight, that the first and last thing he vieweth in all these parts, is this hill.' Amara stood 'in a great plain . . . without other hill in the same for the space of thirty leagues; the form thereof round and circular, the height such that it is a day's work to ascend from the foot to the top. Round about, the rock is cut so smooth and even . . . that it seemeth to him that stands beneath, like a high wall whereon heaven is as it were propped. And at the top it is overhung with rocks, jutting forth off the sides . . . so that it is impossible to ascend it.' 'At the top is a gate with another guard.' 'The soldiers that guard the place dwell in tents.'

Of the prescribed pattern of events between the creation of man and his ejection from Paradise, Milton now has delineated approximately one-half. Specifically, with the catalog of Pareus taken as a guide, he has described 'the creation of man and the animals, the leading of the creatures before man, his assigning their names, the creation of Eve, institution of matrimony, the collocation of Adam and Eve, and the giving of the precept.' There remain, again following Pareus, 'the discourse of Eve with the serpent, the fall of mankind, donning the fig leaves, flight, Divine judgment, God's clothing the first parents, and their expulsion from the Garden.'

CHAPTER VII

THE TEMPTATION

TO the early Seventeenth and preceding Centuries, no theme had greater imaginative appeal than the temptation. It then possessed the four essentials of convincing drama: a concrete setting, a dynamic plot, important and human characters, and above all, universal significance. Because of its great appeal, writers of all nations not only presented the temptation at length, but also enhanced it by addition of a multiplicity of secondary conceptions. These varied conceptions, in keeping with others previously discussed, came largely from men primarily theologians, and passed directly or indirectly from them to a succession of poets. Such is the general history of the ideas and details employed in the temptation scene of *Paradise Lost*.

Nevertheless, Milton once more proved himself a creative poet, and made his own the material which centuries of writers had placed before him. To this material he added the important episode which distinguished his account from all others. I refer to the initial and unsuccessful temptation of Eve. As was the case with the two mountains of Paradise, we cannot be certain why Milton employed two temptations. However, some comprehension may be had of the varied forces which contributed to his revolutionary addition. Chief among these stands the vigorously argued question: How long did Adam remain in Paradise before he sinned and was expelled by God?

To this question the third chapter of Genesis gave no answer. Indefatigable and imaginative theologians then pressed into service generally unrelated verses scattered throughout Scripture. The numerous conclusions reached varied from a half-day to a third of a century, with both minimum and maximum derived from Biblical descriptions of Christ. The shorter period represented the length of His crucifixion, usually given as the twelve hours which elapsed between the deliverance of Christ to Pilate and His removal from the Cross. Somewhat similarly, the contrasting period stood for the number of years Christ had lived as man. The second interpretation developed little influence, but the first became in time the most authoritative of the many diverse conclusions.

A multiplicity of arguments supported the belief that Adam's creation, temptation, and expulsion from Paradise occurred within a period equal to that of the Crucifixion. Christ and Adam both were men. The Crucifixion took place on the sixth day of the week; God created Adam on the sixth day. Christ died the sixth day in atonement for man's sin. A further type of reasoning held that John 8. 44: 'The Devil . . . was a murderer from the beginning,' referred to an attack upon man immediately following his creation. A related argument asserted that Satan tempted man at once because Adam and Eve were then least able to resist. Because of God's command to increase and multiply, commentators believed the parents of mankind cohabited the first evening. Were Adam and Eve then unfallen, the resulting offspring would be untouched by original sin. Andrew Willet concluded his list of ten supporting reasons with the contention: 'That place lastly maketh to this purpose, Psalm 49. 13 [12], "Adam lodged not one night in honor," for so are the words if they be properly translated.'

Various theologians, including Cedrenus, Tostatus, Pererius, and Pareus, could not believe that Adam sinned and was ejected on the day of his creation. Cedrenus, Pareus and others maintained that twelve hours did not provide sufficient time for the creation of man and the animals, the naming of the latter, the institution of marriage, and the remaining related events. A further argument held that since God declared everything 'was very good' at the end of the sixth day, Adam had not been judged and expelled. Pareus and others argued that because God blessed the Sabbath, or seventh day, 'man neither fell nor was ejected on the sixth.' For this and related reasons, this Protestant commentator joined the Jesuit theologian Pererius, and supported the second most influential interpretation—that 'Adam fell on the eighth day of his creation, that day seven-night wherein he was made.'

For his separate temptations, Milton selected the periods advocated by the two most authoritative interpretations, one of which maintained Adam fell on the first day; the other, on the eighth. Satan's initial and unsuccessful seduction, he assigned to the day of Creation; the second and conventional temptation he placed precisely one week later. By adding the unsuccessful seduction, Milton both met and utilized the belief that the Devil attacked man immediately following creation. Moreover, Raphael's instruction of Adam represented in part the natural development of a further conception employed in support of the single day interpretation—that newly created man was untrained in obedience, and unable to resist the Apostate. As I previously stated, Milton accepted and developed the idea that Adam and Eve cohabitated the night of Creation.

It has been mentioned that various theologians made much of the analogy between Christ and Adam, and from the Crucifixion determined the number of hours man remained in Paradise. Continuing the analogy, they built from the Crucifixion a pattern, or schedule, for the allotted half-day. Christ came before Pilate in the morning; there-

fore God created Adam at this time. The Roman soldiers
placed Christ on the Cross the third hour; Satan tempted
man the third hour. Darkness descended the sixth hour
(noon); precisely at this hour Eve ate the fruit. The Son
called unto his Father the ninth hour; God then called
Adam to judgment. In the evening, Christ was taken from
the Cross, and man ejected from Paradise. This schedule
Milton followed rather closely in describing the successful
temptation of the eighth day. During the early morning
of this day, Adam and Eve went separately to their tasks.
Later, the disguised Satan found and accosted Eve. As
'the hour of noon drew on,' Eve had virtually succumbed,
and shortly thereafter took the forbidden fruit. When the
sun stood 'in western cadence low from noon,' the voice
of God called Adam to judgment. At evening, although
God had not ejected man, the Garden had ceased to be
Paradise. Milton's Adam then lamented to Eve:

> The inclement seasons, rain, ice, hail, and
> Snow . . . now the sky, with various face, begins
> To show us in this mountain, while the winds
> Blow moist and keen, shattering the graceful locks
> Of these fair spreading trees; which bids us seek
> Some better shroud, some better warmth to cherish
> Our limbs benumbed.

For the initial and unsuccessful temptation, Milton
neither used nor had available a predetermined pattern.
Its description he divided into two versions, the first of
which opened with Satan discovered:

> Squat like a toad, close at the ear of Eve,
> Assaying by his devilish art to reach
> The organs of her fancy, and with them forge
> Illusions as he list, phantasms and dreams.

'Conjured' to his proper shape by the prick of Ithuriel's
spear, Satan abandoned the temptation, and marched with

his captors to Gabriel. Here conflict threatened, and, exemplifying the idea that within a moment's time spirits
may 'dilate' to what size they choose, the Apostate:

> Collecting all his might, dilated stood,
> Like Teneriff or Atlas, unremoved:
> His stature reached the sky, and on his crest
> Sat horror plumed.

As his follower Belshazzar later discovered, Satan found
himself weighed in the balances and found wanting. For
this conception, which pictured God as setting 'forth in
heaven his golden scales,' Milton drew also upon the
balances of gold wherein Homer's Jupiter had weighed the
fates of Achilles and Hector. Without pausing to question the 'writing' in the heavens, Satan fled from Eden.

The second account of the abortive seduction Milton
gave following the flight of Satan. In what she called a
dream, Eve walked by the tree of knowledge. Beside it
she found an angel: 'shaped and winged like one . . .
from heaven, by us oft seen.' When tempted with the forbidden fruit, Eve first rejected it, then weakened, and
at last could not withstand its fragrance. Immediately she
flew with the angel high into the clouds, and as a superior
being looked down upon the earth.

The poet's first description of Satan as a toad rested in
part upon the general conception that spirits might take
any form they desired. It had also support from the belief
that the Devil appeared disguised as a creature—behemoth
and leviathan, a snake and a lion; an owl, ostrich, lamia
and siren; and as an adder, basilisk and dragon. In that
division of the *Hierarchy of the Blessed Angels* which
Heywood entitled 'The Fall of Lucifer,' Milton's older
contemporary described Satan as expertly informed 'in
the proprieties of creeping things, ants, toads, snakes, ser-

pents.' He also depicted hell as filled with snakes and
toads. Scot wrote in the division termed an 'Inventory
. . . of Devils and Spirits,' that the 'first and principal
king,' whenever he is conjured up, appeareth under three
heads: the first, like a toad.'

Equally authoritative for the day was Milton's picture
of Satan attacking the fancy of Eve. In the *De Lamiis* of
1582, Wier entitled his eighth chapter 'De Phantasia,' and
discussed at length the power of evil spirits over human
fancy and imagination. Psellus declared in *De Operatione
Daemonis*, Chapter XII, that devils whisper to our minds,
not speaking so loudly that our ears may hear them. Quoting loosely from Hermes, Thomas Heywood wrote that
evil spirits:

> Deceived themselves, they others would deceive.
> They waking trouble us, molest our sleep;
> And if upon ourselves no watch we keep,
> Our bodies enter—then distract our brain.

The belief that spirits whispered in the mind of man,
Reginald Scot accepted as a true description of Satan's
machinations. Similarly, he approved the account of the
temptation 'wherein the Devil is resembled to an odious
creature, who, as he creepeth upon us to annoy our bodies;
so doth the Devil there creep into the conscience of Eve,
to abuse and deceive her.' In the *Divine Weeks*, perhaps
our most complete single analogue for *Paradise Lost*, Du
Bartas declared:

> Sometimes, me seems, troubling Eve's spirit, the
> Fiend made her this speaking fancy apprehend . . .
> The evil angels slide too easily, as subtle
> Spirits, into our fantasy.

Milton's conception of Satan tempting Eve in the guise
of a good angel cannot be called widespread, and cer-

tainly was not orthodox. It could, however, be properly and effectively employed precisely as the poet used it—as a fantastic dream. When or where the conception originated, I cannot say, but it had appeared as early as the metrical paraphrase of Genesis at times attributed to Caedmon. In describing her tempter, the Eve of this paraphrase said, 'I by his habit see that he is one of the envoys of the Lord.' This seducer also held before his victim an apple plucked from the tree of knowledge. During Milton's century, Andrew Willet quoted, and rejected, the speculation of Bonaventure that Eve thought her tempter 'a good angel.' The Eve of Andreini's *Adam* declared to her husband she ate the fruit in order that she might carry him to the sky.

The thought of protecting Adam and Eve by angelic guards rested ultimately upon such passages as Psalm 91. 11, wherein the godly are assured: 'For he will give his angels charge concerning thee.' As Thomas Aquinas shows in the *Summa Theologica*, the Thirteenth Century found well-established the idea that Adam enjoyed angelic guardianship in Paradise. In a seventeenth-century repetition of the belief, Thomas Peyton declared to the unfallen Adam of his poem, 'God hath . . . charged the angels for thy fence and guard.' To some degree, Milton's selection of Gabriel as leader of the angelic watch doubtless was influenced by the Hebrew meaning of his name—the strength of God. Gregory the Great and Bonaventure previously had joined in describing this angel as the might of God, who strengthens man. The *Psychozoia* of Henry More referred to him as 'the strong, youthful Gabriel.' In *Paradise Lost*, the guards whom he commanded were the 'youth of heaven.' The *Cornish Creation* pictured Gabriel as the outstanding angelic warrior, and Vondel's *Adam* made him leader of the angels guarding the wedding feast of Adam and Eve.

We perhaps should assume some indebtedness to contemporary descriptions of Mount Amara, the famous hill
which became the second mountain of Paradise. At the
entrance of Amara, guards were posted, who in addition
kept watch over the interior. Only on the second mountain
of Paradise—in effect, on Mount Amara—did Milton place
angelic guards. These watched at the single gate, and
patrolled the garden. Moreover, the atmosphere of the
poet's descriptions, the methods and tactics of the soldiers,
all strongly suggest an organized military unit. With the
chieftain Gabriel, Milton associated one of his three most
important angels, the versatile Uriel. First a warrior against
Satan, and next a Presence and watcher before God's
throne, Uriel later served both as Regent of the sun, and
the revealer of cosmological secrets. As the associate of
Gabriel, he functioned as might a guard over hell, and
carried to Paradise the warning that 'one of the banished
crew . . . hath ventured from the deep to raise new
trouble.' The Uriel of I Enoch, who performed all the
duties of Milton's character, likewise had served as a
watcher over Tartarus.

Meanwhile, Satan's abortive attack had not passed un-
noticed in heaven. Come morning, God sent Raphael to
talk with Adam, as friend with friend, and so instruct him
that the strategems of Satan would prove to no avail. This
angel, later the companion of Tobias, then related to
Adam and Eve the tale of Satan's rebellion, the story of
Creation, and joined with Adam in three dialogues. To his
important discourse with Adam, and much as did Michael
in Book XI, Raphael came in the capacity and with the
majesty of an archangel. 'Archangels,' ran the traditional
description of Thomas Heywood, 'are ambassadors, great
matters to declare.' That Raphael was a distinguished per-
sonage, the Adam of *Paradise Lost* quickly recognized:

Haste hither, Eve, and, worth thy sight, behold
Eastward among those trees what glorious Shape
Comes this way moving; seems another morn
Risen on mid-noon. Some great behest from heaven
To us perhaps he brings, and will voutsafe
This day to be our guest.

A minor result of Satan's attack upon Eve was to bring
forth our 'first' discussion on psychology. The morning
following the attempted seduction, Adam awakened to
find Eve frightened and disturbed, 'with tresses discom-
posed and glowing cheek.' Informed of her vision, he
quieted her fear by a discourse on dreams, giving his major
emphasis to the operations of the mind:

                    In the soul [mind]
Are many lesser faculties, that serve
Reason as chief. Among these Fancy next
Her office holds; of all external things
Which the five watchful senses represent,
She forms imaginations, aerie shapes,
Which reason, joining or disjoining, frames
All what we affirm or what deny, and call
Our knowledge or opinion; then retires
Into her private cell when nature rests.
Oft, in her absence, mimic fancy wakes
To imitate her; but, misjoining shapes,
Wild work produces oft, and most in dreams,
Ill matching words and deeds long past or late.

To a modern reader, Milton's digressive lecture on psychology may appear superficial. However, his ideas were
almost precisely those set forth in Fletcher's *Purple Island*,
a work with some scientific pretensions. Indeed, the two
accounts so resemble each other as to suggest either a common source, or direct borrowing by Milton. In much the

same relative places both writers employed common terms: faculty, next, office, forms, shapes, private, oft, dreams, and retire, the last of which is not included within those fragments to be quoted from Fletcher. Again in the same relative positions we meet a variety of comparable words: external—outward, watchful—pry, our knowledge—memory, together with reason described as chief and as the highest sovereign. Milton named fancy a mimic, imitator, and transformer of shapes; Fletcher exemplified fancy playing these rôles. One writer described reason as choosing what we affirm or deny; the other, as sifting the true from the false. By way of explanation I mention that Fletcher personified reason as the Prince, and fancy or imagination as the character Phantastes. To compare most effectively his extended discussion, I give in prose form a majority of the fragmentary citations from his poem.

Reason or understanding is the 'highest sovereign,' who 'his time in double office spends. The next that' to him 'is placed, Phantastes hight—the active faculty—which to a higher power the object leaves.' 'Five of less dignity have outward courts, and in all actions pry.' Among the senses, 'the eye . . . lets in wandring shapes.' Reason, 'first those forms and fancies . . . admits, which to his court busy Phantastes sends,' and 'clears their dusky shades.' As quickly as the Prince 'these forms hath clearly seen, parting the false from true, the wrong from right . . . he straight commits them to his treasury, which old Eumnestes keeps, father of memory.'

Fancy, continued Fletcher, has its private thoughts, and takes the idea or perceived object (the perception) 'in itself.' Then, 'cunningly changing itself . . . straight itself in selfsame shape adorning, becomes the same [as the perception], with quick and strange transforming.' Fancy, he reiterated, conforms itself to all things, and when meeting 'wandring shapes . . . quickly itself to every sort consorts.' Within the brain of fancy, or those ruled by it:

> Thousand thin forms, and idle fancies flit;
> The three-shaped sphinx, and direful harpy's train,
> Which in the world had never being yet:
> Oft dreams of fire and water, loose delight,
> And oft arrested by some ghostly sprite,
> Nor can he think, nor speak, nor move
> For great affright.

In Milton's discourse on psychology, as in numerous other sections of *Paradise Lost*, the highest possible place is accorded reason. This emphasis on reason we have at times regarded as unusual. However, both early Greek and Roman philosophers had stressed reason, or intellect, as the quality which lifted man above the animal. Its exaltation had entered hexameral literature by the first century, when Philo remarked in his *Creation* that God 'made man partaker of kinship with himself in mind and reason, best of all gifts.' What man shared with God, he of course must share with the angels, the difference being that angelic reason was intuitive, and the human discursive. Discursive reason was external, in the sense that it required the accumulation and weighing of evidence. To name the writers who preceded Milton in stressing the high place held by 'God's image in man' would prove endless, but I may mention Ainsworth, Basil, Damascene, Du Bartas, More, Peter Lombard, Raleigh, Ross, Swan, Thomas Aquinas and Wolleb.

Following his discovery at the ear of Eve, and subsequent flight from Paradise, Satan left the earth. For seven nights, wrote Milton at the opening of Book IX, 'he rode with darkness.' Returning at midnight, Satan entered the Garden through the fountain by the Tree of Life. As he prepared anew for the seduction of man, his first thought was disguise, and the finding of the creature best suited for this purpose:

> Sea he had searched and land
> From Eden over Pontus, and the Pool
> Maeotis, up beyond the river Ob;
> Downward as far antartic; and, in length,
> West from Orontes to the ocean barred
> At Darien, thence to the land where flows
> Ganges and Indus. Thus the orb he roamed
> With narrow search, and with inspection deep
> Considered every creature, which of all
> Most opportune might serve his wiles, and found
> The Serpent subtlest beast of all the field.

Previously, while watching Adam and Eve in Paradise, Satan assumed successively the forms of different animals, his thought being to observe them more closely:

> Then from his lofty stand on that high tree
> Down he alights among the sportful herd
> Of those four-footed kinds, himself now one,
> Now other, as their shape served best his end,
> Nearer to view his prey, and, unespied,
> To mark what of their state he more might learn.

The idea that Satan selected the serpent after choosing from among the animals previously had been used by a variety of writers, including Calvin, Du Bartas, and Vondel. Of these men, the French poet described the Apostate as making trial of numerous creatures before choosing the serpent:

> [Satan] much like, therefore, some thief . . .
> Himself doth ambush in a bushy thorn . . .
> Taking his level, from a hollow tree . . .
> Our freedom's felon, fountain of our sorrow,

Thinks now the beauty of a horse to borrow;
Anon to creep into a heifer's side;
Then in a cock, or in a dog to hide;
Then in a nimble hart himself to shroud . . .
And lest he miss a mischief to effect,
Oft changes mind, and varies oft aspect.
At last remembering that of all the broods,
In mountains, plains, airs, waters, wilds and
Woods, the knotty serpents' spotty generation
Are filled with infectious inflammation . . .
He crafty cloaks him in a dragon's skin,
All bright bespecked.

Having selected, but as yet not entered his instrument
for the temptation, Satan renewed a type of lamentation
uttered in Book IV. In partial contrast with his outburst
there, and as a prelude to the seduction of Eve, the Apostate voiced less his hatred toward God, and more his enmity
toward man. In the lamentation, he praised the beauty of
earth and grieved over his fallen state. Forgetting his spe-
cious and unorthodox expression of sympathy for man,
Satan poured out his envy and jealousy of Adam. In so
doing he vilified man, and promised to himself sweet revenge. To present a more complete picture of Satan's
reaction toward Adam and his Paradise, I include some
few verses previously quoted from Book IV:

[In] this Assyrian garden . . . the Fiend
Saw undelighted all delight, all
Kind of living creatures, new to sight and strange.
Two of far nobler shape, erect and tall . . .
And worthy seemed; for in their looks divine
The image of their glorious Maker shon . . . .:
'Hell shall unfold, to entertain you
Two, her widest gates . . . there will be room,
Not like these narrow limits, to receive

Your numerous offspring. . . .
  'O earth, how like to heaven, if not preferred
More justly, seat worthier of gods, as built
With second thoughts, reforming what was old! . . .
[God] determined to advance into our room
A creature formed of earth, and him endow . . .
With heavenly spoils, our spoils. What he decreed
He effected; Man he made, and for him built
Magnificent this world, and earth his seat,
Him lord pronounced, and, O indignity!
Subjected to his service angel-wings
And flaming ministers. . . . Wrapt in mist
Of midnight vapor, [I] glide obscure. . . .
O foul descent! that I, who erst contended
With gods to sit the highest, am now constrained
Into a beast, and mixed with bestial slime. . . .
Who aspires, must down as low, as high he soared.
[I shall find sweet revenge] . . .on him who next
Provokes my envy, this new favorite
Of heaven, this Man of clay, son of despite.'

Milton's desire to follow versions long established, together with his accuracy in so doing, finds no better illustration than this monologue by Satan. Within it the English
poet of the Seventeenth Century placed the major points
which Moses Bar Cepha had included in the Ninth. As
Milton's epic was later to do, we find that the *Paradise* of
the Syrian Bishop employed comparison and contrast, gave
to Satan a soliloquy (or monologue), emphasized his tor-
menting self-pity, and depicted him as reacting profoundly
to the sight of the fortunate Adam. Bar Cepha's Apostate
specifically described Adam as the recipient of what he asserted rightfully belonged to him, dwelt upon his exile,
and compared the dignity of his nature and first estate
with the baseness of Adam's origin. The character also

followed allusion to his fall with a lament because he now must consort with beasts:

> When Satan fell from his place of high dignity and glory, and saw Adam created from clay (*lutum*), made in the image and similitude of God, and all things on earth subjected to his rule; particularly when he observed the dwelling-place of Paradise filled with all delight, and Adam's enjoyment of the society of angels, while he himself was utterly cast down and dejected, a truly powerful hatred and envy moved him against Adam and Eve, so that he seduced them. Truly, he was tormented by such thoughts as these. 'I who am spiritual am exiled; but Adam, who is corporeal, is taken in. I am driven away and deprived of all glory; Adam is clad and arrayed in glory. I have fallen to the depth; he stands on the height. I move among beasts; he among angels. I haunt desolate solitude; he lives among the delightful trees of Paradise.' . . . Satan knew from what had befallen him, that if Adam sinned . . . he either should die or be driven from Paradise, and afterward . . . he (Satan) would hold rule over Adam and over all his posterity.

The serpent which Milton employed for the temptation, in keeping with that of Beaumont, Grotius, and Murtola, was strikingly beautiful. Neither did he 'walk on his chest or belly,' but 'upright and erect on his feet,' to quote the negative and positive descriptions given by Origen and Basil. The conception of Basil, Pareus accepted without question; Luther, with the reservation that the snake chosen 'did not walk erect as did man.' Among others Bonaventure quoted the belief of Origen; and Bishop Tostatus cited the interpretation of Peter Lombard that 'the Devil selected that kind of serpent which walked erect, that they call Pharias.' Du Bartas described Satan's instrument as 'not groveling on the clay.' However, we may note that Milton's earlier and hard-headed contemporary, the Anglican theologian Andrew Willet, rejected the belief. During the time of temptation, he declared, 'it is not to be supposed with Didymus, Jerome's master, that the serpent . . . was caused by the spirit to stand upright.'

The traditional Satan knew well that Eve was the weaker and more susceptible, and in the representative description of Peter Lombard, 'he first therefore sought to find the woman alone.' This belief, taken verbatim by Peter from Hugo's *De Sacramentis*, is reiterated by Ainsworth, Bonaventure, Calvin, Grotius in his *Adam*, Heywood, Mercer, Pererius, and Purchas. Finding Eve alone and unsuspecting, as was the woman of Peyton and Willet, Satan sought to attract her attention, and approached her with 'blandishments.' More effectively to impress Eve, said Beaumont, 'thrice did he bow his flattering neck.' These more or less common ornaments, including discussion of historically famous serpents, Milton accepted and utilized. He proved equally faithful to tradition in setting forth the temptation proper.

Under the influential analogy of the day of Crucifixion, the seduction of Eve covered a period which extended from nine in the morning until noon. This space of time suggested a lengthy and somewhat complex episode, and as such the temptation commonly was regarded. The good Bishop Babington spoke justifiably when he lamented Eve's 'tittle-tattle too long with the serpent.' The Satan and Eve of *Paradise Lost* maintained admirably this tradition.

As a preliminary to the temptation, Milton's Eve deliberately separated herself from Adam. At the outset of the temptation proper, to quote Philo, the woman was seduced 'by wiles and deceptions.' Satan flattered her, stressing particularly her beauty, intrigued her by speaking as a man, employed a persuasive voice, and in keeping with Genesis 3. 5, promised the fruit would make her a Deity. He urged the tyranny and envy of God, declared he had tasted the fruit, and described the enlightenment and exaltation which followed. As is implied in Genesis 3. 6, the fruit itself was rarely attractive, and, in the words of Swan, 'gave longing to the palate.' Tempted both by Satan and the fragrant apple, frail woman succumbed. Earth shuddered and nature sighed, but undeterred, Eve 'greedily . . . ingorged without restraint.'

For the larger part, Milton's themes and details were conventionalities common to poet and theologian alike. A number appear somewhat rare, among them the picture of Eve gorging the forbidden apple. One partial analogue of the scene comes from Caedmon, whose God declared to Eve, 'thou in that apple erst thyself did gorge.' The idea that nature reacted to Eve's transgression—and also to Adam's—probably stemmed from the Crucifixion analogue. At noon, the time assigned for man's fall, unnatural darkness overshadowed the earth. Later, the veil of the temple split in twain, an event suggestive of an earthquake. The idea had, however, previously been used by Beaumont, by Boehme in the *Three Principles*, Du Bartas, and Grotius in his *Adam*. The closest single analogue for all episodes is probably the *Divine Weeks*, but Professor Taylor's detailed analysis of the Milton-Du Bartas correspondences makes further consideration gratuitous. Beaumont's *Psyche* provides, however, an admirable substitute. Because the description is so extended, I quote only scattered verses, and this without indicating omissions. The opening lines refer to Beaumont's Tempter:

> To Paradise he came, and brought his hell
> Into the earthly heaven, where looking round,

A creature spruce and delicate he found
Upon a bank of flowery pleasures spread,
But far more sweet and beauteous than its bed!

It was the serpent, whose illustrious skin
Played with the sun, and sent him back his beams
With glorious use: that wealth which glisters in
The bosom of the oriental streams;
His sharpest eyes sparkled with nimble flames.

So now the serpent felt his bosom swell
With peevish rage and desperate disdain;
But pondering then how Adam's sober breast
With wisdom's ammunition furnished was,
He shook his head, and thought the match not even.

Thus said, he towards Eve did gently glide,
Whom straying from her husband he espied.
Unhappy error that, which did invite
The jealous tempter to be bold, since she
Had robbed herself of all her spouse's might,
By starting from his holy company.

Love and friendship smiled in his eyes,
Upon his face sat tenderness and care:
Thrice did he bow his flattering neck, and thrice
His silent homage he presented her:
'Why then, fair queen of heaven,' said he,
'Why must the Prince be bound, and subjects free?'

Eve and the Tempter argued at length regarding the truth
and justice of God's precept. Finally, Beaumont's Apostate declared he had eaten the fruit:

'O how it stings my soul, to think that you,
My sovereign, should thus faint-hearted be;
But yesterday, when I began to taste
The spiteful fruit, flames kindled in mine eyes;
My soul awaked, and from my bosom chased

> Those mists of ignorance.'
>   Three times she stepped to the inchanting tree,
> As oft by conscience plucked back again;
> Up went her desperate hand, and reached away
> All the world's bliss whil'st she the apple took:
> When lo, the earth did move, the heavens did stay,
> Beasts and birds shivered.

When Milton turned to the fatal temptation of Adam, he again sought to follow established tradition. Eve advanced the 'false persuasions' of Satan, Adam weighed them seriously, but the decisive force was the 'female charm' of Eve. The first and second steps may be called a literary expression of the interpretation, as set forth by Willet, that Adam was to an important degree 'seduced by the same . . . false persuasions whereby the woman was first beguiled, being carried away with an ambitious desire, in knowledge, not to be equalized, but made like unto God.' The basic conception of the final stage, in the words of Calvin, was that while 'Eve entangled Adam with the same fallacies by which she was deceived, . . . the opinion has commonly been received that he was rather captivated by her allurements than persuaded by Satan's impostures.' This standard belief apparently was dictated by the necessity of providing an explanation of Adam's fall in harmony with 1 Timothy 2. 14: 'Adam was not beguiled, but the woman.'

Coupled with these general correspondences to Milton's account are a number somewhat more detailed. His description of the forbidden fruit as exhilarating man harmonized with that of Valmarana, and may have some indirect connection with the rabbinical legend, discussed by Peyton, that it was actually an intoxicating wine. The conception that eating the apple would make Eve equal or superior to Adam had occurred implicitly in Caedmon, and perhaps in Tostatus. Both Mercer and Willet mentioned, and rejected, a further rabbinical legend which held that Eve tempted Adam lest she die and he marry another woman. Beaumont declared Eve 'played the serpent,' because she desired Adam to share her misery; Willet, to share her happiness; and Tostatus concluded she principally was motivated by 'inordinate love' for her husband—all of which themes were used, and the last stressed by Milton.

When the Eve of *Paradise Lost* finally resolved to tempt Adam, she brought not one apple, but 'a bough of fairest fruit'—a charming expansion of Scripture both comparable and superior to the plurality of 'beauteous apples' offered by Beaumont's temptress, and the undisclosed number which Caedmon's Eve carried 'in her hands,' and 'in her bosom.' Having eaten the fruit, Milton's Adam flamed with 'carnal desire,' and 'on Eve began to cast lascivious eye . . . in lust they burn.' The poet here gave dramatic expression to the ancient belief that carnal lust was a consequence of the fall. We note, however, that in his *Demonomachiae*, or *Battle of the Spirits*, Valmarana related that when Adam tasted the apple, 'immediately he cast his eyes upon his wife, and through his members burned a heat unknown before.'

Our most complete analogue for this section of Milton's epic comes from the previously quoted *Paradise*, or *De Paradiso*, of Moses Bar Cepha. Again we find the Syrian Bishop preceding Milton in linking with commonplace ideas, conceptions that were noticeably unusual. Both writers included the relatively uncommon picture of Eve urging upon Adam the argument that he incurred no danger in eating the fruit. Milton described Eve as presenting many arguments to Adam; Bar Cepha said that she did this. The two writers set forth the customary interpretation that Adam yielded because of physical charm, but followed it with the unusual idea that he and Eve grew intoxicated. Distinctly uncommon was the subsequent emphasis on an immediate and lustful cohabitation, together with the point that because of copulation Adam and Eve 'soon found their eyes how opened.' Two further ideas were wholly conventional in themselves, but their use at this place was not. One held that by sin the first glory of the naked body was destroyed; the second, that by transgression man had forfeited his immaterial but glorious 'ornaments.' The discussion of Bar Cepha, from which I translate only a minor part, covers something more than two folio columns:

> The man inquired concerning the fruit, and the woman repeated to him the arguments (words) which the serpent-Devil set forth to her. . . . Eve replied to Adam that she took the fruit from the serpent, and that not only would they not die, but that without danger they would grow to be as Gods. . . . Master Ephraem wrote truly that Eve urged the man with many entreaties. . . . Adam was not pursuaded by hunger to eat of the tree, but by physical desire (*libido*). . . . Because they partook of the fruit, which in truth they ate, they became inclined toward lechery . . . and at length were made intoxicated . . . Moreover, they were followers of wanton lust, to go whoring, to be defiled with adultery . . . 'And the eyes of both were opened.' . . . Sin had removed from them the garments of glory. . . . They were covered with shame. . . . After they had sinned, the glory of the body was spoiled.

Perhaps the most serious secondary result of the fall, as tradition had it, was its effect upon reason, the image of God within man. In the conventional statement of Philo, 'reason is henceforth ensnared,' and 'becomes a slave.' This belief Milton supported and employed, together with a group of ideas whose importance was more literary than philosophical: intense sorrow on the part of Adam and Eve, loss of desire to live or contemplation of suicide, heated quarrels, and self-recrimination. Descriptions of the quarrelling and self-recrimination of Adam and Eve were not uncommon in literary treatments of the fall, but it probably was less literary influence and more that of commentaries and compendiums which made and kept such disputes traditional. In the latter type of work, quoting Bonaventure, one of the most mooted questions occasioned by the fall was, 'Did the man or the woman sin more grievously?'

In discussions of this question both Adam and Eve were 'indicted' on a varying number of 'counts,' four each with Bonaventure, but with Willet, four against Adam and three against Eve. The representative conclusion appears that set forth by the Saint, who found Eve had transgressed more in the *sinning;* Adam, more in the *sin.* The principal charge against the first was the fault which Milton's contrite Eve confessed to her husband: 'Thou [hast sinned] against God only; I against God and thee.' Similarly, the gravest indictment against Adam—one based upon Romans 5. 12—was that which Milton's Adam emphasized: 'Endless misery from this day onward . . . to perpetuity.' 'All mankind, for one man's fault . . . condemned.' In harmony with Genesis 3. 13 and 1 Timothy 2. 14, the point frequently was made that Eve had been deceived.

Among literary and theological expansions of Scripture, few surpassed in force that based upon a single verse from Paul, Romans 5. 12: 'Wherefore, as by one man, sin entered the world, and death by sin; and so death passed upon all men.' From these two lines, and with some assistance either from general tradition or particular works,

Milton created his powerful picture of Sin and Death coming to waste the world. The following representative verses open with the evil pair waiting before the gates of hell:

>   [Sin] now to Death began:
> 'O Son, why sit we here, each other viewing
> Idly, while Satan, our great author, thrives
> In other worlds, and happier seat provides
> For us, his offspring dear? . . . Let us try—
> Adventrous work, yet to thy power and mine
> Not unagreeable!—to found a path
> Over this main from hell to that new world
> Where Satan now prevails, a monument
> Of merit high to all the infernal host. . . .'
>   Then both, from out hell-gates, into the waste
> Wide anarchy of chaos, damp and dark,
> Flew diverse, and, with power—their power was
>   great—
> Hovering upon the waters, what they met,
> Solid or slimy, as in raging sea
> Tossed up and down, together crowded drove,
> From each side shoaling. . . . The aggregated soil
> Death with his mace petrific, cold and dry,
> As with a trident smote, and fixed as firm
> As Delos, floating once; the rest his look
> Bound with Gorgonian rigor not to move,
> And with asphaltic slime; broad as the gate,
> Deep to the roots of hell the gathered beach
> They fastened, and the mole immense wraught on
> Over the foaming deep high-arched, a bridge
> Of length prodigious, joining to the wall
> Immovable of this now fenceless world,
> Forfeit to Death—from hence a passage broad,
> Smooth, easy, inoffensive, down to hell.

Frequently connected with Romans 5. 12 was Genesis 3. 17-18. Because Adam had sinned, God cursed the ground, and decreed that 'thorns and thistles, shall it bring forth.' From these verses came the belief of Christendom that the Creator so altered the world as to supplant eternal spring:

> [With] pinching cold and scorching heat . . .
> Vapor, and mist, and exhalation hot,
> Corrupt and pestilent. Now from the north
> Of Norumbega, and the Samoed shore,
> Bursting their brazen dungeon, armed with ice,
> And snow, and hail, and stormy gust and flaw,
> Boreas and Caecias and Argestes loud
> And Thrascias rend the woods, and seas upturn.

After Sin, Death, and inclement weather marched famine, sickness, madness and war, together with all the physical evils which long have tested both animal and man.

If Milton's description of Sin and Death provides the most forceful section of Book X, his farewell to Satan affords the most picturesque. The Apostate had returned to hell, and related his achievements to the surrounding peers. Much in the manner of Valmarana's Lucifer, he dramatized his use of an apple to seduce man, and, after a few additional words, stood waiting an outburst of applause. But rather than acclaim, he heard:

> On all sides, from innumerable tongues
> A dismal universal hiss, the sound
> Of public scorn. He wondered, but not long
> Had leisure, wondering at himself now more.
> His visage drawn he felt to sharp and spare,
> His arms clung to his ribs, his legs entwining
> Each other, till, supplanted, down he fell,
> A monstrous serpent on his belly prone,
> Reluctant, but in vain. . . . He would have spoke,
> But hiss for hiss returned with forkèd tongue
> To forkèd tongue; for now were all transformed

Alike, to serpents all, as accessories
To his bold riot.

Here Milton again made use of a favorite rhetorical
device, that of a catalog—now a catalog of snakes. Subsequently, when the serpents sought to eat fruit like that
forbidden, they chewed only bitter ashes. 'Thus they
were plagued,' wrote the poet, 'till their lost shape, permitted, they resumed.'

This episode is one born of rare inventive genius. Standing as such, inquiry regarding its background carries a
special interest. I first may note that no picture was better
known than that which painted hell as alive with serpents. It occurred and recurred, among others, in the
works of Beaumont, Cowley, Fletcher, Heywood, Marini,
and Tasso. In one scene by Beaumont:

> The snakes then hissed, and their poison spit,
> And in a thousand knots tied, and untied . . .
> Huge snakes, fierce vipers, angry adders, fell
> And fiery hydras all discovered were,
> With cockatrices, scorpions, dragons, and
> Of foul chimaeras, a full marshalled band.

So deeply ingrained was the practice of placing serpents in
hell, that Milton had violated custom by omitting them.
Yet the atmosphere and narrative of Books I and II had
no place for snakes. If custom were respected, serpents
must appear during the next and final scene in hell. This
they did.

The idea that by listening to the snake Satan, his hearers
turned into snakes, Fletcher had advanced in the *Purple
Island*. Equally significant is the preceding picture of the
rebellious spirits who rejected God and followed Satan:

> In heaven they scorned to serve, so now in hell
>   they reign.

There turned to serpents, swollen with pride and
   hate,
Their Prince a dragon fell.

Marini, in Crashaw's English translation, related that the
powers of hell greeted the fourth Fury with 'a general hiss.'
As we might expect, the picture of serpents in hell commu-
nicating by hisses represented a commonplace. Beaumont,
whom Milton joined in setting forth a catalog of snakes,
had effectively described discomfited serpents rolling
about, biting both themselves and the ground. Such similarities, coupled with the poet's probable acquaintance
with Beaumont, Crashaw, and Fletcher, would indicate
some indebtedness to them. However, we meet in the
anonymous poem *Genesis*, reprinted in volume XVIII of
the Ante-Nicene Christian Library, the conception that
following Satan's temptation of Eve:

> [God] bid him presently,
> With grovelling breast to crawl,
> And then to bite and chew the soil.

I suggest, therefore, a somewhat different conclusion—
that the tradition of which the English writers formed a
part, contributed those basic themes from which Milton
fashioned his farewell to Satan.

Chapter VIII

THE JUSTIFICATION OF GOD

HAD *Paradise Lost* remained a tragedy, we should now await the fifth and concluding act. Within Books IX and X, comparable to Act IV of the abandoned drama, Satan had seduced Eve, and Eve in turn had beguiled Adam. The temptation completed, Satan returned to hell, there to meet a punishment not unrelated to that accorded the Serpent in Genesis. The monsters Sin and Death invaded the earth, now a place of storm and tumult, conflict and toil. Human reason succumbed to lust, to the broader sin of concupiscence, to passion and misunderstanding. Stricken by Divine condemnation and judgment, Adam and Eve renewed their bitter quarrel. With the passing of hours, a spirit of reconciliation came to them, and at peace with themselves, they sought peace with God.

The objectives of a fourth act achieved, Milton turned in Books XI and XII to the necessary and important finale. Corrupted as he was by sin, only death could purify man and make possible a future life. Because unfit for God's holy Garden, and lest he achieve immortality from the Tree of Life, Adam must depart from Paradise. His expulsion, the Father entrusted to the mightiest warrior of heaven, the archangel Michael. By Divine command, Michael both revealed to man future events, and completed the poet's justification of the ways of God. I shall discuss these two divisions in this order, adding to the last related sections from earlier books of *Paradise Lost*.

It is the judgment of contemporary Miltonic criticism that the historical narrative of Books XI and XII, considered as a whole, forms the least stimulating and signifi-

cant division of the epic. We must question however if
this were the verdict of educated Christian readers perhaps as late as 1750. Among many others, works utilizing
much the same subject-matter had been written by Augustine, Caedmon, Du Bartas, Peyton, and Valmarana, the
last of whom described Michael as sent to eject man from
Paradise, and as instructing Adam concerning future events
of Biblical history. This subject-matter also had appeared
in a legion of commentaries on Genesis and other books of
Scripture, to say nothing of its inclusion in histories, as with
Raleigh; in poetry, as in Cowley's *Davidëis;* and in geography, as in Peter Heylyn's *Cosmography*. When Raleigh
used the word *memorable* in the caption, 'Memorable things
between the Fall of Adam and the Flood of Noah,' he suggested accurately the interest of his contemporaries in amplified paraphrases of Biblical history. There was indeed
good reason why the *Divine Weeks and Works* of Du
Bartas should have reached in approximately fifty years
more than two hundred and thirty editions.

During the Sixteenth and Seventeenth Centuries, by far
the most popular book for commentary, for literary paraphrase, and for incidental use was Genesis. So vast was
the learning expended upon this book, that the last of
the great commentaries, the *Questions on Genesis* of Marin
Mersenne, required more than fifteen hundred large folio
columns to reach discussion of Tubal and Jubal Cain. The
major interest, as in *Paradise Lost*, Books IV, VII-IX, was
in the three opening chapters; the secondary and tertiary
on events from the Fall to the Flood, and from the Flood
to the conclusion. The Book of Exodus, a poor second to
Genesis, apparently received somewhat more attention
than subsequent books of the Old Testament. The four
hundred and ninety lines which Milton devoted to per-
sonages and happenings from the Fall to the Flood, the

one hundred and sixty-three lines allotted to the remainder
of Genesis, the ninety-seven to Exodus, and the brief passages given to other books, reflect not inaccurately the
proportional variations of contemporary interest.

There is some truth in our conventional interpretation
that in *Paradise Lost*, XI-XII, Milton followed the Bible.
A more exact statement, however, is that in the major
part of these books he frequently followed various interpretations of Scripture which had appeared in commentary
and literary paraphrase. It was such works, not Genesis
4. 8, which supported his interpretation that Cain slew
Abel with a stone, and the implication that prior to the
deed Cain dissembled or concealed his anger. A second
illustration comes from the emphasis which he placed
upon Jubal and Tubal Cain, mentioned in passing in
Genesis 4. 21-22 as 'the father of all such as handle the
harp and pipe,' and 'the forger of every cutting instrument of brass and iron.' Genesis said but little of Enoch
or of Nimrod, and did not describe the latter as leader of
those who erected the tower of Babel. In harmony with
much of the commentary literature, Milton stressed both
characters, and made the latter the chief or a chief builder
of Babel.

Because of the poet's deep hatred of oppression, nothing
in the whole of *Paradise Lost* appears more personal and
spontaneous than the digression on tyrants and tyranny
which followed his account of Nimrod. Milton unquestionably believed all that he uttered here, but it was nevertheless a tradition to include with description of the tyrannical Nimrod a discussion or condemnation of tyranny. It
was also the commentaries and related literature which described Abraham as 'bred up in idol-worship.' Had the poet
followed Genesis, and Genesis alone, he would have written
with Caedmon that God called Abraham, not at Ur of Chal-

dea, but at Haran, and that the Patriarch had resided at
Haran for some years before he departed to seek the 'land
unknown.' In extended portions of Books XI-XII Milton
utilized the conceptions of commentary and related literature.

The poet's general indebtedness to such literature raises
a further important question: Did Milton employ it eclec-
tically, creating an individual pattern from widely chosen
details? Our available evidence indicates that he did not.
There existed, for example, much disagreement as to the
manner in which Cain murdered his brother. One theory
held that Cain strangled Abel; another, that he killed him
with a stone. The Protestant commentator Mercer declared
some writers held that Cain used a stone; others, one among
different weapons; and concluded there are a thousand ways
of inflicting death. Two additional disputes centered about
Abraham, the first of which concerned his being reared an
idolater. One group asserted he had been; Syncellus,
Pererius, and others maintained the contrary with equal
vigor. The second dispute arose over the place where
God called Abraham. The Calling in Chaldea, adopted
by Milton, held the support of Du Bartas, Mercer, Pererius,
Raleigh, Syncellus, and Willet. A number of theologians
compromised as to the place, and described Abraham as
called neither at Ur of Chaldea nor at Haran, as Augustine,
or as called at both, as Ainsworth and Tostatus. Augustine
based his interpretation upon the account of Stephen,
Acts 7. 2-3, according to which God called the Patriarch
in Mesopotamia before he had reached the city of Haran.

As a result of these, and other differences of interpretation, complete agreement among poets and theologians
proved much more the exception than the rule. Among the
relatively small group of writers who exactly paralleled Milton on the three points discussed, the best known and most

widely read was the French poet Du Bartas. In that book
of the *Divine Weeks* entitled *The Handicrafts*, the Adam
of Du Bartas saw in a vision important events of the future,
and described 'that which should befall his posterity unto
the end of the first world destroyed by the Flood, according to the relationship of Moses in Genesis in the
fourth, fifth, sixth, and seventh chapters.' In Book XI
of *Paradise Lost*, Adam had a series of visions which opened
with the fourth and closed with the seventh chapter of
Genesis. Both visions were announced to a listener—with
Du Bartas, to Seth; with Milton, to Michael. Each poet
also made explicitly the point that the events envisioned
by Adam were those which involved his posterity. With
these similarities are included differences, but comparison
discloses that Milton utilized a narrative pattern closely
related to that previously employed by Du Bartas.

In his first prophetic vision, Milton's Adam saw the not
far distant murder of Abel:

> Adam, now enforced to close his eyes,
> Sunk down, and all his spirits became entranced.
> But him the gentle angel by the hand
> Soon raised, and his attention thus recalled:
> 'Adam, now ope thine eyes, and first behold
> The effects which thy original crime hath wrought
> In some to spring from thee. . . .'
> His eyes he opened, and . . . thither anon
> A sweaty reaper from his tillage brought
> First fruits, the green ear and the yellow sheaf,
> Unculled, as came to hand. A shepherd next
> More meek, came with the firstlings of his flock . . .
> His offerings soon propitious fire from heaven
> Consumed, with nimble glance and grateful steam;
> The other's not, for his was not sincere:
> Whereat he inly raged, and, as they talked,
> Smote him into the midriff with a stone

That beat out life; he fell, and deadly pale,
Groaned out his soul, with gushing blood effused.
Much at that sight was Adam in his heart
Dismayed. . . . But [Michael replied,] the bloody fact
Will be avenged . . . though here thou see him die,
Rolling in dust and gore.

Du Bartas stated that Cain had concealed his anger, and
in addition, used the word *sight* in describing the bloody
Abel:

Now, the one in cattle, the other rich in grain,
On two steep mountains build they alters twain; . . .
[God] accepts good Abel's gift; but hates the other,
Profane oblation of his furious brother;
Who feeling deep the effects of God's displeasure,
Raves, frets, and fumes, and murmurs out of measure.
But, one day drawing with dissembled love
His harmless brother far into a grove . . .
With both his hands he takes a stone so huge
That in our age three men could hardly budge,
And just upon his tender brother's crown,
With all his might he cruel casts it down.
  The murdered face lies printed in the mud,
And loud for vengeance cries the martyred blood.
The battered brains fly in the murderer's face;
The sun, to shun this tragic sight, apace
Turns back his team.

To Adam's greater horror, he learned from Michael
that there exist 'many shapes of death, and many are the
ways that lead to his grim cave.' Numerous men, the angel
continued, shall die from violence; others by fire, flood,
and famine; but 'by intemperance more, in meats and
drinks.' He displayed to Adam a sad, dark building that
seemed a lazar house, within which tossed and groaned
the sufferers from a catalog of diseases. In this house,

Despair tended the sick. Du Bartas had spoken of 'a thousand kinds of living deaths,' of 'that fearful cave,' and emphasized the part played in death by famine, war, and 'surfeit.' He included a catalog of diseases more extended than Milton's, and wrote of 'mad Despair, that bears about her burning coals.'

The Adam of *Paradise Lost* next envisioned Jubal and Tubal Cain, long celebrated by Christian commentator and poet as the inventors of musical and mechanical instruments. I quote only from Milton's second and longer description, that of Tubal Cain:

> He looked, and saw a spacious plain, whereon. . . .
> In other part stood one who, at the forge
> Laboring, two massy clods of iron and brass
> Had melted. . . . the liquid ore he drained
> Into fit moulds prepared; from which he formed
> First his own tools, then what might else be wrought,
> Fusil or graven in metal.

Du Bartas pictured the mighty Tubal standing at the forge, and described him first as moulding tools; secondly as constructing other instruments:

> Compassed round with smoking cyclops rude . . .
> Sweating Tubal stands, hastening the hot work
> In their sounding hands . . . the unfull harmony
> Of uneven hammers, beating diversely. . . .
> And first perceiving that this scalding metal
> Becoming cold, in any shape would settle
> He casts a hundred plots, and ere he parts
> He moulds the groundwork of a hundred arts . . .
> In two square creases of unequal sizes
> To turn to iron streamlings he devises . . .
> And this a hammer, that an anvil makes;
> And, adding tongs to these two instruments,
> He stores his house with iron implements.

Developing further the second vision of Adam, Milton lamented the marriage of the sons of Seth with the daughters of Cain. In the third vision, he described the tyrannical offspring which resulted from this union. The two episodes rested partially upon Genesis 6. 2, 4: 'The sons of God saw the daughters of men that they were fair; and they took them wives of all which they chose. . . . And they bare children to them; the same became mighty men which were of old, men of renown.' In the two visions, *Paradise Lost* employed a number of conceptions not found in the *Divine Weeks*, but easily available in such works as the *Chronographia* of Syncellus. Having descended to the plain, wrote Milton, the godly sons of Seth:

> Long had not walked when from the tents behold
> A bevy of fair women, richly gay
> In gems and wanton dress! to the harp they sung
> Soft amorous ditties, and in dance came on.
> The men, though grave, eyed them, and let their eyes
> Rove without rein, till, in the amorous net
> Fast caught, they liked, and each his liking chose. . . .
>   He looked, and saw wide territory spread
> Before him—towns, and rural works between,
> Cities of men with lofty gates and towers,
> Concourse in arms, fierce faces threatening war,
> Giants of mighty bone and bold emprise. . . .
> Destroyers rightlier called, and plagues of men.

Du Bartas had included these episodes:

> O strange to be believed! the blessed race,
> The sacred flock, whom God by special grace
> Adopts for his, even they, alas, most shameless
> Do follow sin, most beastly brute and tameless,
> With lustful eyes choosing for wanton spouses
> Men's wicked daughters; mingling so the houses

Of Seth and Cain; preferring foolishly
Frail beauty's blaze to virtuous modesty.
   From these profane, foul, cursed kisses sprung
A cruel brood, feeding on blood and wrong;
Fell giants strange, of haughty hand and mind,
Plagues of the world, and scourges of mankind.

Within Adam's third vision, Milton placed a description of
Enoch not substantiated by Genesis. Like the poet himself, the Patriarch who walked with God, 'spake much of
right and wrong; of justice, of religion, truth, and peace.'
Du Bartas pictured only the conventional Enoch, who
'mounting from form to form, in form of God he happy
doth transform.'

   From the Patriarch Enoch, Milton turned to Noah
and the Flood. This fourth vision proved the last, for
subsequent to its close Michael perceived Adam's 'mortal
sight to fail.' It also unnerved Adam greatly, a point which
Milton emphasized in two successive passages. In the first,
the poet addressed himself directly to his character; in the
second, Adam lamented to Michael. The Archangel voiced
the line last quoted:

            Of mankind, so numerous [of] late,
All left in one small bottom swum embarked.
How didst thou grieve then, Adam, to behold
The end of all thy offspring, end so sad,
Depopulation! Thee another flood,
Of tears and sorrow a flood thee also drowned,
And sunk thee as thy sons; till, gently reared
By the angel, on thy feet thou stood'st at last . . .
And scarce to the angel utteredst thus thy plaint:
'O visions ill foreseen! Better had I
Lived ignorant of future. . . .' 'A world devote
To universal wrack.'

   The *Divine Weeks* made precisely these additions to
Genesis: that Adam saw in a vision the drowning of his

posterity, that this vision disturbed him greatly, and that with it he ceased to fortell the future. Said the distraught Adam of Du Bartas:

> 'Alas! so many nephews lose I here. . . .
> O children, whither fly you? O sonless father!
> O world's decay! O universal wrack!
> O flesh! O blood!' Here, sorrow stopped the door
> Of his sad voice; and, almost dead for woe,
> The prophetizing spirit forsook him so.

The second half of Adam's concluding vision, Milton devoted to the Ark of Noah. More precisely, Michael and Adam collaborated in relating the entire story, with the archangel speaking both first and last. Du Bartas also had given much place to this narrative, and devoted to it that division of the *Divine Weeks* which he entitled *The Ark*. Among other similarities in detail, the French poet spoke of 'shutting heaven's sluices;' the English writer employed the expression, 'now had stopped his sluices, as the heaven his windows shut.' In Genesis 8. 4-5, the Flood subsided slowly, ten weeks elapsing between the time when the Ark touched Ararat, and 'the tops of the mountains [were] seen.' Despite this fact, both Du Bartas and Milton conceived the waters as retreating swiftly. In the lines of *Paradise Lost:*

> The Ark no more now floats, but seems on ground
> Fast on the top of some high mountain fixed.
> And now the tops of hills as rocks appear;
> With clamor thence the rapid currents drive,
> Towards the retreating sea, their furious tide.

Such are examples of major correspondences between Book XI of *Paradise Lost* and comparable sections of the *Divine Weeks,* in particular that division of the second week named by Du Bartas *The Handicrafts.* Equally suggestive similarities occur in the first third of Book XII, and those parts of the *Second Week* which the French writer entitled *Babylon, The Vocation, The Law,* and *The Captains.* As I previously suggested, Genesis provided no justification for the assertion of both poets that Abraham was reared an idolater. Milton and Du Bartas likewise departed from its statement that God called Abraham at Haran, some years after he had left Chaldea. With each writer, the Biblical 'wilderness' of Shur became the 'desert.' Where Exodus stated directly that in crossing the Red Sea the Israelites 'walked upon dry land,' the English and the French poet employed the simile, 'pass as upon dry land.' Again, Joshua 10. 12 declared this leader said the sun should stand upon Gibeon, and the moon in the valley of Ajalon, but both Milton and Du Bartas substituted 'command' for 'said,' 'in' Gibeon for 'upon' Gibeon, and 'vale' for 'valley.' No translation I have met used the phrase 'in Gibeon.'

There existed in Genesis no authority for Milton's statement, given early in Book XII, that the 'black bituminous gurge' employed in building the tower of Babel came from the mouth of hell, or the implication that the tower was constructed adjacent to this opening. The statement and the implication conflict unmistakably with the description which placed the hell of *Paradise Lost* within chaos, far beyond both earth and its encircling cosmos. Milton discussed tyranny in general immediately subsequent to Nimrod and the tower of Babel; Du Bartas attacked tyranny in his introduction to 'the life and manners of Nimrod.' Genesis of course failed to connect Nimrod with the tower of Babel, and indeed gave but little space to him. I quote first from Milton's epic:

> One shall rise . . . who, not content . . .
> Will arrogate dominion undeserved

Over his brethren, and quite dispossess
Concord and law of nature from the earth—
Hunting, and men, not beasts, shall be his game,
With war and hostile snare such as refuse
Subjection to his empire tyrannous. . . .
    He, with a crew, whom like ambition joins
With him or under him to tyrannize,
Marching from Eden towards the west, shall find
The plain, wherein a black bituminous gurge
Boils out from under ground, the mouth of hell.
Of brick, and of that stuff, they cast to build
A city and tower, whose top may reach to heaven;
And get themselves a name, lest, far dispersed
In foreign lands, their memory be lost. . . .
But God . . . them beholding soon . . . in derision
    sets
Upon their tongues a various spirit, to raze
Quite out their native language, and instead
To sow a jangling noise of words unknown.
    Forthwith a hideous gabble rises loud
Among the builders; each to other calls,
Not understood—till, hoarse and all in rage,
As mocked they storm.

In addition to including many words and ideas similar
to those of *Paradise Lost*, Du Bartas exemplified dramat-
ically both Milton's 'hideous gabble,' and his statement that
'among the builders, each to other calls, not understood.'
I do not give from Du Bartas the digression of tyranny
with which he prefaced his account of Nimrod:

[Side caption:] Nimrod's exercises and essays
To make himself master of the rest.
Then Nimrod . . . leaves hunting beasts, and
Hunteth men to trap . . . [employing] darts,
And shafts, and swords, their rage to tame.
    Enthroned thus, this tyrant 'gan devise

To perpetrate a thousand cruelties. . . .
[He] busies them to build a lofty tower . . .
A palace, whose proud front and feet,
With heaven and hell may in an instant meet . . .
Lest . . . dispersed o'er all the regiments . . .
[He said,] at least let's leave memorials . . .
Heap they night and day, the gummy slime
Of chalky waters gray. . . . They dig to hell . . .
[But God struck] them straight with a spirit
Of difference . . . a jangling noise, not much
Unlike the rumors of Bacchus's swains. . . .
 Some speak . . . in the nose . . . some howl, some
Halloo, some . . . strain; each has his gibberish . . .
Bring me, quoth one, a trowel, quickly quick:
One brings him up a hammer. Hew this brick,
Another bids, and then they cleave a tree. . . .
One calls for planks, another mortar lacks:
They bear the first a stone; the last an axe. . . .
Nigh breathless all, with their confused yowling
 . . . the storm arrived.

Subsequent to the expected dissertation upon tyranny which followed his account of Nimrod, Milton described the calling of Abraham. The poet's departure from Genesis in placing the Call in Chaldea had the support of Acts 7. 2-3, but as much may not be said of other variations from the Mosaic version. According to Genesis 11. 31, 'Terah took Abram his son, and Lot . . . and they went forth with them from Ur of the Chaldees, to go unto the land of Canaan; and they came unto Haran and dwelt there.' After Abraham had reached the age of seventy-five, Genesis 12. 5 records that he 'took Sarai his wife, and Lot his brother's son, and all their substance that they had gathered, and the souls that they had gotten in Haran.' Despite these straightforward statements, Milton described Abraham, not Terah, as the leading force in the departure from Chaldea, and neglected to mention his apparently extended residence in Haran. Although Abraham possessed no flocks and herds when he left Chaldea—these being the property of Terah his father—Milton depicted him as departing with all his wealth:

> Tyranny must be,
> Though to the tyrant thereby no excuse. . . .
> Thus will this latter, as the former world,
> Still tend from bad to worse, till God at last
> . . . leave them to their own polluted ways,
> And one peculiar nation to select . . .
> A nation from one faithful man to spring.
> Him on this side Euphrates yet residing,
> Bred up in idol worship—Oh, that men
> (Canst thou believe) should be so stupid grown . . .
> As . . . to worship their own work in wood and stone
> For gods!—yet him God the Most High voutsafes
> To call by vision from his father's house,
> His kindred, and false gods. . . . He straight obeys,
> Not knowing to what land, yet firm believes.
>   I see him, but thou canst not, with what faith
> He leaves his gods, his friends, and native soil,
> Ur of Chaldea, passing now the ford
> To Haran—after him a cumbrous train
> Of herds and flocks, and numerous servitude—
> Not wandering poor, but trusting all his wealth
> With God, who called him, in a land unknown.
> Canaan he now attains.

The earlier French writer named Abraham as leader of the group which left Chaldea. He also referred to idolatry, to those who forsook the true God, stressed the faith of Abraham, mentioned the Euphrates, and alluded to the degeneration of men—details all absent from Genesis. In keeping with Protestant tradition, Du Bartas made idolatry a form of tyranny:

Though profane service of idolatry . . . through
All did tyrannize; yet in Chaldea was their
Chiefest seat . . . and that city great,
Built on the slimy strand of Euphrates. . . .
[Side caption:] The Calling of Abraham.
But God, desirous more for us than him,
In some one stock to save Faith's sacred stem . . .
Marks Abram for his own; and from false rites
To men, to beasts, to stocks, to stones, to sprites,
Him graciously to his own service draws. . . .
    The sacred faith of Abram languished not
In idleness, but always waked and wrought. . . .
Alas! said Abram, must I needs forego
These happy fields where Euphrates doth flow . . .
To seek a country God knows where or whither,
Whose unknown name hath yet scarce sounded
    thither?
Can I thus my native soil forsake? . . .
Farewell Chaldea . . . my friends [and] brothers . . .
But, for all reasons, faith sufficeth me;
Who lodge with God can never houseless be.

Where Du Bartas had pictured the plague of locusts as a 'sable cloud' which 'swarmeth down,' Milton spoke of 'a darksome cloud of locusts swarming down.' In their accounts of the plague of 'thick darkness,' both writers referred to the heavy blackness as 'palpable darkness.' Equally close were their descriptions of the Israelites crossing the Red Sea. According to Exodus 14. 29: 'the children of Israel walked upon dry land in the midst of the sea; and the waters were a wall unto them on their right hand, and on their left.' When Du Bartas retold the story, Moses parted the Red Sea so that the people 'pass through as on dry land,' flanked on right and left by 'walls of crystal . . . two walls of glass.' Milton likewise inserted the word 'as,' and said that the Israelites 'pass as on dry land, between two crystal walls.' As I have mentioned above, both writers utilized precisely the same variations from Joshua 10. 12. At this point, Milton concluded the extended discourse by Michael which opened Book XII of the epic. With conclusion of this revelation, there ended noticeable and repeated similarities to the *Divine Weeks*.

Throughout the seven hundred and fifty verses which began with Adam's first vision of Book XI, and closed with Michael's first revelation of Book XII, Milton's narrative has followed such a pattern as that employed in the *Divine Weeks*. Despite the accepted fact that Milton, as a youth, knew thoroughly the poetry of the French writer, I do not state categorically that he obtained from Du Bartas his structural outline. Rather, my point is this—if Milton did not draw his basic narrative pattern from Du Bartas, he obtained it from a work highly similar to the *Divine Weeks*.

· · · · ·

Milton's most effective justification of God was not his explicit exposition of theological doctrine. It consisted rather of a powerful and dramatic narrative which instructed far more by example than by precept. That the poet desired primarily to address the varied emotions of man requires no evidence other than the preponderance of space devoted to pure narrative. The story was the thing. However, his scattered and relatively limited presentations of doctrine scarcely mean that Milton regarded it as nonessential. Had he done so, he neither would have been Milton, nor a true son of his age.

The poet's explicit or doctrinal justification of God is as noteworthy for its simplicity as for its relative brevity. Indeed, this justification rested ultimately upon four basic conceptions. Both angel and man were created just and

right, able to have withstood temptation. Their fall resulted from exercise of the free will which God gave them,
and refused to take away. Divine foreknowledge neither
influenced nor occasioned their tragic error. Through His
grace, and Christ's Atonement, God brought good out of
evil, and by redeemed man repaired the damage wrought
in heaven by the rebellious angels.

These few beliefs had long stood as fundamentals of
Christian thought. With minor variations, they had been
reiterated by theologians of all major creeds, a condition
perhaps adequately illustrated by Augustine, Calvin, and
the Angelican divine, Andrew Willet. The excerpt from
Augustine will be found in that paragraph which opens
The City of God, Book XXII, Chapter I. I use the translation of the Reverend Marcus Dods:

> Of the Creation of Angels and Men: It is He who
> gave to this intellectual nature free will of such a kind,
> that if he wished to forsake God; that is, his blessedness,
> misery should forthwith result. It is He who, when He
> foreknew that certain angels would in their pride desire
> to suffice for their own blessedness, and would forsake
> their great good, did not deprive them of this power,
> deeming it to be more befitting His power and good-
> ness to bring good out of evil than to prevent evil from
> coming into existence. . . . It is He who with very
> just punishment doomed the angels who voluntarily fell
> to everlasting misery. It is He who made also man him-
> self upright, with the same freedom of will—an earthly
> animal, indeed, but fit for heaven if he remained faithful
> to his Creator. . . . When He foreknew that man would
> in his turn sin . . . did not deprive him of the power
> of free will, because He at the same time foresaw what
> good He himself would bring out of evil, and how from
> this mortal race, deservedly and justly condemned, He
> would by his grace collect, as now He does, a people

so numerous, that He thus fills up and repairs the blank
made by the fallen angels; and that thus that beloved
and heavenly city is not defrauded of the full number
of its citizens, but perhaps may even rejoice in a still
more overflowing population.

Again within a single paragraph, one found in his *Commentary on Genesis*, Calvin wrote in not dissimilar vein.
His digressive discourse included a multiplicity of secondary themes and ideas which Milton later utilized:

Though Moses begins in this book with the creation of
the world, he nevertheless does not confine us to this
subject. For these things ought to be connected together:
that the world was founded by God, and that man, after
he had been endued with the light of intelligence, and
adorned with so many privileges, fell by his own fault,
and was thus deprived of all the benefits he had obtained. Afterwards, by the compassion of God, he was
restored to the life he had forfeited, and this through the
loving-kindness of Christ. . . . This is the argument of
the Book: After the world had been created, man was
placed in it as in a theatre, that he, beholding above
him and beneath the wonderful works of God, might
reverently adore their Author. Secondly, that all things
were ordained for the use of man, that he, being under
deeper obligation, might devote and dedicate himself
entirely to obedience towards God. Thirdly, that he was
endued with understanding and reason, that being distinguished from brute animals he might meditate on a
better life, and might even tend directly towards God,
whose image he bore engraven on his own person.
Afterwards followed the fall of Adam, whereby he
alienated himself from God; whence it came to pass
that he was deprived of all rectitude. Thus Moses represents man as devoid of all good, blinded in understanding,
perverse in heart, vitiated in every part, and under sen-

tence of eternal death; but he soon adds the history of his
restoration, in which Christ shines forth with the benefit
of redemption. . . . After Adam had by his own desperate fall ruined himself and all his posterity . . . we,
being rescued out of profound darkness, have obtained a
new life by the mere grace of God; . . . and all the
pious who have since lived were sustained by the very
same promise of salvation by which Adam was first
raised from the fall.

Twelve centuries after Augustine, and less than a century after Calvin, Andrew Willet set forth compactly the
four major conceptions. He said nothing however of man's
repairing the damage done in heaven:

A question will here be moved: why the Lord gave
this precept to Adam, which he knew he would not keep.
For answer whereunto, first we say, that God gave him
a precept which was possible to be kept, and Adam had
power to keep it, if he would. It was then not God's
fault, that gave him free will, but his own, that abused
that gift. Secondly, if it be replied, why God did not
give him grace and stay him from the transgression: I
answer that God could have given him such grace, and
to the angels likewise, that they should not have fallen.
But it was fit that God should leave the creatures to their
free will, and not hinder the course of nature, which he
had made. Thirdly, though God foresaw man's transgression, yet that was no reason to withhold the precept;
for then God should neither have made the angels, nor
man, because he saw that some of both should be repro-
bates. . . . Fourthly, as God foresaw man's transgression,
so he knew how to turn it to good, as in showing mercy
to sinners, and in sending Christ to restore what man had
lost. So that notwithstanding God's foresight of Adam's
transgression, he was not to forbear to charge Adam
with this commandment, in regard of the great good
which God also did foresee should ensue.

With the elements fundamental to a justification of God, Milton naturally, and perhaps inevitably intermingled the less vital themes which long had clustered about them. In fact, the first point made in Book III consisted of the secondary conception that God gave to Adam but one commandment. The single pledge, as Milton afterwards stated, was both simple and easily obeyed. This argument, employed at least as early as Tertullian, appeared during the Seventeenth Century in the writings of Beaumont, Grotius, and Willet. Equally orthodox was the picture of man as an ingrate, together with the beliefs voiced subsequently through the Deity of *Paradise Lost:*

> I made him just and right,
> Sufficient to have stood, though free to fall.
> Such I created all the ethereal powers
> And spirits, both them who stood and them who failed;
> Freely they stood who stood, and fell who fell.
> Not free, what proof could they have given sincere
> Of true allegiance, constant faith, or love . . .
> When will and reason . . . both, had served necessity,
> Not Me? They, therefore, as to right belonged,
> So were created, nor can justly accuse
> Their Maker, or their making, or their fate,
> As if predestination overruled
> Their will, disposed by absolute decree
> Or high foreknowledge. They themselves decreed
> Their own revolt, not I. If I foreknew,
> Foreknowledge had no influence on their fault.

The basic theological problem involved in these verses is that of explaining the appearance of evil in a world ruled by a provident God who is both all-knowing and all-powerful. But one orthodox answer could be made: that God created perfect man and angel, and gave to them complete freedom of choice. Such was the answer of all

Fathers who did not assume an uncontrolled principle of
evil, of the Lateran Council, and of Protestant theology.
Prior to *Paradise Lost*, literally thousands of compendiums,
commentaries, and works chiefly literary had stressed this
solution. There existed in Christendom, one may say, no
better known nor more widely accepted belief.

Continuing his exposition, Milton reiterated the point
that God had made man free, and then turned to a further
link in the complete argument. This point held that the
angels, self-depraved, would find no mercy; man, however,
having been tempted by another, would receive grace. The
poet again spoke through God:

> I formed them free, and free they must remain
> Till they enthrall themselves. I else must change
> Their nature, and revoke the high decree
> Unchangeable, eternal, which ordained
> Their freedom; they themselves ordained their fall.
> The first sort by their own suggestion fell,
> Self-tempted, self-depraved; Man falls, deceived
> By the other first. Man, therefore, shall find grace;
> The other, none. In mercy and justice both,
> Through heaven and earth, so shall my glory excel;
> But mercy, first and last, shall brightest shine.

Although moved by pity, the mercy of God did not immediately overcome the claims of either Divine justice or
wrath. As Milton later wrote, mercy, justice, and wrath
remained long in conflict. When the Redeemer had observed the Father 'more to pity inclined,' the angelic chorus
sang that Christ offered himself:

> To appease thy [God's] wrath, and end the strife
> Of mercy and justice in thy face discerned.

Among other theologians, Abelard, Bonaventure, Damascene, and Gregory the Great discussed with approval the

idea that Divine grace would be accorded man, but not
the fallen angels. On occasion, the extension of grace to
mankind often was thought to produce a temporary conflict between such Divine attributes as God's justice and
mercy. As a result, a number of writers which included
Du Bartas and Joseph Fletcher pictured these or related
qualities as if in debate. Fletcher, author of *The Perfect,
Cursed, Blessed Man*, wrote in 1629:

> To express and set forth this wonderful work of God
> for the redemption of mankind, we imagine him first to
> be moved by his compassion or pity; his pity to stir
> up his mercy; his mercy for truth and justice's sake to
> submit herself to his wrath; his wrath to be assuaged by
> his peace: and so one grace to advise and deal with
> another, till at last they sweetly agree and join all in one,
> how to perfect and effect a work for the deliverance of
> all mankind out of its misery.

Following the announcement of Milton's God that his
mercy should rule his justice, Christ praised the grace of
the Father, and in this fashion instituted the consultation
which brought forth the Divine plan for redemption. As a
first step, God declared his decree of election and reprobation:

> Upheld by me, yet once more he shall stand
> On even ground against his mortal foe—
> By me upheld, that he may know how frail
> His fallen condition is, and to me owe
> All his deliverance, and to none but me.
> Some I have chosen of peculiar grace,
> Elect above the rest; so is my will:
>   The rest shall hear me call, and oft be warned
> Their sinful state, and to appease betimes
> The incensèd Deity, while offered grace
> Invites; for I will clear their senses dark

What may suffice, and soften stony hearts
To pray, repent, and bring obedience due.
To prayer, repentance, and obedience due,
Though but endeavored with sincere intent,
Mine ear shall not be slow, mine eye not shut.
And I will place within them as a guide
My umpire Conscience; whom if they will hear,
Light after light well used they shall attain,
And to the end persisting safe arrive.
     This my long sufferance, and my day of grace,
They who neglect and scorn shall never taste;
But hard be hardened, blind be blinded more,
That they may stumble on, and deeper fall;
And none but such from mercy I exclude.

One who attempts discussion of the doctrine of predestination—especially one so inadequately prepared as the
writer—invites the fate of those speculative devils whom
Milton described in *Paradise Lost*, Book II. These fallen
angels 'reasoned high of providence, foreknowledge . . .
free will, foreknowledge absolute, and found no end, in
wandering mazes lost.' Nevertheless, I shall venture some
few conjectures.

     In the plan set forth by Milton, all mankind depended
upon the grace of God for deliverance from sin and eternal
death. One group of men, necessarily smirched by original
sin, God arbitrarily elected or predestined to salvation.
These two phases of the poet's doctrine, the latter of which
had the support of Romans 8. 29-30; 9. 22-23; 11. 29; 2
Timothy 2. 20; Titus 3. 5; and related passages, appear
orthodox commonplaces generally accepted by Protestant
and Roman Catholic. We should recall, however, that Milton seemingly regarded election as wholly absolute, an interpretation not held by such an influential theologian as
Thomas Aquinas. Glossing 2 Peter 1. 10, Thomas wrote

that 'the predestined must strive after good works and prayer; because through these means predestination is most certainly fulfilled. . . . Predestination can be furthered by the creatures, but it cannot be impeded by them.'

If, as I have remarked, Milton conceived election as absolute, he also went beyond Calvin. In the discourse on predestination given in the celebrated *Institutes*, this theologian declared that Paul himself, 'in another place, cautions against carelessness, saying, "Let him that thinketh he standeth, take heed lest he fall." Again: "Art thou grafted among the people of God? Be not high minded, but fear. God is able to cut thee off again, and graft in others." Lastly, experience itself teaches us that vocation and faith are of little value, unless accompanied by perseverance, which is not the lot of all.' Whether conceived as absolute, or in some measure conditional, the poet's conclusion conflicted directly with the not unimportant interpretation of Origen. Explicating 2 Timothy 2. 20-21, the Greek Father stated that 'the Creator makes vessels of honor and vessels of dishonor, not from the beginning according to his foreknowledge, since he does not condemn or justify beforehand according to it; but makes those into vessels of honor who purged themselves, and those into vessels of dishonor who allowed themselves to remain unpurged.'

To a further group, likewise sinful, the Deity of *Paradise Lost* made a general call, including within the vocation aid sufficient for repentance. Of this group, some members heard the call; others retained their stony hearts. The first and repentant type may constitute such an addition to the elect as was suggested by one translation of Deuteronomy 1. 11: 'The Lord God adds to this number many thousands.' Considered somewhat differently, the two divisions represent Paul's vessels of honor and dishonor, as Origen interpreted the Apostle's words. More important

however is the fact that, as Origen had done in the passage
quoted, Milton believed no man absolutely predestined to
damnation. In short, his doctrine of predestination included only the elect.

From one point of view, the division of mankind into
elect and reprobate displayed the goodness and grace of
the Father. The sin of Adam had made all men reprobate,
with the result that predestination caused no man to be
lost, and many men to be saved. As Giovanni Diodati said
in his *Pious Annotations*—a work printed in translation by
order of the Commons of England—'the sentence of condemnation was generally passed against them all; but it was
God's pleasure to appropriate it only to a part of Adam's
race.' I mention in passing that this Diodati was the respected theologian whom Milton paused to visit as he
returned to England from Italy.

From a second point of view, the division appears un-
justifiable. Christ died for all men, in atonement for their
sins. Were mankind composed only of those eternally predestined either to election or reprobation, the Saviour died
in vain. In keeping with predecessor and contemporary,
Milton left this problem untouched when he turned from
the doctrine of predestination to that of the Atonement.
Once more in harmony with Christian thought, he made
the Atonement a prerequisite for the granting of Divine
mercy to mankind:

> But yet all is not done. Man disobeying,
> Disloyal, breaks his fealty, and sins
> Against the high supremacy of heaven,
> Affecting Godhead; and, so losing all,
> To expiate his treason hath naught left . . .
> Die he, or justice must; unless for him
> Some other, able, and as willing, pay
> The rigid satisfaction, death for death.

Such words may sound harsh today, but their meaning is that of Gregory the Great when he said: 'This sin cannot be removed except by sacrifice (. . . *talis culpa, sed nisi per sacrificium deleri non poterat*).'

The consultation of Father and Son, opened somewhat earlier, had now reached its major objective. To Milton's contemporaries, Christ unquestionably would intercede for man, and offer his life in atonement. Nevertheless, so skilfully did the poet develop the situation that the expected became the dramatic. The author's picture of God in consultation with the Son may seem somewhat unusual, but it had flourished since the early days of Christianity. Lactantius set forth such a conception in the *Divine Institutes*, a work which the Seventeenth Century regarded highly. Because it includes other interesting similarities with *Paradise Lost*, I quote a major part of the paragraph which concluded with the description here in point. The translation is that of the Reverend William Fletcher:

> Since God was possessed of the greatest foresight in planning, and of the greatest skill for carrying out in action, before He commenced this business of the world . . . in order that goodness might spring as a stream from Him, and might flow forth afar, He produced a Spirit like to himself, who might be endowed with the perfections of God the Father. . . . Almighty God begat His Son. . . . Then He made another being, in whom the disposition of the divine origin did not remain. Therefore he was infected with his own envy, as with poison, and passed from good to evil; and at his own will, which has been given to him by God unfettered, he acquired for himself a contrary name. From which it appears that the source of all evils is envy. For he envied his predecessor, who through his steadfastness is acceptable and dear to God the Father. This being, who from good became evil by his own act, is called by the Greeks

diabolus; we call him the accuser, because he reports to
God the faults to which he himself entices us. God,
therefore, when He began the fabric of the world, set
over the whole work that first and greatest Son, and used
Him at the same time as counsellor and artificer, in
planning, arranging, and accomplishing, since He is complete both in knowledge, and judgment, and power.

A contemporary picture by Joseph Fletcher depicted
God in consultation regarding man's redemption, not however with Christ, but with himself:

> For man's redemption, as God at first consulted with
> himself how, and after what manner he might make
> man . . . surely much more did he now consult with
> Himself, and by what means he might set man on his
> feet again; and so restore him and his whole race into
> their former state and happy being. This being a work,
> if we may compare God's works one with another, of
> greater glory, difficulty, and labor than that of Creation.
> Which consultation I mention not here, for . . . I be-
> lieve, as God's all-seeing eye did foresee the Fall, so his
> insearchable wisdom did provide for the same, even from
> all eternity. . . . Deliverance of all mankind out of its
> misery . . . was put upon Christ, the annointed Messiah,
> who cheerfully undertook it, and for his part effectively
> performed. And as many of all mankind, as according to
> God's purpose, do receive this blessed and gracious
> Mediator . . . so many are freed from their thralldom
> and misery, and are restored to the inheritance and par-
> ticipation of life and felicity.

The offer of Milton's Christ to die in atonement for
erring man necessarily brought forth both revelation of the
future Incarnation and the decree of Exaltation. As I
mentioned in Chapter II, many ancient and contemporary
theologians held that God announced to the angels the
coming Incarnation of Christ. Once again, as on that fate-

ful day when Satan determined to revolt, the Father commanded the assembled angels to bow before the Son:

> Here shalt thou sit incarnate, here shalt reign
> Both God and Man, Son both of God and Man,
> Anointed universal King. All power
> I give thee; reign for ever . . . as Head Supreme,
> Thrones, Princedoms, Powers, Dominions, I reduce:
> All knees to thee shall bow of them that bide
> In heaven, or earth, or, under earth in hell.

In the chronologically earlier Book V, Milton's Deity had promulgated the same decree of Exaltation, one drawn in both instances from Philippians 2. I shall discuss later some implications of the poet's impropriety in describing God as twice announcing to the angels an immutable and eternal decree.

This important decree concluded, its Author promised that in time hell should be forever shut, the sinful world should burn, and from its ashes spring a new heaven and new earth—Biblical themes strongly reiterated in Book XII. However, prior to the final justification of this book, Milton paused either to present new arguments or to repeat the old. Book V set forth the theory that God protected Adam against the violence of Satan, a point previously made by Bonaventure, Peter Lombard, and Tostatus. To guard him against the deceit of the Tempter, Raphael both warned man concerning his danger, and informed him of the revolt in heaven. The warning given by Raphael exemplified the idea of Calvin and others that 'Adam was admonished in time.' His tale of the rebellion gave flesh and blood to the belief cited by Willet and urged by Catharinus that man received instructions concerning the fall of Lucifer. Through the angel, Milton stressed the doctrine of free will, and commended the happy immortality which would follow obedience to the one simple precept.

Book VII described God as having created man to replenish the vacant rooms of the fallen angels, a well-
known conception indicative of Divine interest in mankind.
In Book XI, the poet developed the idea that sinful man
must die in order to receive the purification necessary for
immortality, an argument which made death not a curse,
but a blessing. In passing, he again mentioned the future
new heaven and earth of Peter and John. As a part of his
resumé of Biblical history, Milton drew a dramatic yet
simple picture of the Messiah, employing here the conception set forth by Willet and others that Adam knew of the
Christ. Subsequent to reiteration of the Biblical themes that
Satan should be bound and the world dissolved, he came
to the final and basic argument of his justification.

With this weighty argument Augustine and Willet had
closed the epitomized justifications of Divine Providence
previously quoted in the present chapter. In brief, it held
that because of his grace and mercy, God had brought good
out of evil. Implicit within the argument stood the even
more vital conception that the Father in part permitted evil
because he planned from it to produce good. As the 'Church
sang,' to quote Marin Mersenne, the fall of Adam then became 'the fortunate sin (*foelix culpa*).' This important
secondary conception of the 'happy fall' the editor Newton dismissed two centuries ago as patristic rant. During
the last decade, however, it was noted by Mr. E. M. W.
Tillyard in his *Milton*, and first described as a conventional
idea common to Milton and Du Bartas by Mr. George
Coffin Taylor. Quite recently, Mr. Arthur O. Lovejoy
showed with illumination and understanding the significant
place which the 'happy fall' has occupied in Christian
thought.

When the world had dissolved, so ran the promise of
Paradise Lost, Divine Providence would reward the faithful,

and bring good out of evil. The latter act of God, to quote from Joseph Fletcher, should be 'a work . . . of greater glory . . . than that of Creation.' This supporting theme Milton also accepted and emphasized:

> 'Earth shall all be Paradise, far happier place
> Than this of Eden, and far happier days.'
>   So spake the archangel Michael; then paused,
> As at the world's great period; and our Sire,
> Replete with joy and wonder, thus replied:
> 'O Goodness infinite, Goodness immense,
> That all this good of evil shall produce,
> And evil turn to good—more wonderful
> Than·that which by creation first brought forth
> Light out of darkness! Full of doubt I stand,
> Whether I should repent me now of sin
> By me done and occasioned, or rejoice
> Much more that much more good thereof shall
>   spring—
> To God more glory, more good will to men
> From God—and over wrath grace shall abound.'

As we approach the conclusion of *Paradise Lost*, the poet again repeated God's promise to create:

> From the conflagrant mass, purged and refined,
> New heavens, new earth, ages of endless date
> Founded in righteousness and peace and love,
> To bring forth fruits, joy and eternal bliss.

Such emphasis upon a new heaven and earth, one distinguished school of contemporary criticism regards as infallible proof that with the Restoration Milton grew dispirited and pessimistic. However, the theme had the full support of 2 Peter 3. 13; not to mention Revelation 21. 1, where it appears in the final book of the Bible. To the Scriptural precedent for stressing the theme within the last sections of *Paradise Lost*, we may add that provided by numerous authoritative writers. Among others, Augustine

had so employed it in *The City of God;* Hugo of St. Victor
in his *Sacraments of the Christian Faith;* Lactantius in the
Divine Institutes; and John Swan in *Speculum Mundi.* Certainly, these men could not have been broken and dispirited by the failure of the Commonwealth.

The story of *Paradise Lost* reached its end as Adam and
Eve, 'with wandering steps and slow, through Eden took
their solitary way.' Prior to this episode, Milton had closed
his justification of God and presented to mankind a final
admonition. Into that final admonition, voiced by the
Archangel and prefaced by Adam's last words, he poured a
dynamic passion which throbbed within the verses. This
is the true finale of his poem:

> Adam last replied:
> 'How soon hath thy prediction, Seer blest,
> Measured this transient world, the race of time,
> Till time stand fixed! Beyond is all abyss—
> Eternity, whose end no eye can reach.
> Greatly instructed I shall hence depart,
> Greatly in peace of thought, and have my fill
> Of knowledge, what this vessel can contain. . . .'
> To whom thus also the Angel last replied:
> 'This having learned, thou hast attained the sum
> Of wisdom; hope no higher, though all the stars
> Thou knew'st by name, and all the ethereal powers,
> All secrets of the deep, all nature's works,
> Or works of God in heaven, air, earth, or sea,
> And all the riches of this world enjoy'dst,
> And all the rule, one empire. Only add
> Deeds to thy knowledge answerable; add faith;
> Add virtue, patience, temperance; add love,
> By name to come called Charity, the soul
> Of all the rest. Then wilt thou not be loth
> To leave this Paradise, but shalt possess
> A Paradise within thee, happier far.'

PART II

CHAPTER IX

THREE SOURCES OF THE DIALOGUE ON ASTRONOMY

THOSE who find Milton the master voice of English poetry face a difficult problem in discussing immediate sources. The modern concept of literary originality being what it is, unfortunate misunderstanding may result. Few readers of the present age know the hexameral literature, particularly its long tradition of imitation and borrowing. Again, we forget easily the historical commonplace that from pre-Chaucerian days through the Seventeenth Century, poets drew freely from Scripture, from the Classics, and from whatever additional sources might prove most desirable. As a result, acquirements which once contributed to strength and universality, now may be judged a mark of weakness.

Despite this powerful deterrent I shall suggest that when Milton composed his celebrated dialogue on astronomy, he employed immediate sources. In brief, these sources consisted of three contemporary English books, two of which were bound in one volume. The earliest of the three works is *The Discovery of a World in the Moone*, or, as entitled in the third edition of 1640, *The Discovery of a New World . . . tending to prove, that 'tis probable there may be another habitable World in the Moone*. Second in appearance, but greater in importance, is the *Discourse That the Earth May Be a Planet*, or, *A Discourse Concerning a New Planet*, first published with the third edition of the *Discovery*. The author of these related works, Bishop John Wilkins, requires no introduction to students of the Seventeenth Century, but I mention in passing that he was

brother-in-law of Oliver Cromwell, more than any other
Englishman founder of the Royal Society, and ultimately
Bishop of Chester.

The third book, a determined and vehement answer to the
Discourse of Bishop Wilkins, is *The New Planet no Planet:
or, The Earth no Wandring Star* of Alexander Ross. To
the limited comment made in Chapter V, I may add that
to his age Ross was the well-known headmaster of the
Free School at Southampton and Chaplain in Ordinary
to King Charles. An encyclopedic writer who took all
knowledge as his province, he held among contemporaries,
to quote David Masson, 'the reputation of being "a divine,
a poet, and an historian." ' His *Mel Heliconium*, 'gathered
from the weeds of Parnassus,' is said to have been recognized by a laudatory poem from Milton, and the *Christ-
iados*, Foster Watson remarked, 'has a distinct analogy to
Milton's great epic cast in the classical mould—however
wide apart their media and respective merits may be.'
Ross was in all things champion of the ancients, and as he
said, judged it his duty 'to honor and defend their reputation . . . and not with too many in this loose and wanton
age slight all ancient doctrines and principles, hunting
after new conceits and whimsies, which . . . dissolve like
the apples of Sodom into dust.'

The principal immediate sources of Milton's dialogue,
the *Discourse*, the *Discovery*, and *The New Planet no
Planet* are three closely related works. Not only are the
first two books allied in theme, in purpose, and have a common author, but the *Discourse* attacked vigorously Ross's
Latin *Commentary on the Circular Motion of the Earth*.
Since the third edition of the *Discovery* and the initial
edition of the *Discourse* appeared as one volume, any person
who read this book during Milton's age held the *Discovery*
in his hand. As a detailed rejoinder to Wilkins's *Discourse*

Frontispiece of Bishop Wilkins's
Discovery and *Discourse*

which included not a few slighting references to the *Discovery*, *The New Planet no Planet* stands in a different but equally vital manner, intimately connected with the two earlier books. It cannot be said that every contemporary who read Ross read Wilkins, or *vice versa*, but those who sought to obtain quickly the major arguments of the opposed camps may have done so.

In the pages following I shall first compare passages from the three works by Wilkins and Ross with related sections of Books VIII and IX. This comparison digests a more detailed and inclusive study available in 'Milton's Dialogue on Astronomy,' *Publications* of the Modern Language Association, LII (1937), 728-762. Subsequent to a resumé of the international conflict epitomized by the Ross-Wilkins controversy, I consider briefly the apparent purpose of the dialogue, together with the question of Milton's objective in basing it primarily upon the *Discovery* and *Discourse* of Bishop Wilkins, and *The New Planet no Planet* of Alexander Ross.

The poetry of Milton will be found on the left hand page; the prose of his two contemporaries on the right. The single passage taken from Wilkins's *Discovery* is that which discussed the world in the moon. Since a complete analysis of the dialogue may be had in the *Publications*, I partially reduce the typographical unsightliness incident to parallels by employing italicized words, as well as the conventional dots, to indicate omissions. I emphasize the point that the excerpts from Wilkins and Ross consist primarily of selected fragments, and that the order of sentences has been altered to conform to the sequence of *Paradise Lost*. Quotation marks are used only for secondary citations. In the first passage from *Paradise Lost*, Milton set forth in poetry major arguments by which Wilkins had supported the daily axial rotation of the earth:

When I behold this goodly frame, this world,
Of heaven and earth consisting, and compute
Their magnitudes—this earth, a spot, a grain,
An atom, with the firmament compared,

And all her numbered stars, that seem to roll
Spaces incomprehensible (for such
Their distance argues, and their swift return
Diurnal) merely to officiate light

Round this opacous earth, this punctual spot,
One day and night, in all their vast survey
Useless besides—

                                    reasoning, I oft admire
How nature, wise and frugal, could commit
Such disproportions, with superfluous hand
So many nobler bodies to create,
Greater so manifold, to this one use,
For aught appears, and on their orbs impose
Such restless revolution day by day
Repeated, while the sedentary earth,
That better might with far less compass move,
Served by more noble than herself, attains

Her end without least motion, and receives,

As tribute, such a sumless journey brought
Of incorporeal speed, her warmth and light:
Speed, to describe whose swiftness number fails. . . .
And Raphael now to Adam's doubt proposed
Benevolent and facile thus replied: . . .
From man or angel the great Architect
Did wisely to conceal, and not divulge
His secrets. . . . Or, if they list to try

Appearances would be the same, in respect of us, *as* if the vast frame of the world . . . were moved. The heavens themselves, *are* of such strange bigness, with so many stars which do so far exceed the magnitude of our *earth* —this earth, that is but a point or center to them . . . all those stars of such number and bigness. Every star in the equator must move 42,398,437½ miles in an hour. *But* the distance of the orbs, and . . . consequently their swiftness, seem . . . incredible. The first motion *is* the diurnal . . . to distinguish between night and day, and so consequently serve . . . the habitable world. The earth *is* an opacous substance. *Yet*, what is this unto the vast frame of the whole universe, but punctulum, such an insensible point . . . a small sand. The heavens do not by this *diurnal* motion attain any farther perfection.

Shall we not think that nature hath as much providence *and* wisdom as not to put any motion in . . . which is superfluous, *and will* so much deviate from that usual harmony and proportion? Can we imagine she should appoint those numerous and vast bodies, the stars, to compass us with such a swift and restless motion . . . when *all* this might be done by the revolution of this little ball of earth? Sun and stars seem to be of a more excellent nature than the other parts, *and* motion is not so noble a condition as rest. 'Tis not likely *that* the heavens, which do so much exceed our earth in perfection, should be put to undergo so great *a* work in the service of our earth. The chief end of the diurnal and annual motions *is* to distinguish betwixt night and day, winter and summer, and *so* serve *the* habitable world. *How is it* any material body should be moved with such a swiftness. An arrow *of* the same swiftness *must* compass this *earth* 1884 times in an hour.

The whole fabric of the heavens *does* so much exceed

Conjecture, he his fabric of the heavens
Hath left to their disputes—
                              perhaps to move
His laughter at their quaint opinions wide,
Hereafter. . . . Consider first, that great
Or bright infers not excellence. The earth,
Though in comparison of heaven, so small,
Nor glistering, may of solid good contain
More plenty than the sun that barren shines,
Whose virtue on itself works no effect,
But in the fruitful earth; there first received,
His beams, unactive else, their vigor find.
Yet not to earth are those bright luminaries
Officious, but to thee, earth's habitant.
And, for the heaven's wide circuit, let it speak
The Maker's high magnificence, who built
So spacious, and his line stretched out so far,
That man may know he dwells not in his own—
An edifice too large for him to fill,
Lodged in a small partition, and the rest
Ordained for uses to his Lord best known. . . .

   [God] placed heaven from earth so far, that earthly
Sight . . . might err in things too high. . . .What if the
Sun be center to the world; and other stars,
By his attractive virtue and their own
Incited, dance about him various rounds?
Their wandering course, now high, now low, then hid,
Progressive, retrograde, or standing still,
In six thou seest; and what if, seventh to these,
The planet earth, so steadfast though she seem,
Insensibly three different motions move?
Which else to several spheres thou must ascribe. . . .

   Or save the sun his labor, and that swift
Nocturnal and diurnal rhomb supposed;
Invisible else above all stars, the wheel
Of day and night; which needs not thy belief,

our earth in magnitude and perfection. In the world, *there* will be always some particulars left *for* dispute. [Ross] God doth punish them *with* contradictory opinions. Who can sufficiently laugh to hear their jars and dissensions? You think *the* sun and stars *are* of a more excellent nature. Is not heaven fitter to undergo *a* constant work than the earth, so small, so dull, so heavy? Yet, as it is the center and habitation of the noblest creature, it is placed in the middle, as being the noblest place. The sun was made chiefly for the earth's sake, and the inhabitants thereof; neither do the stars need so much his light and heat as we, without which we can neither live, nor procreate. Neither was heaven made to serve this ball, but to serve him who was made lord of this ball. [Wilkins] That incredible swiftness *they* imagine *to* manifest the infiniteness of the Creator. [Ross] That immense and stupendious bigness . . . we may admire God's greatness. God himself asketh Job, Who is it *that* hath stretched the line? How much man is inferior to Him, in that not only he cannot do the works that God hath done, but also that he hath *not* knowledge of them.

[Wilkins] *In* the world, there are six planets . . . granted to move. As for the sun and the earth *it* is yet in question. The earth *may* be turned about in its diurnal revolution *by* some motive power of its own. That opinion of Kepler is not very improbable, that all the primary planets are moved round by the sun. The sun *may* send forth a magnetic, motive virtue, whose power may continue to the farthest planets . . .: all which are thus made to appear direct, stationary, and retrograde, by the motion of our earth, without the help of those epicycles and eccentrics, and such unnecessary wheelwork.

The diurnal arches *are* bigger than the nocturnal. For the difference betwixt days and nights, 'tis evident, that this may be caused as well *by* revolution of the earth, as the motion of the sun, since the heavenly bodies

If Earth, industrious of herself, fetch day,
Travelling east, and with her part averse
From the sun's beam meet night, her other part
Still luminous by his ray.
                            What if that light,
Sent from her through the wide transpicuous air,
To the terrestrial moon be as a star,

Enlightening her by day, as she by night
This earth—reciprocal;

                            if land be there,
Fields and inhabitants?
                            Her spots thou seest
As clouds, and clouds may rain, and rain produce
Fruits in her softened soil, for some to eat
Allotted there; and other suns, perhaps,
With their attendant moons, thou wilt descry. . . .
Stored in each orb perhaps with some that live:
   For such vast room in nature unpossessed
By living soul, desert and desolate,
Only to shine, yet scarce to contribute
Each orb a glimpse of light, conveyed so far
Down to this habitable, which returns
Light back to them, is obvious to dispute.
   But whether thus these things, or whether not—
Whether the sun, predominant in heaven,
Rise on the earth, or earth rise on the sun;
He from the east his flaming road begin,
Or she from west her silent course advance
With inoffensive pace that spinning sleeps
On her soft axle, while she paces even,
And bears thee soft with the smooth air along—
Solicit not thy thoughts with matters hid:
Leave them to God above; him serve and fear. . . .

must needs seem after the same manner to rise and
set. The earth does pass *from* west to east. As the
earth *is* in Aries we see its nocturnal hemisphere; . . .
in Libra it turns only the enlightened part towards us.
    As their world is our moon, so our world is their moon.
They should *have* night and day as we have. The 'earth is
nothing else but another moon or star. . . . I believe that
this globe of earth and water would appear like some
great star to any one, who should look upon it from the
moon.' As she doth most illuminate the earth when the
sunbeams cannot, so the grateful earth returns to her
as great, nay greater light, when she most wants it.
They have all things alike with us, as sea and land,
with dews and gentle moisture *for* inhabitants and plants.
'A certain blackish spot discerned *in* the moon,' *you* might
conjecture *was* some dilated cloud, being pregnant with
showers. Such fumes . . . may cause winds, and why not
such also as may cause rain. The sun *has* some lesser clouds
moving about him. Saturn, he hath two moons on each side;
Jupiter hath four that encircle him with their motion.
    It *would* conclude a great improvidence of nature in mak-
ing such a multitude of those lesser stars . . . lately discovered by the perspective. There may be elsewhere *other*
inhabitants, by whom these lesser stars may be more plainly
discerned. Should so many lights be created for the
use of man, since his eyes were not able to discern them?
    [Ross] Take heed you play the anatomist upon these ce-
lestial bodies, whose inward parts are hid from you. In the
curious and needless search of them . . . you shall never find
God. Let us not then spend that time in vain . . . speculations
which we should employ in knowing God, and in working out our salvation with fear and trembling. You answer
that there is no reason why this motion should *cause* sound.
The softest ground is in the lowest parts . . . of the earth.
You answer, 'the subject, medium, and object, are all carried with the same equal motion.' Heaven is a smooth body.

Dream not of other worlds,

what creatures there live,

In what state,
condition,
or degree—

Contented that thus far ˈhath been revealed
Not of earth only, but of highest heaven.
To whom thus Adam, cleared of doubt, replied: . . .
    That not to know at large of things remote . . .
But . . . that which before us lies in daily life,
Is the prime wisdom. What is more is fume,
Or emptiness, or fond impertinence,
And renders us in things that most concern
Unpracticed, unprepared, and still to seek.
Therefore from this high pitch let us descend
A lower flight, and speak of things at hand
Useful; whence, haply, mention may arise
Of something not unseasonable to ask,
By sufferance, and thy wonted favor, deigned.
    [From Satan's soliloquy, Book IX]
Terrestrial heaven, danced round by other heavens,
That shine, yet bear their bright officious lamps,
Light above light, for thee alone, as seems,
In thee concentring all their precious beams
Of sacred influence! As God in heaven
Is center, yet extends to all, so thou
Centring receiv'st from all those orbs; in thee,
Not in themselves, all their known virtue appears,
Productive in herb, plant, and nobler birth
Of creatures animate with gradual life
Of growth, sense, reason—all summed up in man.

[Wilkins] What can such little creatures as we discern, *or* they in the moon know of us. He that dwelleth above *may* only understand *things* in the height of the heavens. There may be inhabitants in this other world, but *it* is uncertain *whether* men *or* some other kind of creatures; . . . whether there in a blessed estate, . . . infected with Adam's sin *or* some of their own. *It* may be . . . that the inhabitants of that world, *are* mixed natures *or* a middle nature between . . . men and angels. [Ross] I reprove the vain curiosity of men, who cannot be content to know with sobriety things revealed, *but* must . . . meddle with *the* heavenly bodies. We know not the earth's measure.

Astronomers . . . gaze and stare on the stars, and dispute. So expert they are, and quick-sighted in these things that are so remote, and yet cannot perceive the things that be hard at hand. Anaximines *was* checked . . . for his curiosity in things beyond his reach, and neglecting that which most concerned him. Even in the opinion of Socrates, it's to be mad, to inquire curiously into these celestial things, which are not to be found out by us. They are furious and mad men, et cetera, saith Lactantius. The knowledge *of* these heavenly bodies . . . in this life is denied us, as being a part of Adam's punishment.

The wise God placed the earth in the midst of this great system of the world, not only for man's sake, who being the lord of this universe, and the most honorable of all the creatures, deserved to have the most honorable place, *the* middle; but chiefly that man with all other animal and vegetable creatures, might by an equal distance from all parts of heaven have an equal comfort and influence. And if the place be it which conserves the creatures, what place more fit for conservation, than that *in* the midst of the world? Having an equal relation to all parts of heaven, and all the powers of the universe uniting themselves together in the earth, as in a small epitome.

It is just to assume that a number of these correspondences and verbal similarities are fortuitous. I also am aware
of the inconclusive nature of such evidence, and of Mr.
George Whiting's earnest protest against the 'heresy' of
depicting Milton as 'literally following first one source and
then another.' Heresy or no heresy, there can be little
probability that Milton could have duplicated so exactly
numerous passages from the *Discourse* unless he had used
the work. It is scarcely possible that chance would have
guided him to duplicate sections from two books published
in one volume. To have utilized by chance the ideas,
phrases, and words of the *Discovery* and *Discourse*, and
by chance to have brought against their specific ideas,
phrases, and words, the specific ideas, phrases, and words
which Alexander Ross so vehemently raised against them,
is far beyond the realm of possibility. The astronomical
dialogue of Book VIII stands largely as a composite of
adapted and selected passages from the *Discourse* and *Discovery* of Bishop John Wilkins, and *The New Planet no
Planet* of Alexander Ross.

. . . . .

Establishment of at least the more extended correspondences from the *Discovery*, the *Discourse*, and *The New
Planet* as the principal immediate sources of Milton's dialogue brings in its train a number of important questions.
I shall discuss only a few of these, taking up first the question: Was the poet's reprimand of cosmological speculation closely connected with the current defense of Revelation against the Copernican hypothesis, the theory of the
earth's axial rotation, and the doctrine of a plurality of
worlds? A survey of this bitter controversy suggests an
affirmative answer.

Among the basic causes which led both Church and
churchman to support the traditional geocentric or Ptole-

maic astronomy, perhaps the most vital was the conviction that Scripture, literally interpreted, provided the final
word in cosmology. If the judgment of Thomas Campanella may be trusted, this belief unquestionably proved
the most fundamental, for he built his courageous *Defense*
around the question: 'Is that kind of philosophy made
famous by Galileo in harmony with or is it opposed to
the Sacred Scriptures?' The conflict between Scriptural
literalism and 'new' astronomical theories was markedly
intensified by the discoveries of Galileo, but it was not
occasioned by them. It had existed and had been growing
in vigor for many decades. In the *Narratio Prima* of 1539,
Rheticus was clearly aware that Biblical objections would
be brought against heliocentric astronomy; and in dedi-
cating to Pope Paul III the *Revolutions* of 1543, Copernicus went so far as to challenge these objections and rebuke those who might raise them:

> I care not if perchance idle talkers, who, although . . .
> ignorant of all mathematical sciences, nevertheless . . .
> should dare to criticize and attack this hypothesis of
> mine, because of some passage of Scripture which they
> have distorted falsely for their purposes—I shall even
> despise their judgment as inane. It is not unknown that
> Lactantius, otherwise an able writer . . . spoke most
> foolishly regarding the shape of the earth when he ridi-
> culed those who declared it has the form of a sphere.

Because Copernicus presented this challenge in his dedi-
catory preface to Paul III, he apparently feared the opposition of Roman Catholics. It was however the Protestants
who first became vocal. Indeed, the dynamic leader of the
German reformation, Martin Luther, vigorously castigated Copernicus some four years prior to publication of
the *Revolutions*. 'A new astrologer is risen,' he asserted,

'who presumeth to prove that the earth moveth and goeth about, not the firmament, the sun, moon, nor the stars. . . . This fool will turn the whole art of astronomy upside down, but the Scripture showeth and teacheth him another lesson, where Joshua commanded the sun to stand still and not the earth.' Although less denunciatory than Luther, Calvin held with equal certainty that Scripture represented the final word on cosmological systems, and in his *Commentary on Genesis* cited the first verse of the ninety-third Psalm with the inquiry: 'Who will venture to place the authority of Copernicus above that of the Holy Spirit?'

More extended, but similar in conclusion, was the comment of Melanchthon, who devoted an entire section in the *Initia Doctrinae Physicae* to attacks upon heliocentric astronomy. He maintained that the Copernican theory affected adversely the status of man, and perhaps more significantly, contradicted various passages in Psalms and Ecclesiastes. He could find nothing desirable in the hypothesis:

> The eyes are witnesses that heaven revolves in twenty-four hours. Yet certain men, either because they love novelty or desire to make a display of ingenuity, have asserted that the earth moves, and maintain that neither the sun nor the eighth sphere revolves. . . . It is a want of decency and honesty to declare publicly such notions, and the example is pernicious. It is the proper part of a good mind to accept truth as it is revealed by God, and to acquiesce in it.

During the final quarter of the Sixteenth Century, the practice of rejecting and attacking the new astronomy because of its incompatibility with Scripture became increasingly common, and made its way into the works of professional Roman Catholic astronomers. It was followed, for example, in the most authoritative and widely used com-

mentary on Sacro Bosco, one extant in many editions between 1581 and 1611, the Latin *On the Sphere of John
of Sacro Bosco* of Christopher Clavius. However, professional Catholic astronomers and mathematicians did not
stand alone in rejecting the motion of the earth because
of adherence to the literal word of Scripture. In complete agreement with Clavius was the important Protestant
astronomer Tycho Brahe. Tycho not only found the
Copernican hypothesis unacceptable because of its conflict
with Holy Writ, but went so far as to assert that since
Moses called the moon the lesser light, he must have known
astronomy. A decade after Tycho, the Englishman Thomas
Hill declared that 'Both holy Scriptures confirm and phys-
ic's reasons prove . . . earth abideth fixed and unmoveable in
the middle of the world.' Hill then cited in the somewhat
unusual order of Clavius the three passages from Psalm
103, Ecclesiastes 1, and Psalm 18 quoted by the Jesuit astronomer.

In keeping with past eras, the Democritian doctrine of
a plurality of worlds continued anathema to the orthodox.
Among its first opponents during the century preceding
Paradise Lost stood the powerful Philip Melanchthon, followed by George Buchanan, Lambert Daneau, Conrad
Gesner, Caesar Baronius, Edward Guilpin, John Rainolds,
William Bucan, and Clavius. Against the doctrine Melanchthon raised four principal arguments, the first and second
of which contended with Aristotle that the earths of the
plural worlds would move together, and that a vacuum
would exist between their enclosing spheres. Furthermore,
Scripture had said God ceased his labor after creating this
world. The most vital argument to Melanchthon proved his
last, wherein he stated that there is but one Son of God,
our Lord Jesus Christ, who was sent into the world, was
dead, and was resurrected. He did not appear in other

worlds; nor was he dead and resurrected there. Nor is it to be thought that if many worlds exist, a thing not to be imagined, Christ often was dead and resurrected. Nor should it be considered, held the Lutheran theologian, that in any other world, without the sacrifice of the Son of God, men could be brought to eternal life. As Melanchthon reasoned, to accept a plurality of worlds was to deny or make a travesty of the Atonement.

Buchanan condemned the doctrine without argument, while Gesner asserted that an infinite universe could not move circularly—which heaven does, and that heavy substances would progress to the center, and the light from it. Daneau imagined that under the doctrine we should have no night, and 'never almost' any eclipses of the sun and moon, 'since one sun or another . . . of the worlds . . . would shine in' the heavens. Regarding the inhabitants of other globes, he asked rhetorically: 'What is their . . . condition, fall . . . Savior and Jesus,' and 'from whence cometh' their salvation? He concluded with the 'ancient Fathers' that there is but one world because there is but one God, and that both an infinite universe and a plurality of worlds contradict Scripture. Baronius stated that belief in a plurality of worlds was heresy; Gilpin satirized 'the infinity of Anaxarchus' worlds,' and Rainolds censured the theme in passing. Bucan rejected the conception because 'the word of God maketh mention, Acts 17. 24, of but one Creator and Governor of the world, not many worlds; and saith, John 3. 17, that the Son was sent into the world, not into the worlds.' With this writer, as with Melanchthon, Daneau, and Baronius, the doctrine of a plurality of inhabited globes offended not so much Aristotelian physics as their religious beliefs. Christopher Clavius found it repugnant to both, and although he introduced the *potentia absoluta* of God, and agreed that Deity could create an infinity of worlds, he nevertheless held with Aristotle and *theologi nostri* that the world is one and finite.

English attacks upon the Copernican hypothesis were not confined to the strictures of astronomers and mathematicians. The statesman Thomas Overbury held that 'astronomy was first taught by God . . . and therefore the first must needs have been the most excellentest.' In 1612 the Prebendary of Salisbury, Nicholas Fuller, set forth in *Three Books of Theological Miscellanies* a detailed list of Scriptural texts which assert the mobility of the sun and heavens, and the immobility of the earth. Less widely read, but equally indicative of the vogue of literalism, was the *Brief Discovery* of Fuller's friend and colleague, William Barlow, Archdeacon of Salisbury. The Archdeacon sought chiefly to discomfit his contemporary Marke Ridley, but his devotion to the letter of Scripture is none the less obvious:

> [Ridley] must be ruled by reason, and afford all those his patience that do believe the holy Scriptures, which flatly deny the earth's motion, and affirm the motion of the sun, moon and stars, in the whole current thereof, as Psalms 19. 6; 104. 5; Joshua 10. 12-14; Isaiah 38. 8 et cetera. . . . [He] will not be offended with those who do pitifully laugh at his magnetical astronomy, with those topsyturvy motions. . . . But although such [reasons] as these are, may go current in a mechanical tradesman shop, yet they are very insufficient to be allowed for good, by men of learning and Christians by profession. . . . God hath ordained the motion of the sun, moon, and stars . . . and the unmoveableness of the earth.

It was inevitable that advocates of the Copernican and related theories should challenge those who proclaimed Scripture, literally construed, the final authority in astronomy. As a result, conflict over the mobility of the earth became to an important degree conflict over the interpretation of Scripture. Catholic and Protestant, cleric and layman, declared abroad their variant glosses of Biblical passages, and Holy Writ was tossed and buffeted on the winds of controversy. That such a conflict would arise was foreshadowed in 1590, when Christopher Rothmann differed sharply with his friend Tycho Brahe regarding the authority of Scripture in astronomy. Their discussion also indicated that the controversy would bring in review passages unrelated to Copernicanism, for Rothmann pointedly asked Tycho if he believed in the windows of heaven which Scripture mentioned in the account of the Flood.

More significant, in the sense that it came before more readers, was Edward Wright's prefatory epistle to Gilbert's *On The Magnet*. His invocation of the doctrine of accommodation was entirely conventional, but his use of it in defense of the motion of the earth quite the contrary. 'It was not,' he declared, 'the purpose of Moses or the Prophets to set forth any mathematical subtleties, but rather to accommodate themselves to the understanding of the vulgar and to ordinary methods of speech, much as nurses are accustomed to accommodate themselves to their infants.' In the slightly later *New Philosophy*, Gilbert himself directly censured literalism, and stated that although it is urged 'the earth is not moved because of the testimony of Psalm 74: "I have established the borders of the earth," the Sacred Book accommodates its phrases to human capacity.' Continuing, Gilbert rejected the authority of two passages frequently emphasized by the slavishly orthodox: 'He hath established the earth; it shall not be moved,' and, 'The earth abideth forever.'

In the years 1609 and 1615 there followed the important challenges to literalism enunciated by Kepler, Foscarini, and Galileo. To his denial of the assumption that the Holy Ghost intended moot passages in Scripture to be literally true, Kepler added vigorous comment upon the fallibility of Saints and Fathers of the Church:

> There are many men so devoted to holiness, that they dissent from the judgment of Copernicus, fearing to give the lie to the Holy Ghost speaking in the Scriptures, if they should say that the earth moves and the sun stands still. . . . Now as touching the opinions of the Saints about these natural points, I answer in one word, that in theology the weight of authority, but in natural philosophy the weight of reason is to be considered. Therefore sacred was Lactantius, who denied the earth's rotundity; sacred was Augustine, who granted the earth to be round, but denied the antipodes; sacred is the liturgy of our moderns, who admit the smallness of the earth, but deny its motion: but to me more sacred than all these is truth.

With the appearance of the *Epistle* of Foscarini, the conflict over the authority of Scripture, literally interpreted, entered a final stage. Earlier opponents had confined themselves to short refutations included in scientific or theological works. The *Epistle* however devoted itself to an extended and carefully organized attack upon literalism, and discussed in six classes 'all authorities of Divine Writ which seem to oppose' the heliocentric hypothesis. Of these several classes the last consisted 'rather of Fathers and Divines, than of the Sacred Scriptures.' Similar in purpose and emphasis to Foscarini's *Epistle* was the lengthy *Letter* which Galileo addressed to the Grand Duchess Cristina di Lorena. Its forthright declarations could not but irritate ecclesiastical authority, and Galileo's impeachment of both the integrity and intelligence of those who differed with him may have made doubly objectionable his error as a Roman Catholic layman in presenting his personal interpretation of Holy Writ:

> They have resolved to try whether they could make a shield . . . of a feigned religion and of the authority of the Sacred Scriptures. . . . This therefore being granted, methinks that in the discussion of natural problems, we ought not to begin at the authority of places of Scripture; but at sensible experiments and necessary demonstrations: for, from the Divine Word, the Sacred Scripture and nature did both alike proceed. . . . Nor does God less admirably discover himself unto us in nature's actions than in the Scriptures' sacred dictions, which peradventure Tertullian intended to express in those words: . . . 'God is known first by nature, and then again more particularly by doctrine.' . . . The prohibiting of the whole science, what other would it be but an open contempt of an hundred texts of the Holy Scriptures, which teach us that the glory and greatness of Almighty God is admirably discerned in all his works, and divinely read in the Open Book of heaven.

In his *Concerning the New Star*, and four years prior to the *Starry Messenger* of Galileo, John Kepler had attacked Bruno for his dreams of other worlds. Then from the telescope and his friend Galileo came the implication that Bruno might be in some measure correct, and we find Kepler in his prefatory *Dissertation* to the *Starry Messenger* giving more energy and thought to the problem of a plurality of worlds than to the scientific data presented by Galileo. His ultimate conclusions are difficult to determine, but he came to regard the moon and Jupiter as similar to the earth.

During succeeding decades, increased acceptance of the doctrine of a plurality of worlds intensified attack upon it. This was at times based on scientific grounds, as in the case of von Guericke, more frequently upon Scripture and theology, as in the case of Alexander Ross and Father Kircher, but normally consisted largely of adverse pronouncements. A fitting example of the last type, and one that illustrates the growing tendency to employ the word 'world' with the meaning of earth, John Donne afforded in the *Devotions upon Emergent Occasions*:

> Men that inhere upon nature only, are so far from thinking that there is anything singular in this world, as that they will scarce think that this world itself is singular, but that every planet, and every star, is another world like this. They find reason to conceive, not only a plurality in every species in the world, but a plurality of worlds. God, and nature, and reason concur against it.

For a variety of reasons, chief among which was probably the distraction of approaching and actual civil war, English literalism became somewhat less vigorous after the first third of the century. However, until both the achievement and prestige of the Royal Society had disarmed opposition, this literalism was by no means inactive. I have mentioned the attacks by Ross in 1634 and 1646, and to these we may add the direct and indirect challenges of Elias Ashmole, William Bagwell, Robert Burton, Viscount Conway, John Goad and John Swan. Ashmole attacked indirectly, but we may infer that to him, as to these other writers, religion and complete acceptance of Scriptural authority in cosmology went together:

> Such men . . . although they, like Xerxes, pull not down religion with hands openly, yet they are of another sort as dangerous, that undermine it with wrong opinions. If our men avowed such plain untruth, as

. . . Nicetas of old, with some of late [Side caption: Copernicus, Gilbert, Campanella, Galileo, Wright] that the earth, the only unmoveable thing in the world, moved, and such like ugly and misshapen lies.

Closely related to the literalists of the late Sixteenth and Seventeenth Centuries was the Raphael of Milton's dialogue on astronomy:

> Whether the sun, predominant in heaven,
> Rise on the earth, or earth rise on the sun . . .
> Solicit not thy thoughts with matters hid . . .
> Be lowly wise . . . Dream not of other worlds . . .
> Contented that thus far hath been revealed
> Not of earth only, but of highest heaven.

A more difficult problem is that of determining the apparent reasons which led Milton to turn to Ross and Wilkins for the source material of his dialogue. At least three are of major importance, the first being that the poet sought to reprimand the Bishop's personal beliefs and speculations. Such a reason would explain why Milton followed his work so closely that Wilkins, or indeed any contemporary well read in the *Discourse* and *Discovery*, would easily recognize the source. This reason is strengthened by the fact that Milton opposed strongly the cause to which *Discourse* and *Discovery* were dedicated—the stimulation of cosmological inquiry and speculation. The essential conflict between poet and bishop over the value of astronomy is well illustrated by comparing the conclusions of Raphael and Adam with those set forth by Wilkins in the last thirteen pages of the *Discourse*. I quote a few representative lines:

> By way of conclusion, I endeavor to stir up others unto these kind of studies. . . . There is nothing either better in itself, or more convenient for us, than this

kind of learning. . . . Certain it is, that amongst the
variety of objects, those are more eligible which conduce unto the welfare of that which is our best part,
our souls. . . . Were it not for the contemplation of
philosophy, the heathen Seneca would not so much as
thank the gods for his being. . . . The Object. It is no
less than the whole world—since our earth also is one
of the planets; more especially those vast and glorious
bodies of the heavens. . . . For the demonstrations of
astronomy, they are as infallible as truth itself; and for
this reason also does it excel all other knowledge. . . .
God gave to man an upright face, that he might view
the stars, and learn astronomy. . . . This knowledge
may conduce to the proving of a God, and . . . so likewise may it serve to confirm unto us the truth of the Holy
Scriptures. . . . Again, when I consider with myself
the strange immensity and bigness of this great universe,
in comparison to which this earth of ours is but as an un-
discernable point . . . then methinks it must needs
argue a degenerateness and poverty of spirit, to busy my
faculties about so ignoble, narrow a subject as any of
these earthly things.

In view of Milton's employment of the Biblical story
of the creation, and his exhortation that man be 'Contented
that thus far hath been revealed . . . of highest heaven,'
the poet may well have resented Wilkins's extended attempt
to demonstrate that Scripture possessed no validity in the
realm of science. Indeed, the major purpose of the *Discourse* was to prove that where Scripture and astronomy
differed, astronomy should stand as the authority:

'Tis not the purpose . . . to set down an exact treatise
of this [Copernican] kind of astronomy; but rather to
remove those common prejudices, which usually deter
men from taking any argument tending this way, into
their considerations. In the search of theological truths,

it is the safest method, first of all to look unto Divine Authority; because that carries with it as clear an evidence to our faith, as anything else can be to our reason. But on the contrary, in the examination of philosophical points, it were a preposterous course to begin at the testimony and opinion of others, and then afterwards to descend unto the reasons that may be drawn from the nature and essence of the things themselves. Why then may we not think that those primitive Saints, who were the penmen of Scripture . . . might yet be utterly ignorant of many philosophical [scientific] truths, which are commonly known in these days?

In proof of his belief that Scripture is uninspired where it conflicts with science, Bishop Wilkins devoted the first half of the *Discourse* to examination of some eighty Biblical passages, and pointed out that their literal meaning could not be accepted. The eighty included a number utilized by Milton, among them the miracle of the sun standing over Gibeon, the conceptions of the earth hanging upon nothing, waters above the firmament, the earth founded upon the waters, rising from the waters, and the sun and moon as two great lights. The idea of the earth hanging, said Wilkins, 'is a metaphor,' and that of the waters above the firmament, 'an opinion, together with both its reasons . . . now accounted absurd and ridiculous.' It is unnecessary to examine the question of Milton's literal acceptance of any or all of these conceptions, for he did reverence them, and could not have found their exposure on a public whipping-post other than distasteful. Because of the Bishop's subjection of Scripture to science, the high value which he placed upon astronomical inquiry, and his earnest exhortation that men practice cosmological speculation, Milton had good reason for attacking Wilkins personally.

The second of the three probable reasons which may have led Milton to utilize the works of Wilkins and the book which so vigorously attacked them was the desire to rebuke, through the Bishop, a movement of which Wilkins was an outstanding representative. It is a commonplace, not to be labored over, that the period from Milton's birth to the publication of *Paradise Lost* stands in history as the great age of organization and expansion of both formal and informal scientific societies. That Milton would possess adequate information regarding the English Royal Society seems unquestionable. His statement in the *Areopagitica* that while travelling in Italy he visited Galileo suggests some interest in the new philosophy. Samuel Hartlib, for whom he wrote the *Of Education* (1644), associated actively with the London group which did much to bring the Society into being. To be sure, Milton said nothing of Galileo in the *Second Defense* (1654), where he enlarged upon the Italian journey. However, during this decade, he corresponded not infrequently with Henry Oldenburgh, who with Bishop Wilkins became one of the two secretaries of the chartered Royal Society. He may not have known of the invisible college at Oxford, but must have been aware of the stated meetings which began at Gresham College, London, shortly after the Restoration. Similarly, he could not have been ignorant of the protection, and in 1662, of the charter given the Society by the King, or of the reputation which it early acquired of being inimical to religion. Milton would have known that the brother-in-law of Cromwell, John Wilkins, was a leader and first chairman of the group, and that to challenge the speculations of Wilkins was indirectly to challenge those of the organization sponsored by the King. Although criticism of the authority of Scripture is unusually extended in the *Discovery*, and particularly so in the *Discourse*, we have noted that advocates of the new philosophy had attacked such authority with increasing vigor throughout the century. Because of the widespread movement to dispense with Scripture in 'philosophical disputes,' the rapid development of scientific groups in London and on the Continent, the poet had, from his point of view, adequate occasion to rebuke a powerful and growing interest in cosmological speculation as well as to reprimand its perhaps most outstanding English advocate.

Although Milton's use of the *Discourse*, the *Discovery*, and *The New Planet* may well have been motivated by a desire to reprimand Wilkins's personal beliefs and speculation, and by a wish to rebuke a movement of which Wilkins was an important representative, he also could have selected the works as convenient sources for material essential in attacking contemporary astronomical inquiry and speculation. As every reader of *Discourse* and *Discovery* has observed, these books would have provided Milton with an admirable background of the ideas, beliefs, and conclusions of early seventeenth-century advocates of advanced cosmological thought. Not only did they present all major phases of current astronomical theories and speculations, but were well documented and gave by reference and quotation unusually complete accounts of the history of the various ideas discussed. In the 1640 edition, the *Discourse* and *Discovery* were printed in rather large, readable type, approximately one hundred and eighty words to the page, had an attractive and simple style, and a few portions of the *Discourse* excluded, were sufficiently nontechnical to be easily comprehended by the layman of the period. Regardless of Wilkins's personal views, and the fact that these views so well typified those of other advocates of astronomical inquiry, his books invited any reader interested in a relatively complete source for conceptions common to advanced cosmological thought of the first half of Milton's century.

With the difference that it represented beliefs still sacred to the conservative, what has been said of *Discovery* and *Discourse* may be said of *The New Planet*. It was in addition a helpful book to be used in connection with the *Discourse*, for it followed this work chapter by chapter, and with minor exceptions, point by point. Essentially a dialogue, wherein Ross quoted and answered the arguments of Wilkins, *The New Planet* harmonized well with this phase of Milton's technique. Many other of its features could not but commend it to a poet engaged in the justification of God's ways to men, particularly the exaltation of Scripture above astronomy with which Ross concluded the work:

> *The Excellence of Divinity above Astronomy, and an Exhortation to the Study of it.* Whereas you say, 'that astronomy serves to confirm the truth of the holy Scripture,' you are very preposterous, for you will have the truth of Scripture confirmed by astronomy, but you will not have the truth of astronomy confirmed by Scripture. Sure one would think that astronomical truths had more need of the Scripture confirmation, than the Scripture had of them. And indeed, all learning besides the Scripture is but . . . mere contention and strife of words not to be reconciled. Let us not then spend that time in vain and needless speculations, which we should employ in knowing God, and in working out our salvation in fear and trembling. . . . Small and mean is all human knowledge compared to the Scripture: for whatsoever learning is nought, it is condemned here; whatsoever is profitable it is to be found here.

As I suggested above, it is apparently impossible to evaluate the relative importance of the several factors which seemingly led to Milton's use of the *Discourse*, the *Discovery*, and *The New Planet*. The poet had good reason for reprimanding the personal beliefs of Wilkins, for utilizing his views as representative of a movement which he desired to rebuke, and for selecting him with Ross as convenient and authoritative sources for the arguments presented by opposing factions. Milton's prior acquaintance with many of the conceptions discussed would have enabled him to see quickly the utility of the three works.

One cannot pass from Milton and Wilkins without noting a curious turn of fate. The scientific movement which the Bishop urged has survived, but his two books long since passed into the limbo. The poet's philosophical beliefs died before his century, but the civilized world has continued to read *Paradise Lost*.

CHAPTER X

MINOR STRUCTURAL PATTERNS

FROM ancient and contemporary hexameral literature came the five basic divisions of *Paradise Lost:* Satan's rebellion and the battle in heaven, the council in hell, creation of the world, the temptation and fall of man, and the extended paraphrase of subsequent Biblical history. In building the narrative of these divisions Milton at times apparently fabricated his own outline, on occasion employed that established by tradition, and in some instances made use of structural patterns similar to those previously utilized by Spenser, Valmarana, Du Bartas, and other writers. The dialogue on astronomy duplicated both the method and ideas found in *The New Planet no Planet,* where Alexander Ross first set forth and later challenged the ideas urged by Bishop Wilkins. Unquestionably, it would seem, an appreciable group of the major structural patterns used in *Paradise Lost* resemble closely those employed in a number of related works.

As much may be said of various minor patterns included within larger structural units, now as an integral part, and on occasion as perhaps an interpolation. That students of Milton's epic have done relatively little to isolate and trace to their origin these minor structural patterns, scarcely implies they are unimportant or non-existent. It suggests rather acceptance of the undemonstrated conception that Milton created within himself the patterns which h' employed. The power of this dominant conception is adequately illustrated by its capacity to mislead such a distinguished and open-minded scholar as Mr. James Holly Hanford.

In discussing the morning prayer which Adam and Eve offered in Book V, Mr. Hanford wrote that this prayer, 'fervid and spontaneous, needing no set form, no temple, no musical accompaniment, is a magnificent descant on the great theme, "The Heavens declare the glory of God." This, far more than his metrical paraphrases, is Milton's true poetic version of the Psalms, and it shows how deeply he had entered into the majesty of Hebraic religious feeling.' The beautiful prayer voiced by Adam and Eve, however, is not a spontaneous poetic discourse based loosely on the general theme of the 19th Psalm. On the contrary, it consists of an expanded and partially 'modernized' paraphrase of Psalm 148, wherein the psalmist invoked the whole creation to praise Jehovah.

This paraphrase followed exactly the three divisions of the Psalm noted in the King James Version: 'The psalmist exhorteth the celestial, the terrestrial, and the rational creatures to praise God.' Moreover, Milton made use of the internal organization of the three divisions. I give in italic type the line or phrase cited from the Psalm, and in the customary roman type the appropriate verses from *Paradise Lost:*

Praise ye the Lord. Praise ye the Lord from the heavens; praise him in the heights.

These are thy glorious works, Parent of good,
Almighty! thine this universal frame,
Thus wondrous fair: Thyself how wondrous then!
Unspeakable! who sitt'st above these heavens
To us invisible, or dimly seen
In these thy lowest works; yet these declare
Thy goodness beyond thought, and power divine.

Praise ye him, all his angels; praise ye him, all his hosts.

Speak, ye who best can tell, ye Sons of Light,
Angels—for ye behold him, and with songs

And choral symphonies, day without night,
Circle his throne rejoicing—ye in heaven;
On earth join, all ye creatures, to extol
Him first, him last, him midst, and without end.

*Praise ye him, sun and moon; praise him, all ye stars
of light.*

Fairest of stars, last in the train of night . . .
With thy bright circlet, praise him in thy sphere
While day arises, that sweet hour of prime.
Thou sun, of this great world both eye and soul,
Acknowledge him thy Greater; sound his praise . . .
Moon, that now meet'st the orient sun, now fliest,
With the fixed stars, fixed in their orb that flies;
And ye five other wandering fires, that move
In mystic dance, not without song, resound
His praise who out of darkness called up light.

*Praise him ye heavens of heavens, and ye waters that
be above the heavens. Let them praise the name of the
Lord: for he commanded, and they were created. He
hath also established them for ever and ever; he hath
made a decree which shall not pass.*

Air, and ye elements, the eldest birth
Of nature's womb, that in quaternion run
Perpetual circle, multiform, and mix
And nourish all things, let your ceaseless change
Vary to our great Maker still new praise.

*Praise the Lord from the earth, ye dragons, and all
deeps . . . snow and vapor.*

Ye mists and exhalations, that now rise
From hill or steaming lake, dusky or gray,
Till the sun paint your fleecy skirts with gold,
In honor to the world's great Author rise;
Whether to deck with clouds the uncolored sky,
Or wet the thirsty earth with falling showers,
Rising or falling, still advance his praise.

Stormy wind fulfilling his word; mountains and all
hills; fruitful trees and all cedars.

His praise, ye winds, that from four quarters blow,
Breathe soft or loud; and wave your tops, ye pines,
With every plant, in sign of worship wave. . . .

Beasts, and all cattle; creeping things, and flying fowl.

Join voices, all ye living souls. Ye birds,
That, singing, up to heaven-gate ascend,
Bear on your wings and in your notes his praise.
Ye that in waters glide, and ye that walk
The earth, and stately tread, or lowly creep.

Both young men, and maidens; old men, and children:
let them praise the name of the Lord.

Witness if I be silent, morn or even,
To hill or valley, fountain, or fresh shade,
Made vocal by my song, and taught his praise.
Hail, universal Lord! . . . So prayed they innocent.

As the conclusion of Chapter II suggested, Milton's description of the rebellion and battle in heaven utilized in
general those patterns which either were traditional or
had been employed by writers well-known during the
Seventeenth Century. There remained, however, a number of apparently unique themes and episodes, one group
of which concerned Satan; the other, the angel Abdiel.

When the God of *Paradise Lost* unexpectedly decreed
to the assembled angels the Exaltation of the Son, Satan
concealed his dissatisfaction. At the hour of midnight, he
enlisted the aid of one called 'companion dear,' and plotted
rebellion. Under his plan, he would proceed to his kingdom as an harbinger, to prepare for a progress by 'our
King.' Satan's true purpose, however, was to proclaim
himself ruler, and prepare an attack upon God. To this
plan one angel objected, the faithful Abdiel. After a
wordy dispute with Satan, 'his back he turned,' and has-

tened southward toward the throne of God. His declared purpose was that of warning God to prepare an army, but upon reaching the throne, found this action had been taken. Deity then requested Abdiel to return and attack the Apostate. This the angel did, and proved the first to meet Satan in single combat.

As I have implied, these themes and episodes apparently stand unique in descriptions of the rebellion and battle in heaven. In addition, some few are unexpected, if not out of place. Such is the idea that God, 'our King,' would go on an Elizabethan progress through heaven. Because the angel, as well as Milton, knew of the 'Eternal Eye,' Abdiel's burning desire to warn Deity was as forced as it proved unnecessary. Equally out of character was God's special appeal to this angel that he return to the north and join the battle against Satan. In the subsequent conflict, the right to meet and overthrow the Apostate belonged by tradition to Michael. This honor Milton bestowed upon Abdiel, and gave the second combat to the leader of the angelic host.

These inter-related structural patterns, seemingly unique in accounts of the battle in heaven, have an unmistakable analogue in a tragedy well-known to Milton. This drama, the *Macbeth* of Shakespeare, Milton frequently echoed in the lines of *Paradise Lost*. As the Trinity manuscript informs us, he once planned to compose a tragedy of *Macbeth*, 'beginning at the arrival of Malcolm at Macduff' (Act IV, Scene III of Shakespeare's drama). Moreover, the circumstance which occasioned the revolt of Milton's Satan inevitably would have called to the poet's mind the plot of *Macbeth*. In the drama, as in the epic, the immediate efficient cause of rebellion was the King's unexpected and formal proclamation elevating the rank of his son. This royal decree placed under the 'Prince' the leader who had stood in power next to the King.

In keeping with the Satan of Milton, the Macbeth of
Shakespeare concealed his displeasure at the exaltation of
Malcolm, named by Duncan the Prince of Cumberland.
Macbeth rode before Duncan's progress ostensibly as an
harbinger, but his actual purpose was to prepare for rebellion. His first overt act, as that of Milton's Satan, took
place at night. He had also the assistance of an accomplice
—his 'dearest love.' In Shakespeare's drama, personified
Sleep prevented Macbeth from completing all details of
his criminal act, and led him to reject his wife's emphatic
request that he do so. Milton's Satan complained because
the sleep of his companion *dissented*, and held apart the
two who 'waking . . . were one.'

As Shakespeare's tragedy progressed, Macduff became
the one principal and outspoken opponent of Macbeth. He
defied the command brought by the tyrant's agent; and
in so doing, said this agent, 'with an absolute "Sir, not
I," . . . turns me his back.' He fled southward toward
London, there 'to pray the holy King' that he assemble
an army and attack Macbeth. Having reached England,
Macduff found his mission anticipated, and preparations for
war complete. In Act IV, Scene III, Malcolm invited him
to return and fight the rebel Macbeth. The first encounter
of Macduff proved to be with Macbeth, who admonished
him to 'let fall thy blade on vulnerable crests.' In the comparable conflict of *Paradise Lost*, the sword of Abdiel 'fell
on the proud crest of Satan.'

Less important, but perhaps suggestive are three additional details. Milton's statement that the 'great hier-
archal standard was to move'—an action important in the
rebellion in heaven—he preceded by the repetition of *ere*
in a description of the time of night. Shakespeare had
preceded his 'deed of dreadful note' by a similar repetition
of *ere* while describing the hour of the evening. In only

one sentence of *Paradise Lost* did Milton repeat the word *new* more than twice, and here he employed it four times. Satan directed this sentence against Deity and the Son, and followed it with the declaration that 'more in this place to utter is not safe.' In describing the tyrannous actions of his king, Macduff four times repeated the word *new* in a single sentence. Some twenty lines later, the cautious Malcolm declared 'mine own safeties' occasioned his reticence. There can be no question as to Milton's acquaintance with and interest in this scene, for it was here that he planned to open his proposed drama of *Macbeth*. In short, the Shakesperian tragedy which most interested Milton placed before him a structural pattern for the related sections of the rebellion and battle in heaven apparently unique among descriptions of these major events.

Among the many enumerations or catalogs which Milton employed in *Paradise Lost*, perhaps the most compact is his survey of the cities and empires of the world. In Book XI, as a prelude to the paraphrase of Biblical history, Milton caused Michael to lead Adam up the highest hill of Paradise, from whose top:

> The hemisphere of earth in clearest ken
> Stretched out to the amplest reach of prospect lay.

This compressed catalog, in which Adam glimpsed many cities not yet in being, various editors of *Paradise Lost* have roundly criticized. Indeed, the learned Richard Bentley refused to believe Milton composed the enumeration, and credited it, with other sections of the epic, to his imaginary editor. However, Milton indirectly presented here the dispersion of the sons of Noah, and in some measure satisfied this requirement of Biblical history.

To this explanation we may add the point that such a catalog was not unique in religious poetry. Joseph Beaumont had devoted five stanzas of his *Psyche* to a not dissimilar enumeration. This list he gave under the caption, 'A Brief History of Events:'

> Heroic were these spectacles. . . .
> The first, subdued Asia did display. . . .
> The second, generous Europe did present . . .
> Hot sandy Africk boiled in the third. . . .
> The fourth, was but prophetic yet, in which
> Deciphered was a strange, untutored world,
> In golden mines, and veins of silver rich.

Milton likewise employed the four conventional divisions of Asia, Africa, Europe, and America. The first three continents Adam viewed directly; the last he saw 'in spirit perhaps.' Since all the continents theoretically had no inhabitants at this time, the differentiation may appear forced. Nevertheless, we note that Beaumont had set America apart from the remaining three, and described it as 'but prophetic yet.'

The sequence utilized in *Paradise Lost*—Asia, Africa, Europe, and America—is not that followed by Beaumont. Neither is it that of Heylyn or the other geographers who began with Europe. Again, the order can scarcely be called Biblical. The King James caption of Genesis 10 had the sequence of Japheth (Europe), Ham (Africa), and Shem (Asia). Genesis 10. 1 stated: 'These are the . . . sons of Noah, Shem, Ham, and Japheth.' The actual account of the dispersion and descendants of Noah's three sons, set forth in Genesis 10. 2-32, followed the order used in the caption: Japheth (Europe), Ham (Africa), and Shem (Asia). Why Milton ran counter to the major account in Scripture, together with that of various geographers, one cannot say. Chance may be the explanation. However, Du Bartas had provided Milton with a not inadequate precedent in *The Colonies*, where he used the order of Shem (Asia), Cham (Africa), Japheth (Europe). The fourth place he also gave to America, 'the newfound world.'

Mr. Allan H. Gilbert, E. N. S. Thompson, George W. Whiting, and other scholars have amply demonstrated Milton's wide knowledge in the field of geography. As a result of his unusual learning, the information compressed into the catalog doubtless came from many sources. We may, nevertheless, illustrate the fidelity with which he followed one or more books by comparing his exposition with that of Heylyn's representative *Cosmography*. I give first the poetic account of Milton; secondly, appropriate fragments from Heylyn, taking up Asia, Africa, and America in this order. Milton included only a passing mention of Europe:

> His eye might there command wherever stood
> City of old or modern fame, the seat
> Of mightiest empire, from the destined walls
> Of Cambalu, seat of Cathaian Can,
> And Samarchand by Oxus, Temir's throne,
> To Paquin, of Sinaean kings, and thence
> To Agra and Lahor of Great Mogul,
> Down to the golden Chersonese, or where
> The Persian in Ecbatan sat, or since
> In Hispahan, or where the Russian Ksar
> In Mosco, or the Sultan in Bizance,
> Turchestan-born.

That city of the Cathayans . . . the chief seat of his empire . . . had the name of Cambalu, that is to say, the seat or city of the Cham. Marachanda . . . on the north side of Oxus . . . afterwards called Samarchand, the seat royal of Tamerlane . . . Tamir-Cutlu, Tamir. The chief city of China had the name of Pequin, signifying in that language the court or city of the King. Lahor . . .

honored for a while with the ordinary residence of the
Great Mongul; till . . . he removed his court . . . at last
to Agra. India Extragangem . . . one tract of it had the
name . . . of the golden Chersonese. Ecbatama . . . for
beauty and magnificence little inferior to Babylon . . .
In former times, the ordinary residence of the monarchs
of the Medes and Persians. Hispaan . . . the regal city
of these parts. Russia . . . Mosco, the Imperial Seat, and
See of the Patriarch. [The city was] first founded by
one Byza, and from him named Byzantium . . . But the
discourse thereof we will defer till we come to Tur-
comania, a province of Asia from whence they made
their first inundations.

> Nor could his eye not ken
> The empire of Negus to his utmost port
> Ercoco, and the less maritime kings,
> Mombaza, and Quiloa, and Melind,
> And Sofala (thought Ophir), to the realm
> Of Congo, and Angola farthest south,
> Or thence from Niger flood to Atlas mount,
> The kingdoms of Almansor, Fez and Sus,
> Marocco, and Algiers, and Tremisen;

Erocco, another noted port on the Red Sea . . . subject
both to the Great Neguz . . . and the Grand Signior of
the Turks. Melinde is to the south of the realm of
Adea. Mombaza is the name of another of these petit
kingdoms. In a little island of twelve miles compass
Quiloa lieth on the south of Mombaza. Sofala lieth on
the south of Mosambique . . . is by some thought to be
that land of Ophir. Congo or Manicongo, the principal
of those many kingdoms which are united in this name.
Angola, bounded on the south with Cafraria. In our
way from Barbary to Lybia Interior, we must pass over
Mount Atlas. Terra Nigritarum . . . exceedingly fruitful, specially in those parts which lie within the compass
of the overflowings of the river Niger. The kingdom

of Fesse. . . . Rabut, built by Mansor, or Almonsor, a king of Morocco. West . . . lieth the province of Sus. The kingdom of Morocco. . . . of Tremesen. . . . called also the kingdom of Algiers, from the city so named.

> On Europe thence, and where Rome was to sway
> The world. In spirit perhaps he also saw
> Rich Mexico, the seat of Montezume,
> And Cusco in Peru, the richer seat
> Of Atabalipa, and yet unspoiled
> Guiana, whose great city Geryon's sons
> Call El Dorado.

Mexico . . . a rich and wealthy city. Montecuma . . . [the] king. The country is inferior to Peru in the plenty and purity of gold and silver. But the greatest riches of this country [Peru] is most out of sight . . . gold and silver. Atabilaba, or Athnalpa, the last king of this country. Cusco . . . once the seat-royal of the Ingas or Peruvian kings. Guiana . . . the great and famous city Manoa, which the Spaniards call Eldorado . . . from the abundance of gold . . . said to be in it. Spaniards and the English have severally sought . . . to find out this city; yet none of them have.

For a further structural analogue we turn back to the opening book of *Paradise Lost*. As we observed in Chapter V, the great council in hell demanded a fitting edifice, and such a building Mammon and Mulciber set out to provide. The material chosen appropriately was gold, and the province of the first spirit became that of locating, mining, and smelting the precious metal. The necessary ore Mammon quickly found within a hill, 'whose griesly top belched fire and rolling smoke.' Here, one crew of devils, 'opened . . . a spacious wound, and digged out ribs of gold.' It had been Mammon, said Milton by way of digression, that taught the avaricious men who:

Ransacked the center, and with impious hands
Rifled the bowels of their mother earth
For treasures better hid.

Once the first crew had brought forth the golden ore:

Nigh on the plain, in many cells prepared,
That underneath had veins of liquid fire
Sluiced from the lake, a second multitude
With wondrous art founded the massy ore,
Severing each kind, and scummed the bullion-dross.
A third as soon had formed within the ground
A various mould, and from the boiling cells
By strange conveyance filled each hollow nook;
As in an organ, from one blast of wind. . . .

When the gold of hell had been refined and wrought:

Anon out of the earth a fabric huge
Rose like an exhalation, with the sound
Of dulcet symphonies and voices sweet—
Built like a temple, where pilasters round
Were set, and Doric pillars overlaid
With golden architrave; nor did there want
Cornice or frieze . . . the roof was fretted gold.

The second builder, and the architect who designed the
golden palace of Pandemonium, was the pagan deity generally known as Vulcan or Hephaestus. Milton chose, however, to identify him by the less common name of Mulciber.
Builder and architect having completed the edifice, trumpets
proclaimed the council. Swiftly the fallen angels came to
their golden seats, while above them:

High on a throne of royal state, which far
Outshon the wealth of Ormus and of Ind,
Or where the gorgeous East with richest hand
Showers on her kings barbaric pearl and gold,
Satan exalted sat.

I previously mentioned that in describing Satan's revolt because of the Exaltation, Milton used in a structural sequence episodes and themes unique among works closely related to *Paradise Lost*. As much now may be said of the structural pattern which began with Mammon and closed with Satan exalted upon Pandemonium's royal throne. An analogue again is not lacking in secular literature. It comes from a work the poet unquestionably knew and loved—the *Faerie Queene* of Edmund Spenser. Of Milton's intimate acquaintance with this analogue, we cannot doubt, for he wrote in his *Commonplace Book:*

> [This] was the reason why our sage and serious poet Spenser, whom I dare be known to think a better teacher than Scotus or Aquinas, describing true temperance under the person of Guyon, brings him in with his palmer through the cave of Mammon . . . that he might see and know, and yet abstain.

All details which make up the analogue occur in Book II, Canto VII, which Spenser summarized in this fashion:

> Guyon finds Mammon in a delve,
>   Sunning his treasure hoar:
> Is by him tempted, and led down,
>   To see his secret store.

As Spenser related the story, Sir Guyon, champion of temperance, first encountered Mammon surrounded by heaps of gold. Some of the metal, Guyon found, was yet crude ore, not purified by 'Mulciber's devouring element' —an interesting implicit association of the name Mulciber with the refining of gold. Subsequently, Mammon informed Sir Guyon that the antique world had enjoyed happiness, but in later ages:

> Then 'gan a cursed hand the quiet womb
> Of his great grandmother with steel to wound,

And the hid treasures in her sacred tomb
With sacrilege to dig.

As he advanced, Guyon reached the gate of hell, and
both adjoining and in immediate contact with the opening,
found a passage which led to a golden edifice, one wherein
'both roof, and floor, and walls were all of gold.' Led by
Mammon, he came shortly to a smoke-filled room:

[Wherein] an hundred ranges weren pight,
And hundred furnaces all burning bright:
By every furnace many fiends did bide,
Deformed creatures, horrible in sight;
And every fiend his busy pains applied,
To melt the golden metal, ready to be tried.

One with great bellows gathered filling air,
And with forced wind the fuel did inflame;
Another did the dying brands repair
With iron tongs, and sprinkled oft the same
With liquid waves, fierce Vulcan's rage to tame,
Who mastering them, renewed his former heat;
Some scummed the dross, that from the metal came,
Some stirred the molten ore with ladles great. . . .

Having passed through a gate of beaten gold—Pandemonium possessed golden doors—Spenser's knight entered
a hall so vast that it appeared a 'solemn temple.' Within
the great hall:

Many great golden pillars did upbear
The massy roof, and riches huge sustain,
And every pillar decked was full dear
With crowns, and diadems. . . .

Within the temple had gathered a great concourse of people, who moved toward the upper section. Here, wrote
Spenser:

was advanced high
A stately siege of sovereign majesty;
And thereon sat a woman gorgeous gay,
And richly clad in robes of royalty,
That never earthly prince in such array
His glory did enhance and pompous pride display.

In this canto of the *Faerie Queene*, we find a narrative sequence which opened with Mammon, and described men who for 'hid treasures' were wont 'with sacrilege to dig' into the womb of the great grandmother earth. Then followed a picture of fiends subject to Mammon refining gold. These fiends, like the devils working under Milton's Mammon, 'scummed the dross,' and employed forced air in their operations. In immediate contact with hell stood Mammon's palace, built entirely of gold, and containing a vast, temple-like hall supported by golden pillars. Within the hall, a high raised and stately seat held a sovereign more gorgeously arrayed than any earthly prince. With the refining of gold, Spenser twice associated Mulciber, identified once by this name, and later by the more commonly used Vulcan.

The gorgeously arrayed sovereign Spenser called Philotime, 'love of honor.' In her hand she held 'a great gold chain,' whose upper end was attached to heaven, and 'whose lower part did reach to lowest hell.' In keeping with Satan, Philotime had lived in heaven. While there she had been exceedingly beautiful, and, according to Mammon, had been cast out because of God's envy. Despite preceding stanzas that placed his golden palace immediately next to hell, Mammon's description of Philotime definitely suggests that her royal seat stood within hell itself.

Nath'less most heavenly fair in deed and view
She by creation was, till she did fall. . . .

> 'And fair Philotime she rightly hight,
> The fairest wight that wonneth under sky,
> But that this darksome nether world her light
> Doth dim with horror and deformity,
> Worthy of heaven and high felicity,
> From whence the gods have her for envy thrust.'

I may add that Spenserian scholars consider the fall of Philotime as 'the fall of Lucifer.'

The chief differences between the accounts of Spenser and Milton are five, three complete, and two partial. The fiends of Spenser's Mammon dug no gold within hell. The golden palace had been erected for an indeterminate period, and Mulciber was not described as having had a part in its construction. As partial differences, Spenser placed Mammon's edifice 'but a little stride' from hell, but at the same time in the 'nether world.' The gorgeously clad occupant of the throne was Philotime, not Satan. However, as I have noted, she was closely allied to the Apostate, and to some degree representative of him. These differences are not unimportant, but the variations from Spenser are little greater than those Milton made when he adapted the 148th Psalm as a prayer for Adam and Eve.

Among the interesting associations utilized by Milton in describing the erection of Pandemonium is that wherein he brought together the moulding of gold and music:

> A third as soon had formed within the ground
> A various mould, and from the boiling cells
> By strange conveyance filled each hollow nook;
> As in an organ, from one blast of wind,
> To many a row of pipes the sound-board breathes. . . .
> The sound of dulcet symphonies and voices sweet.

As Mr. George Coffin Taylor noted some years past, and as the quotation in Chapter VIII has shown, the Du Bartian

description of Tubal Cain previously had 'blended . . .
music and the mechanic arts.'

The account of Pandemonium contained, in addition, a
closer and more detailed correspondence with Du Bartas.
To facilitate comparison, I italicize and repeat two lines of
the related passage from *Paradise Lost*. The italicized lines,
it will be noted, may be used in either position:

> By him [Mammon] first
> Men also, and by his suggestion taught,
> Ransacked the center, and with impious hands
> Rifled the bowels of their mother earth,
> For treasures better hid. *Soon had his crew*
> *Opened into the hill a spacious wound,*
> *And digged out ribs of gold.* Let none admire
> That riches grow in hell; that soil may best
> Deserve the precious bane. *Soon had his crew*
> *Opened into the hill a spacious wound,*
> *And digged out ribs of gold.* And here let those
> Who boast in mortal things. . . .

These verses, whose words at times duplicate those used
by Spenser, include a greater number of terms employed
by Du Bartas. Their sequence, with one exception, is the
reverse of that used in the *Divine Weeks*:

> [Men] ransacked deeply in her bosom tender,
> With sacrilegious tools we rudely rend her,
> O odious poison! for the which we dive
> To Pluto's dark den; for the which we rive
> Our mother earth . . . for this dire bane.
> With these, our grandam's fruitful paunch he pulls,
> Whence many an ingot of pure gold he culls . . .
> On a high rock, better his thefts to keep . . .
> He guards . . . his treasure-trove.

To compare in detail such obvious similarities seems
gratuitous. However, I mention: ransacked the center—

ransacked deeply in her bosom; with impious hands—with sacrilegious tools; rifled the bowels of their mother earth—rive our mother earth, grandam's fruitful paunch; hell—Pluto's dark den; the precious bane—this dire bane; ribs of gold—many an ingot of pure gold; treasure—treasure-trove. The one important variation between the backward sequence of Du Bartas and the forward sequence of Milton consists of the lines from *Paradise Lost* both italicized and twice printed. Although the poet employed them in the first position, they can be shifted to the second without any alteration of line, and with improved continuity. In short, they easily could have been written for the second position and later moved to the first. Employed in the second place, we have almost precisely the sequence or structural pattern of Du Bartas.

Unless we may assume that within seven lines Milton could use by chance an equal number of words, phrases, and ideas employed by Du Bartas in double the number, this passage from *Paradise Lost* was heavily indebted to the *Divine Weeks*. Such indebtedness, however, need not exclude conscious or unconscious employment of a section from the *Faerie Queene* as a larger structural pattern into which might be fitted a smaller unit drawn largely from Du Bartas. We have an echo of Spenser in Milton's 'treasures . . . hid,' and perhaps in the word 'digged,' to say nothing of Mammon. Indeed, the law of association indicates that use of Spenser's account would recall the similar and more detailed description of Du Bartas. It is of course beyond question that Milton knew equally well both the *Faerie Queen* and the *Divine Weeks*.

In his *Milton's Use of Du Bartas*, Mr. Taylor has cited from the *Divine Weeks* such an extended number of small units comparable to short passages in *Paradise Lost*, that supplementary illustration has little point. I shall, however, add one further illustration. Milton had departed from tradition by retaining Adam and Eve in the Garden during the first night following their fall. This he apparently did in order to permit Michael to come to Paradise and reveal future events prior to the expulsion of man. However, Divine judgment had been pronounced and the Garden had ceased to be Paradise, so that Adam and Eve were subjected to the vicissitudes and perturbation which tradition had assigned to them. Milton's Adam, although yet within the Garden, found himself miserable the night following his fall:

> Thus Adam to himself lamented loud
> Through the still night—not now, as ere Man fell,
> Wholesome and cool and mild, but with black air
> Accompanied, with damps and dreadful gloom;
> Which to his evil conscience represented
> All things with double terror. On the ground
> Outstretched he lay, on the cold ground, and oft
> Cursed his creation; death as oft accused
> Of tardy execution. . . . Why comes not death,
> Said he, with one thrice-acceptable stroke
> To end me. . . . Our limbs benumbed. . . .

Du Bartas, who adhered firmly to tradition, described Adam and Eve as driven from Paradise the day of the fall. His picture of Adam was, nevertheless, much the same as that drawn by Milton:

> [Side caption:] An elegant comparison representing the lamentable condition of Adam and Eve driven out of Paradise.
> The bitter smoke exhales abundantly,
> From his before-unsorrow-drained brain,
> The brackish vapors of a silver rain:
> Where Usherless, both day and night, the North
> South, East, and West winds, enter and go forth . . .
> He weeps and sighs, and, shunning comforts aye,

> Wisheth pale death a thousand times a day . . .
> Lie languishing near Tigris's grassy side,
> With numbed limbs, and spirits stupified.

Among the important but traditional results of the fall, mentioned in passing in Chapter VII, was the coming to earth of sin, death and inclement weather, as well as the beginning of strife and conflict. These unfortunate events Milton described in Book X, 586-822, closing with a lam- -entation by Adam. His narrative order followed closely that employed by Du Bartas in *The Furies*, lines 4-275, the one noteworthy difference being that the sequences are exactly reversed—that is, Du Bartas opened this section with a lament. I may mention that both poets described God as calling the Furies to earth subsequent to the fall, and that Du Bartas caused these hideous figures to advance from hell over a bridge. Milton's characters, in passages not cited, built their own bridge or causeway, over which they came to earth. The accounts are quite long, but since discussion would obscure the relationship of their structural patterns, I present them without break or comment. The sections from the *Divine Weeks*, given first and identified by italic type, appear in exactly the reverse of their proper order:

> *First comes Dearth, the lively form of Death . . .*
> *With sharp lean bones piercing her sable skin:*
> *Her empty bowels may be plainly spied*
> *Clean through the wrinkles of her withered hide . . .*
> *Insatiate orque . . . whose greedy gorge. . . .*
>
> Death close following pace for pace . . . half-starved . . .
> 'To me, who with eternal famine pine,
> Alike is hell, or paradise, or heaven—
> There best where most with ravin I may meet:
> Which here, though plenteous, all too little seems
> To stuff this maw, this vast unhidebound corpse.'

And suddenly Avernus's gulf did swim . . .
Hydras and Harpies 'gan to yawn and yell . . .
[Side Caption:] The Furies with their . . . train.
Already all roll on their steely cars
On the ever-shaking ninefold steely bars
Of Stygian bridge . . . and dire Cerberus. . . .

See with what heat these dogs of hell advance
To waste and havoc yonder world, which I [God]
So fair and good created, and had still
Kept . . . had not the folly of Man
Let in these wasteful furies.

God . . . summoned up with thundering call
The damned crew, that sup of . . . bloody Cocytus,
Muddy Acheron. Come, snake-tressed sisters,
Come . . . Come, parbreak here your foul, black,
Baneful gall.

I [God] called and drew them thither,
My hell-hounds, to lick up the draff and filth
Which Man's polluting sin with taint hath shed
. . . till, crammed and gorged, nigh burst,
With sucked and glutted offal. . . .

The sun with heat, the moon with cold doth vex him,
The air with unlooked-for sudden changes checks him:
The stars conjured through envious influence,
By secret hangmen punish his offense.

The sun had . . . precept so to move, so shine,
As might affect the earth with cold and heat . . .
To the blanc moon, her office they prescribed . . .
And taught the fixed their influence malignant
When to shower.

The tumbling sea, the air with tempests driven,
Thorn-bristled earth, the sad and lowering
Heaven . . . revenge on him [man] . . .

The winds they set . . . with bluster to confound
Sea, air, and shore; the thunder when to roll
With terror through the dark aerial hall.

The first moved heaven . . . rapped with all his
Course . . . all the other spheres [and changed]
The world's great vessel, sailing yerst at ease,
With gentle gales . . . on quiet seas.

Some say he bid his angels turn askance
The poles of earth twice ten degrees and more
From the sun's axle . . . else had the spring
Perpetual smiled on earth.

His hail, his rain, his frost and heat,
Doth parch and pinch . . . hoars with snows . . .
The sullen, envious earth from blackest
Cells of her foul breast sends forth
A thousand foggy fumes.

Pinching cold and scorching heat . . .
Vapor, and mist, and exhalation hot,
Corrupt and pestilent . . . and snow and hail,
And stormy gust and flaw.

[Side captions:] Of the Discord that Sin
Hath brought among all things.
Sundry notable Antipathies.

Began outrage from lifeless things; but Discord
First, daughter of Sin, among the irrational
Death introduced through fierce antipathy.

The grief of mine afflicted spirits;
This sea I sail, this troubled air I sip,
Are not the First Week's glorious workmanship . . .

'Tis but a dungeon and a dreadful cave,
Of that first world the miserable grave.

[Adam] in a troubled sea of passion tossed,
Thus to disburden . . . with sad complaint:
'O miserable of happy! Is this the end
Of this new glorious world.'

Having stated that 'meanwhile in Paradise the hellish pair too soon arrived,' and later, 'they both betook them several ways' on earth, Milton wrote: 'which the Almighty seeing . . . uttered . . . "See with what heat these dogs of hell advance, to waste and havoc yonder world." ' There was little point in describing Sin and Death as advancing upon 'yonder world' when they not only had reached earth, but had separated. Similarly, the expression, 'See with what heat . . .' is not justified by the preceding lines, for none of these contain any suggestion of a heated advance. We may note however that the furies of Du Bartas move upon earth in a decidedly heated fashion, and that utilization of the structural pattern cited from the *Divine Weeks*—in backward sequence—would have resulted in a description of Death and the furies advancing upon earth *after* they had arrived in Paradise.

If this present chapter has appeared to suggest, as it does, that Milton consciously or unconsciously adapted to his purposes the minor structural patterns of other writers, I doubtless have committed the heresy which Mr. Whiting has condemned. However, Milton had a good memory, and, with the possible exception of Heylyn, he knew well the authors cited in this chapter. Such circumstances indicate that some use of their works might be expected. This point has the support of unimpeachable external evidence.

Milton's anonymous biographer, who unquestionably knew the poet intimately, and has been identified by Miss Helen Darbishire as John Phillips, stated plainly that his friend (or uncle) read books with the conscious purpose of making use of them. According to this biographer of Milton: 'The evenings he likewise spent in reading some choice poets, by way of refreshment after the day's toil, and to store his fancy against morning. . . . And he waking early . . . had commonly a good stock of verses ready against his amanuensis came.' The portion of the account which implied that Milton worked out verses during the night or early morning has the support of Thomas Ellwood and the poet. The young Quaker remarked that on occasion he would 'lie awake all night, striving, but unable to make a single line.' Again, the verses came with a rush, and he would call his daughter from her bed to take down his words. In the introduction to Book IX, Milton indirectly confirmed this account of nocturnal composition by alluding to his Celestial Patroness:

> who deigns
> Her nightly visitation unimplored,
> And dictates to me slumbering.

From John Aubrey came the definite statement that Milton intermingled reading and composition: 'At seven his man came to him again, and then read to him and wrote until dinner; the writing was as much as the reading.' An author with a normal memory who mixed writing and reading, and who read at night with the expressed purpose of storing his imagination for the composition of the morning, certainly should have carried over details and minor structural patterns from those books which he perused with care. That Milton knew well the Scripture, Shakespeare, Spenser, and Du Bartas, has not been questioned.

CHAPTER XI

ADAM UNPARADISED

IN a double sense, *Paradise Lost* is a mature epic. The child of hexameral and classical literature, it sprang from ancient roots. As a poem completed after 1662, its verses carried the thought of a man grown old for poetry. Yet the strength of maturity did not lack warm vitality, for both to Milton and the period his chosen subject exemplified the noble, the grave, and the majestic. Equal power flowed from a second spring. This source was the tried devotion which resulted from four decades of preparation, kept always alive by the resolution to build a poem which mankind would not willingly let die.

From the days of early childhood Milton had rejected the philosophy of gracious living, a creed best distinguished by satisfaction with leisure and a preference for veneer. His high aspiration demanded courage and discipline, self-denial, and patient, unremitting toil. From these and other personal qualities, strengthened by the conflicts to which they inevitably led, came the sturdy fibre which gave enduring life to *Paradise Lost*. In this poem, if ever, both style and the work are the man.

Because of both the man and his work, the chrysalis which became *Paradise Lost* will never lack interest. Its story began with an ideal—untried, and unsure of the direction it should take, but nevertheless an ideal not to be abandoned. Problems of the language to be used, of the proper subject and literary form, were faced and resolved. Then followed a long and slow period of evolution, wherein the chosen subject passed from stage to stage, changing from one species of drama to another, and at last emerged as an epic. Of the intermediate stages, the best known, and perhaps the most important, is the early draft entitled *Adam Unparadised*.

As his work slowly developed, Milton discarded much of the old. The greater part he retained, for he was no wastrel of idea or episode. What he kept, he largely altered—externally by a change in relative position; internally, by a shifting of rôles, by a fresh interpretation, and by the skilful blending of new material with old. Above all, his poem became less a thing of types, and more an instrument which voiced the fears and hopes of living characters. This achieved, the beauty and truth of Renaissance Christianity became as one.

At the age of nineteen, Milton hoped to employ the English language in a grave and noble subject. His transported mind should rise above the cosmos, and look through the gates of heaven. Here he would behold Hebe, graceful cupbearer of the gods, bringing rich nectar to her lord. He then proposed to traverse the celestial spheres, and relate secret events which took place before Beldam Nature rose from her cradle. These imagined episodes foreshadowed the happy angels of *Paradise Lost* who quaffed nectar before the throne of God, and gave some promise of the flights of Satan and Raphael through the spheres of heaven. The secret things which preceded the birth of nature call to mind 'the secrets of another world' which the Archangel revealed to Adam—the world which existed when 'Chaos wild reigned . . . where earth now rests.' We may believe it more than coincidence that in Book V of *Paradise Lost*, Milton first described Raphael as winging his way through the celestial spheres; somewhat later as revealing the secrets of another world; and fifty lines subsequently, as informing Adam that the angels of heaven quaffed ruby nectar from cups of pearl and massive gold.

The following year Milton reiterated his interest in the grave and sublime. When he wrote *Elegia Sexta* to Charles Diodati on 13 December, 1629, he rejected the light and trivial elegy. In doing this, he described such a poet as might have composed *Paradise Lost.* He who writes of weighty themes, said Milton, must live sparingly, and find his simple food in herbs. His drink shall be crystal water in a beechen cup. His youth will embrace no evil; his standards will be unyielding. This poet lives as the sacred priest of the gods. The circumstance which had moved Milton so to speak was the composition of a poem whose central figure possessed an ideal character, and therefore required such a character from all who sincerely praised him. The poem, he wrote Diodati, represented his gift to the birthday of Christ.

We know Milton's elegy as the *Ode on the Nativity.* Here the youthful poet first uttered the organ tones which rolled majestically through the lines of *Paradise Lost.* This Christian theme, in keeping with humanistic tradition, Milton adorned with classical learning. The enumeration of the pagan gods who fled upon the Savior's birth brought in addition more than a suggestion of the catalog of heathen deities who marched in Book I from the fiery lake of hell. Some few of the verses will bear repetition:

> The lonely mountains o'er
> And the resounding shore,
> A voice of weeping heard and loud lament;
> From haunted spring, and dale
> Edgèd with poplar pale,
> The parting Genius is with sighing sent;
> With flower-interwoven tresses torn
> The nymphs in twilight shade of tangled
> thickets mourn.

Peor and Baälim
Forsake their temples dim,
With that twice-battered god of Palestine;
And moonèd Ashtaroth,
Heaven's queen and mother both,
Now sits not girt with tapers' holy shine:
The Lybic Hammon shrinks his horn;
In vain the Tyrian maids their wounded
Thammuz mourn.

And sullen Moloch, fled,
Hath left in shadows dread
His burning idol all of blackest hue;
In vain with cymbals' ring
They call the grisly king,
In dismal dance about the furnace blue;
The brutish gods of Nile as fast,
Isis, and Orus, and the dog Anubis, haste.

Nor is Osiris seen
In Memphian grove or green,
Trampling the unshowered grass with lowings loud;
Nor can he be at rest
Within his sacred chest:
Nought but profoundest hell can be his shroud;
In vain, with timbreled anthems dark,
The sable-stolèd sorcerers bear his worshiped ark.

So, when the sun in bed,
Curtained with cloudy red,
Pillows his chin upon an orient wave,
The flocking shadows pale
Troop to the infernal jail,
Each fettered ghost slips to his several grave,
And the yellow-skirted fays
Fly after the night-steeds, leaving their moon-
loved maze.

Despite occasional fruitful returns to prosody during
the next decade, Milton became temporarily more the

student and less the poet, a perhaps inevitable result of completing the Master's degree, the six years spent in study at Horton, and the comparative solitude of his life there. At the age of thirty, when Wordsworth, Byron, Shelley, and Keats had completed much of their best work, Milton read avidly from history. In September, 1637, he informed Diodati he had covered the works of the Greek historians, and buried himself in the obscure history of the early Italians under the Lombards, Franks, and Germans. The great favor sought from his friend was that Diodati obtain in London the work of Giustiniani, historian of Venice. Milton had not wholly forgotten poetry, but as his studies and the beautiful lines which open *Lycidas* remind us, he had postponed it to an undetermined future period:

> Yet once more, O ye laurels, and once more
> Ye myrtles brown, with ivy never sere,
> I come to pluck your berries harsh and crude,
> And with forced fingers rude
> Shatter your leaves before the mellowing year.
> Bitter constraint and sad occasion dear
> Compels me to disturb your season due,
> For Lycidas is dead, dead ere his prime,
> Young Lycidas, and hath not left his peer.

But the forced fingers which composed *Lycidas* did not lack an echo in *Paradise Lost*. The epic's 'grievous wolves' who 'shall succeed for teachers,' had lived in the monody as the 'grim wolf' who daily devoured apace the neglected sheep.

Fortunately for English prosody, the secluded existence of Horton came to an end, and in 1638 the poet embarked for a tour of the Continent which brought him to Paris, Florence, Rome, Naples, and Geneva. The active world of men and affairs so challenged Milton that the Lady of Christ's became the man of action. He debated religious and political problems; visited and contributed to informal meetings of critics and writers. Manso, inspiring friend of Torquato Tasso, particularly stimulated him, and turned his aspirations toward poetry. Influenced by Homer, Virgil, and Tasso, together with Spenser and his own historical studies, Milton dreamed of an Arthurian epic which should honor his native England. Before he departed from Naples, he wrote Manso that with such support as the patron had given Torquato, 'I shall sing of the high-souled heroes of the Table invincible.'

Having returned to England in August, 1639, and established himself on Aldersgate Street, Milton 'renewed with rapture' his literary pursuits. A year later, so he wrote in *Epitaphium Damonis*, the Arthurian epic still ruled his thought. He promised to sing of the hoary kingdom of Imogene, of Brennus, Arviragus, of ancient Belinus, and of the Armoricans who came under the rule of the Britons. This national poem would describe Igraine made pregnant with Arthur through the wiles of Merlin, and spread abroad the exploits of the legendary king. Applause from the world at large he renounced, and found contentment in the thought that England would memorize his verses.

But Milton's interest in the epic form did not remain an exclusive one. He considered the possibilities of the drama, and about 1640-41 jotted down in the Trinity manuscript a list of approximately one hundred subjects. A goodly number were British themes which apparently derived from Holinshed, Malmsbury, and kindred writers; others he termed 'Scotch stories,' and included among them the tragedy *Macbeth*, to be opened with the episode where Malcolm met Macduff.

To national subjects, Milton added a larger group of religious themes. He contemplated a drama entitled 'Adam in Banishment,' and outlined more or less completely various others, 'Christus Patiens,' 'Phineas,' 'Abraham from Morea,' 'Sodom Burning,' 'Baptistes,' and 'The Deluge.' Although he had not made the subject his choice, Milton displayed unmistakable interest in giving dramatic treatment to the fall of man. Three drafts of such a tragedy he outlined on page thirty-five of the manuscript, and a fourth on page forty. The final draft, well-developed and bearing the title *Adam Unparadised*, provided in time the principal foundation for *Paradise Lost*.

Despite the numerous dramas contemplated in the Trinity manuscript, Milton by no means abandoned his aspiration to write a national or Arthurian epic. Within the Preface to the second book of *The Reason of Church Government*, published in 1642, he considered at length the merits of the national epic together with those of other subjects and other literary forms. Here he advanced the truly Miltonic hope:

> That what the greatest and choicest wits of Athens, Rome, or modern Italy, and those Hebrews of old did for their country, I, in my proportion—with this over and above, of being a Christian—might do for mine; not caring to be once named abroad, though perhaps I could attain to that, but content with these British islands as my world; whose fortune hath hitherto been, that if the Athenians, as some say, made their small deeds great and renowned by their eloquent writers, England hath had her noble achievements made small by the unskilful handling of monks and mechanics.
>
> Time serves not now, and perhaps I might seem too profuse to give any certain account of what the mind at home, in the spacious circuits of her musing, hath liberty to propose to herself, though of highest hope and hardest attempting: whether that epic form whereof the two poems of Homer, and those other two of Virgil

and Tasso, are a diffuse, and the book of Job a brief model; or whether the rules of Aristotle herein are strictly to be kept, or nature to be followed, which in them that know art, and use judgment, is no transgression, but an enriching of art; and lastly, what king or knight, before the conquest, might be chosen in whom to lay the pattern of a Christian hero.

And as Tasso gave to a prince of Italy his choice whether he would command him to write of Godfrey's expedition against the Infidels, or Belisarius against the Goths, or Charlemain against the Lombards; if to the instinct of nature and the emboldening of art aught may be trusted, and that there be nothing adverse in our climate, or the fate of this age, it haply would be no rashness, from an equal diligence and inclination, to present the like offer in our own ancient stories.

Milton immediately questioned whether 'those dramatic constitutions, wherein Sophocles and Euripides reign, shall be found more doctrinal and exemplary to a nation.' He found also 'a divine pastoral drama in the Song of Solomon, consisting of two persons, and a double chorus, as Origen rightly judges. And the Apocalypse of St. John is a majestic image of a high and stately tragedy, shutting up and intermingling her solemn scenes and acts with a sevenfold chorus of hallelujahs and harping symphonies.' Nor did he fail to think upon 'those magnific odes and hymns, wherein Pindarus and Callimachus are in most things worthy.'

While Milton favored slightly a national epic in 1642, he had reached no final decision. What his discourse in *The Reason of Church Government* shows most clearly is that the visit to Italy had moved him to write an immortal work, one which should glorify God and prove doctrinal to man. This great work he would write in English, and base upon extensive reading:

In the private academies of Italy, whither I was favored to resort, perceiving that some trifles which I had in memory, composed at under twenty or thereabout—for the manner is, that everyone must give some proof of his wit and reading there—met with acceptance above what was looked for. And other things, which I had shifted in scarcity of books and conveniences to patch up amongst them, were received with written encomiums, which the Italian is not forward to bestow on men of this side the Alps. I began thus far to assent both to them and divers of my friends here at home, and not less to an inward prompting which now grew daily upon me, that by labor and intense study—which I take to be my portion in this life—joined with the strong propensity of nature, I might perhaps leave something so written to aftertime, as they should not willingly let it die.

These thoughts at once possessed me, and these other: that if I were certain to write as men buy leases, for three lives and downward, there ought no regard be sooner had than to God's glory, by the honor and instruction of my country. For which cause, and not only for that I knew it would be hard to arrive at the second rank among the Latins, I applied myself to that resolution, which Ariosto followed against the persuasions of Bembo, to fix all the industry and art I could unite to the adorning of my native tongue; not to make verbal curiosities the end—that were a toilsome vanity—but to be an interpreter and relater of the best and sagest things among mine own citizens throughout this island in the mother dialect.

Perhaps more significant with regard to the ultimate choice of *Paradise Lost* was Milton's broadening conception of the ideal poet. Poetry now represented an art inspired of God, and rightly employed contained the power to implant within 'great people the seeds of virtue and public civility, to allay the perturbations of the mind, and set the affections in right tune.' It should 'celebrate in glorious and lofty hymns the throne and equipage of God's almightiness, and what he works, and what he suffers to be wrought with high providence in his church.' Its song portrayed 'the victorious agonies of martyrs and saints, the deeds and triumphs of just and pious nations, doing valiantly through faith against the enemies of Christ.' True poetry deplored 'the general relapse of kingdoms and states from justice and God's true worship.' Lastly, he declared, 'whatsoever in religion is holy and sublime, in virtue amiable or grave; whatsoever hath passion or admiration in all the changes of that which is called fortune from without . . . these things' poetry will describe with weight and beauty.

His basic theory of art followed that classical conception urged by Sir Philip Sidney, according to which prosody should please and instruct the reader. Wrote Milton: 'Teaching over the whole book of sanctity and virtue, through all the instances of example, with such delight to those especially of soft and delicious temper—who will not so much as look upon Truth herself, unless they see her elegantly dressed—that whereas the paths of honesty and good life appear now rugged and difficult, though they be indeed easy and pleasant; they will then appear to all men both easy and pleasant, though they were rugged and difficult indeed.' The great work proposed by Milton in *The Reason of Church Government* was not one to be raised from the heat of youth. It rather would rest upon extended selected reading and observation of human affairs. Toward its development he promised to labor with unwearied spirit and unabated zeal. Completion of the work— so he warned the too optimistic—could not be realized 'for some few years.'

Two passages within this preface definitely foreshadowed fragments of Milton's introductions to Books I and IX of *Paradise Lost*. He wrote in the first that his contemplated work should 'be raised' by 'devout prayer to that eternal Spirit, who can enrich with all utterance and knowledge, and sends out his seraphim with the hallowed fire of his altar, to touch and purify the lips of whom he pleases.' To this Spirit Milton called in the opening invocation of *Paradise Lost:*

> And chiefly Thou, O Spirit, that dost prefer
> Before all temples the upright heart and pure,
> Instruct me, for Thou knowest.... What in me is
> Dark, illumine; what is low, raise and support.

Following discussion of the proposed national or Arthurian epic, Milton wrote in the pamphlet that he held high hopes of completing his work, if 'there be nothing adverse in our climate, or the fate of this age.' Although amplified in detail, and approbation of the subject replaced by disapproval, the introduction to Book IX unmistakably echoed this passage:

> Since first this subject for heroic song
> Pleased me, long choosing and beginning late,
> Not sedulous by nature to indite
> Wars, hitherto the only argument
> Heroic deemed. . . . [To] me, of these
> Nor skilled nor studious, higher argument
> Remains, sufficient of itself to raise
> That name, unless an age too late, or cold
> Climate, or years, damp my intended wing.

By the year 1642 Milton had determined to compose a literary work which the world should not willingly let die. In this work, be it epic or tragedy, he proposed to glorify God and instruct mankind in the paths of justice and righteousness. By way of fitting preparation, he pledged devotion to abstemious living, high thinking, and years of serious reading and patient study. The great contribution would honor his native tongue; and, if the promise of the *Ode on the Nativity* and *Lycidas* met fulfillment, its lines would sound with an organ tone unheard in English prosody.

Conclusions equally important follow comparison of the poet's early writings with those of later years. He definitely manifested a tendency to carry phrases, ideas, and patterns of thought from one composition to another. Under proper conditions, as we noted in the preceding chapter, the ideas, phrases and thought patterns which use, reading, and reflection had fixed in his mind appeared or reappeared in his writing. Related to this trait of intellectual and poetic economy was a pertinacity which led Milton to complete the several major literary types foreshadowed in the Trinity manuscript, and discussed in *The Reason of Church Government*. As all readers have observed, *Paradise Lost* is adorned with 'magnific odes and hymns,' and its partial sequel, *Paradise Regained*, constitutes the short epic. True it is that the national epic did not survive in this form, but it nevertheless received being in the *History of Britain*. The outlined drama of *Adam Unparadised* became a related, intermediate stage of the epic *Paradise Lost*, and the gap thus created Milton filled with the tragedy *Samson Agonistes*.

As we return to the year 1642, we find two themes favored above all others. First and somewhat more prominent stood the national or Arthurian, conceived as an epic. The second subject was the fall of man, to be given the form of tragedy. Between 1642 and 1649 Milton apparently abandoned the first of the two plans, for by the latter year the national epic had taken definite shape as the *History of Britain.* At this time, he wrote in the *Second Defense,* four books of the history had been completed. The drama outlined as *Adam Unparadised* then stood alone among the subjects which he tentatively had selected for the work which posterity should long cherish.

The Trinity manuscript, which included the four early drafts of Milton's epic, was discovered by the Woodwardian professor at Cambridge, Dr. Mason, among other neglected papers belonging to Sir Henry Newton Puckering. It contained two drafts of a letter to a friend who had plead with Milton to take holy orders, the outlines of numerous tragedies, a number of which have been mentioned, and complete copies of many minor poems, including corrections which he had made. Much of the manuscript is written in Milton's hand, and thus provides more than a record of literary aspiration and evolution.

Of the four drafts which Milton devoted to the contemplated drama on the fall of man, the first three occur on a single sheet of the Trinity manuscript. Apparently struck off at much the same time—the two first drafts being cancelled—these three outlines are so closely related that without inaccuracy they may be termed stages of a single draft. Acts I and II of the concluding version constitute a development of the four groups of characters active in Drafts I and II. In reproducing the opening acts of Draft III, I omit the greater part of the prologue:

Draft I	Draft II
Michael	Moses
Heavenly Love	Wisdom, Justice, Mercy
Chorus of Angels	Heavenly Love
	The Evening Star Hesperus
	Chorus of Angels

Draft III

Prologue. Moses recounting how he assumed his true body.

Act I. Justice, Mercy, [and] Wisdom, debating what should become of man if he fall.
Chorus of angels sings a hymn of the creation.

Act II. Heavenly Love. Evening Star.
Chorus sings the marriage song and describes Paradise.

Minor exceptions excluded, the characters and incidents found in the two first acts of these drafts foreshadowed sections from Books III and IV of *Paradise Lost*. Book III of the epic presented extended discussion of the fate of man, then unfallen, but soon to succumb to the machinations of Satan. Two of God's attributes, his Justice and his Mercy, are described as in conflict, and in his historical rôle of Wisdom, Christ interceded for man. This he did, said Milton later in the epic:

To appease thy [God's] wrath, and end the strife
Of mercy and justice in thy face discerned.

Under the decision which was reached, the Father promised 'heavenly love shall outdo hellish hate.' Shortly thereafter the angelic host praised the creating Son, and in the final lines of Book III, Uriel related the brief secondary account of Creation discussed in the closing paragraphs of Chapter V.

Within the compass of one hundred verses, Book IV of the epic described the evening star Hesperus, and spoke of angels singing the marriage hymn. With the latter Milton included an account of the nuptials of Adam and Eve somewhat repetitive of and withal somewhat different

from that given Raphael by Adam. Few sections of the
poem are more charming than the lines on the evening
star and the bower where Adam and Eve first lodged:

> Now came still evening on, and twilight gray
> Had in her sober livery all things clad;
> Silence accompanied, for beast and bird—
> They to their grassy couch, these to their nests
> Were slunk; all but the wakeful nightingale.
> She all night long her amorous descant sung:
> Silence was pleased. Now glowed the firmament
> With living sapphires—Hesperus, that led
> The starry host, rode brightest, till the moon,
> Rising in clouded majesty, at length
> Apparent queen, unveiled her peerless light,
> And o'er the dark her silver mantle threw.
>
> When Adam thus to Eve: 'Fair consort, the hour
> Of night, and all things now retired to rest,
> Mind us of like repose. . . . Alone they passed
> On to their blissful bower. It was a place
> Chosen by the sovran Planter, when he framed
> All things to man's delightful use. The roof
> Of thickest covert was inwoven shade,
> Laurel and myrtle, and what higher grew
> Of firm and fragrant leaf. . . . In close recess,
> With flowers, garlands, and sweet-smelling herbs,
> Espousèd Eve decked first her nuptial bed,
> And heavenly choirs the hymenaean sung.

In the third draft, Acts III and IV again added detail to
the corresponding parts of the two preceding outlines:

Draft I	Draft II
Lucifer	Lucifer
Adam [and] Eve with the serpent	Adam [and] Eve
Conscience	Conscience

Draft III

Act II.   Lucifer contriving Adam's ruin.
           Chorus fears for Adam, and relates Luci-
           fer's rebellion and fall.

Act IV.   Adam [and] Eve fallen.
           Conscience cites them to God's examina-
           tion.
           Chorus bewails, and tells the good Adam
           hath lost.

The relationship between *Paradise Lost* and these sections of the early drafts is extremely close. Book IV of the
epic opened with a lament for innocent, frail man, and
later described the entrance of Satan, bent upon revenge.
The latter third of Book V, and the following Book VI
recounted the story of the rebellion and battle in heaven.
Book IX told of the Fall; and in Book X a guilty conscience tormented Adam. However, Milton rejected for
use in *Paradise Lost* the episode of the third draft where
'Conscience cites them to God's examination.' This episode,
I mention in passing, suggests the section from Du Bartas's
Imposture entitled 'Description of the horrible effects of
a guilty conscience, summoned to the presence of God.'
The formal lamentation of the angelic chorus likewise
failed to pass into the epic.

The remaining characters of the two cancelled drafts
Milton utilized with little change in the final act of Draft
III:

Draft I	Draft II
Mutes:	*Mutes:*
Death, Labor, Sickness	Labor, Sickness, Discontent
Discontent, Ignorance,	Ignorance, Fear, Death
with others	Faith, Hope, Charity
Faith, Hope, Charity	

Draft III

Act V.   Adam and Eve, driven out of Paradise, pre-
          sented by an angel with Labor, Grief,
          Hatred, Envy, War, Famine, Pestilence.
          Mutes: Sickness, Discontent, Ignorance,
          Fear, Death.
          Likewise Winter, Heat, Tempest etc. en-
          tered the world.
          Faith, Hope, [and] Charity comfort him
          [Adam] and instruct him.
          Chorus briefly concludes.

The most significant survival from these drafts occurred in the closing sections of *Paradise Lost*. In the
doctrinal finale of the epic, the angel Michael comforted
Adam by giving him reason for hope, and instructed him
to have faith and love, the last by name to come called
charity. Book X described forcefully winter, heat, tempest and inclement weather entering the world. In Book
XI, Michael presented Adam with visions of death, sickness, hatred and war. The chief difference between the
episodes of the epic and their counterparts of the third
draft lies in the narrative order, that of the epic placing
the entrance of heat and cold prior to the vision of death
and disease. In a further difference, both the epic and
Adam Unparadised brought these and other distressing
visions before Adam prior to his ejection from Paradise.
I mention here that Du Bartas set forth his comparable
descriptions in *The Furies*, the division of the *Second
Week* which followed immediately expulsion of Adam
and Eve from the Garden.

How much time elapsed between composition of Drafts
III and IV can only be conjectured. The closely related
first, second, and third drafts occurred on page thirty-five
of the Trinity manuscript. *Adam Unparadised*, the fourth
draft, appeared on page forty. Notable differences exist,

and at the close of Draft IV, Milton penned the words, 'compare with former draft.' The intervening space in the manuscript, the important variations, and the notation that comparison be made suggest that Milton composed *Adam Unparadised* some time after he had completed Draft III. Of the more vital differences, a number consist of omissions; others, of additions. The former include the elimination of all characters and episodes which partially foreshadowed Book III of the epic, together with the description of the evening star of Book IV. Additions consisted in part of episodes which expanded the rôle of Satan, including the Apostate's 'discourse of enmity' with the angelic chorus, and descriptions which pictured Adam and Eve less as types and more as human beings. Lucifer's 'rebellion and fall' became 'the battle and victory in heaven,' a title reminiscent of Rupert's *De Victoria Verbi Dei.*

Adam Unparadised had no act divisions, but following the corrected precedent established by Peck in 1740, these may be supplied from the third draft.

Act I.   The angel Gabriel, either descending or entering—showing, since this globe was created, his frequency as much on earth as in heaven —describes Paradise.

Next the chorus, showing the reason of his coming: to keep his watch in Paradise after Lucifer's rebellion, by command from God, and withal expressing his desire to see and know more concerning this excellent and new creature, man.

Act II.   The angel Gabriel, as by his name signifying a prince of power, tracing Paradise with a more free office, passes by the station of the chorus, and desired by them relates what he knew of man, as the creation of Eve, with their love and marriage.

Act III. After this Lucifer appears, after his overthrow; bemoans himself; seeks revenge upon man.

The chorus prepares resistance at his first approach. At last, after discourse of enmity on either side, he departs.

The chorus sings of the battle and victory in heaven against him and his accomplices, as before, after the first act was sung a hymn of the Creation.

Act IV. Here again may appear Lucifer, relating and insulting in what he had done to the destruction of man.

Man next and Eve, having been by this time seduced by the serpent, appear confusedly, covered with leaves. Conscience, in a shape, accuses him; Justice cites him to the place whither Jehovah called for him.

In the meantime, the chorus entertains the stage, and is informed by some angel of the manner of his fall.

Here the chorus bewails Adam's fall.

Act V. Adam then and Eve return and accuse one another; but especially Adam lays the blame to his wife—is stubborn in his offense.

Justice appears, reasons with him, convinces him. The chorus admonishes Adam, and bids him beware Lucifer's example of impenitence.

The angel is sent to banish them out of Paradise; but before causes to pass before his eyes in shapes a masque of all the evils of

this life and the world. He is humbled, re-
lents, despairs.

At last appears Mercy, comforts him,
promises him the Messiah; then calls in Faith,
Hope, Charity; instructs him. He repents,
gives God the glory, submits to his penalty.

The chorus briefly concludes.

Compare this with the former draft.

Upon completion of Draft IV, *Paradise Lost* began to
take definite form. Foreshadowed are the first half and
final quarter of Book IV, the battle in heaven of Books
V and VI, the account of Creation given in VII, and
those sections of Book VIII which described the creation
of man. Then follow a majority of the themes and episodes
vital to Books IX-XII. In keeping with both *Paradise
Lost* and the three preceding drafts, *Adam Unparadised*
introduced Faith, Hope, and Charity in the closing lines.
It presaged unmistakably the promise of the Messiah subsequently developed in the epic, and depicted Adam as
repentant and submissive following his discourse with the
angel sent by God. As I shall emphasize in the concluding
chapter, Milton's early decision to employ the Messianic
vision bears heavily upon one important phase of contemporary criticism—that which regards the poet as dispirited and pessimistic following the Restoration.

A number of the variations between Draft IV and the
completed poem also are incidental. In *Adam Unparadised*,
the angel Gabriel entered with the expressed purpose of
describing Paradise, and both viewing and describing Adam
and Eve. In the epic, Satan performed comparable functions. It is through his eyes that we first glimpse the
heavenly spot known as the Garden in Eden. Within the
Garden, where the distraught fiend first gazed upon all
kind of living creatures, he at last saw:

> Two of far nobler shape, erect and tall
> Godlike erect, with native honor clad
> In naked majesty, seemed lords of all.

To the Apostate of the epic, as doubtless to the Gabriel of the draft, Adam and Eve appeared:

> Creatures of another mould, earth-born perhaps,
> Not Spirits, yet to heavenly Spirits bright
> Little inferior—whom my thoughts pursue
> With wonder, and could love; so lively shines
> In them divine resemblance, and such grace
> The hand that formed them on their shape hath
>   poured.

This description, I may add, is precisely what we should expect from Gabriel, particularly the speaker's declaration that he could love Adam and Eve because they so closely resembled God. It well may be that the non-traditional admiration and sympathy which at times crept into Satan's discourse resulted in part from a transfer of Gabriel's role to the Apostate.

The angelic chorus of *Adam Unparadised* recounted the rebellion and victory in heaven, creation of the world, and acted as auditor of the story of man's creation. In the epic, the angel Raphael performed these three functions. Subsequently, Eve assumed in *Paradise Lost* the rôle formerly played by Justice, and Michael took the parts of Mercy and the unidentified angel. The verbal conflict between Lucifer and the chorus of angels of the draft became in the epic a contest between Satan and the leading angels of the guard assigned to Paradise. Conscience ceased to be a 'shape,' but nevertheless remained to accuse at length the sorrowing Adam.

With this type of variation I may include a curious circumstance. In Act III of *Adam Unparadised*, Milton wrote that after the departure of Satan from the garden, the chorus sang of the battle and victory in heaven against him and his accomplices, *as before after the first act was sung a hymn of the Creation.* Although Milton's first thought apparently was not to use the Creation at this place, nevertheless he did make his one reference to it immediately following the celestial battle. As we know, he carried this sequence into *Paradise Lost.*

In addition to having omitted themes found in Book III and other sections of the epic foreshadowed in the third draft, *Adam Unparadised* said nothing suggestive either of Books I-II or of the untraditional and unsuccessful first temptation of Eve. The latter omission necessarily excluded all themes of Book V which precede the rebellion in heaven, for these themes and associated episodes resulted directly from this temptation. We may only surmise when Milton added the unsuccessful seduction, but similarities between Caedmon's account and the dream related by Eve suggest a date later than 1651. At this time, Milton's acquaintance Junius received from Bishop Usher the manuscript of the *Genesis.* The poet doubtless could not read the Caedmon, but we may be sure that he knew of the manuscript and inquired eagerly concerning its contents. In a further variation, Draft IV gave no suggestion of the last half of Book XI and the immediately following first half of Book XII.

The three initial drafts which Milton penned in the Trinity manuscript suggest the Italian *sacre rappresentazione*, a type of drama which set forth Biblical themes and episodes by means of allegory. Combined with the influence of this form was that of classical tragedy. The chorus concluded each act of the third draft, and the outline indicates that Milton purposed to maintain the unities of time and place. Draft IV likewise followed the classical form, but abandoned largely the allegorical characters of the *sacre rappresentazione*. Such of these characters that remained were in addition personifications not uncommon to hexameral literature. Indeed, it was this literature rather than allegorical religious drama which dominated episode and characterization within *Adam Unparadised*.

'Several years' prior to beginning *Paradise Lost*, Milton still thought of his chosen subject in terms of the dramatic form given it in the *Adam*. At this time, however, he introduced some changes, only one of which we know. The known change moved the entrance of Satan to 'the very beginning' of the tragedy—in short, to much the same position which it was to occupy in Book IV of *Paradise Lost*. In addition, the lamenting Apostate uttered to the sun the ten verses which later he voiced in IV, 32-41. The single difference consisted in the use of *glorious* King rather than the later *matchless* King.

By assigning to Satan the opening episode of the lost tragedy, Milton indicates elimination of those themes from Acts I-II of the *Adam* which later found no place in *Paradise Lost*. Subsequent to Satan's entrance, the tragedy doubtless employed the several episodes which follow the coming of the Apostate in both the preceding *Adam* and the later epic. Its narrative sequence apparently was remarkably close to that of the poem. Moreover, if Milton continued in *Paradise Lost* the trends shown unmistakably in *Adam Unparadised* and the lost tragedy, he began work upon the epic with the themes and episodes which open Book IV.

The extent to which this tragedy, and particularly the *Adam*, contributed to the narrative sequence and episodes of *Paradise Lost*, becomes clear from tabulated comparison. In this comparison, the bracketed inserts will emphasize further Milton's habit of poetic economy by altering what was at hand rather than by beginning anew. The most important parts of *Paradise Lost* unforeshadowed by the fourth draft are Books I-III, the third quarter of Book IV, the first two-thirds of Book V and the first third of VIII, together with the final half of Book XI and slightly more than the initial half of XII. As I mentioned earlier, Milton omitted from Draft IV all themes common to the third draft and Book III of the epic. With the exception of the first quotation, the citations from *Adam Unparadised* follow the sequence of this draft.

Paradise Lost	*Adam Unparadised*
IV, 13 ff.	Lucifer appears after his overthrow, bemoans himself, seeks revenge on man.
IV, 131 ff.	The angel Gabriel [*cf.* Satan] . . . describes Paradise.
IV, 285 ff.	[The angel Gabriel] coming to . . . Paradise after Lucifer's rebellion [*cf.* Satan] . . . to see and know more concerning this excellent and new creature man.
IV, 440 ff. VIII, 250 ff.	The angel Gabriel . . . passes by the station of the chorus, and . . . relates [*cf.* Eve-Adam; Adam-Raphael] what he knew of man, as the creation of Eve, with their love and marriage.
IV, 799 ff., 878 ff.	The chorus [*cf.* Gabriel and his guards] prepares resistance at his first approach. After discourse of enmity on either side, he departs.
V, 577 ff., VI.	The chorus [*cf.* Raphael] sings of the battle and victory in heaven.

VII, 192 ff.	. . . was sung [by the chorus] a hymn of the Creation [cf. Raphael].
IX, 97 ff., 412 ff. Cf. X, 460 ff.	Here again may appear Lucifer, relating and insulting in what he had done to the destruction of man.
IX, 1051 ff., 1101 ff.	Man next and Eve . . . seduced by the serpent, appear confusedly, covered with leaves.
X, 842 ff.	Conscience . . . accuses him.
IX, 412 ff.	. . . the manner of his fall.
X, 21 ff.	The chorus [cf. the ethereal people] bewails Adam's fall.
Cf. X, 101 ff.	Justice cites him to the place whither Jehovah called for him.
IX, 1131 ff. X, 863 ff.	Adam then and Eve return and accuse one another, but especially Adam lays the blame to his wife.
X, 909 ff.	Justice [cf. Eve] appears, reasons with him, convinces him.
XI, 126 ff.	The angel [cf. Michael] is sent to banish them out of Paradise.
XI, 421 ff.	But before, causes to pass before his eyes . . . a masque of all the evils of this life and the world.
XI, 448 ff., 754 ff.	He [Adam] is humbled, relents, despairs.
XI, 868 ff., XII, 360 ff.	Mercy [cf. Michael] comforts him, promises him the Messiah.
XII, 582 ff., 574 ff.	Calls in Faith, Hope, Charity; instructs him.
XII, 552 ff., 610 ff.	He repents, gives God the glory, submits to his penalty.

CHAPTER XII

A DECADE OF COMPOSITION

TO the mind that delights in obscure problems, few are more inviting than the long unanswered question: When did Milton write *Paradise Lost?* In general, we have repeated the secondary account of John Aubrey, interpreting his words to mean that Milton began active composition in 1658, and in 1663 concluded the epic. As supplements to Aubrey's version, we frequently add the first-hand records of Edward Phillips and the anonymous biographer, usually read in the light of the second-hand account. So interpreted, these men describe Milton as initiating preparatory work upon *Paradise Lost* during the years 1655-56.

Evidence at hand should provide conclusions more detailed and apparently more trustworthy. I list first our knowledge of the poet's activities, his own statements, and those made by his nephew Edward Phillips. To these data we may add internal evidence from *Paradise Lost*, supplemented by that from a variety of sources. This body of evidence will advance the probable date of first composition to 1652-53, and suggest strongly that the order in which Milton published the books of his poem was not the order in which all were composed.

That *Paradise Lost*, published in 1667, was complete in 1665, is the statement of Thomas Ellwood. During this plague year, wrote the young Quaker:

> Some little time before I went to Alesbury Prison I was desired by my quondam Master Milton to take an house for him in the neighborhood where I dwelt, that he might go out of the city for the safety of himself

Paradiſe loſt.

A
POEM

Written in
TEN BOOKS

By *JOHN MILTON*.

Licenſed and Entred according
to Order.

LONDON

Printed, and are to be ſold by *Peter Parker*
under *Creed* Church neer *Aldgate* ; And by
Robert Boulter at the *Turks Head* in *Biſhopſgate-ſtreet* ;
And *Matthias Walker*, under St. *Dunſtons* Church
in *Fleet-ſtreet*, 1 6 6 7.

and his family, the pestilence then growing hot in London. I . . . intended to have waited on him and seen him well settled in it, but was prevented by that imprisonment. But now being released and returned home, I soon made a visit to him to welcome him into the country.

After some common discourses had passed between us, he called for a manuscript of his; which being brought he delivered to me, bidding me take it home with me and read it at my leisure, and when I had so done, return it to him with my judgment thereupon. When I came home and had set myself to read it, I found it was that excellent poem which he entitled *Paradise Lost.*

Of greater importance to the general problem is Milton's own testimony, but this and other evidence best follows tabulation of both the poet's major activities and various events which directly affected him. With these I include some dates of incidental interest:

1608.   9 December. John Milton born.

?1620.   Entered St. Paul's School.

1625.   9 April. Matriculated Christ's College, Cambridge.
         March. Charles I acceded to the throne of England.

1629.   26 March. Received degree of A.B.
         25 December. *Nativity Ode.*

1632.   3 July. Received degree of A.M.
         Took up residence at Horton.

1634.   29 September. *Comus* performed.

1637.   November. *Lycidas.*

1638–39. Tour of the Continent, including Paris, Florence, Naples, Rome, Geneva.

1639.　　August. Returned to England. Lodged in St. Bride's Churchyard, London; soon removed to Aldersgate Street. Resumed literary pursuits.

1640.　　?Summer. Began tutorship of his nephews Edward and John Phillips, then ten and nine years of age.

?1640.　　*Adam Unparadised*, and other dramatic outlines.

1641–42.　　Five anti-prelatical pamphlets.

1642.　　Married Mary Powell, who soon deserted him. Accepted additional pupils.
23 October. Preparations for civil war.

1643–45.　　Four tracts on divorce, the first of which appeared August, 1643 (second edition, enlarged, February, 1644), and the last, May, 1645.

1644.　　June. *Of Education.*
November. *Areopagitica.*

1645.　　July-August. Reconciliation with Mary Milton. Removed to larger home in Barbican.
June. Victory of Cromwell at Naseby.

1645–46.　　Collected and published first book of poems.

1646.　　29 July. Anne, the first child, born.
Powell family took shelter with Milton.

1647.　　15 March. John Milton, Sr. died.
Moved to smaller quarters in High Holborn.
Abandoned teaching.
Army occupied London.

1648.　　25 October. Mary, the second child, born.
Probably completed Books I-IV, *History of Britain.*

1649–53.　　The Commonwealth.

1649.　　February. *Tenure of Kings and Magistrates.*

March. Appointed Latin Secretary to Council of State, for which he wrote numerous official Latin letters, one hundred and fifty-six of which are extant. Approximately one-third date from the years 1649-52. Allowed chambers in White-hall and annual salary a few shillings less than £290.

Observations on the Articles of Peace.

October. *Eikonoklastes.*

1651.   February. *Defense of the English People (De-fensio pro Populo Anglicano).*

16 March. John, the third child born. Died shortly thereafter.

Total blindness; granted assistance in office.

Deprived of Whitehall lodgings; removed to Petty France, Westminster.

1652.   2 May. Deborah, third daughter, born.

5 May. Death of Mary Powell Milton.

Sonnets to Cromwell and Sir Henry Vane.

1653.   Psalms I-VIII.

1653–58. The Protectorate.

1654.   Spring. *The Second Defense (Defensio Sec-unda).*

July. Letter to Henry Oldenburgh: 'If my health . . . and the cries of these imposters will permit, I shall readily be led to engage in other undertakings, which I know not whether they can be more noble or more useful; for what can be more noble or more useful than to vindi-cate the liberty of man? An inactive indolence was never my delight, but this unexpected contest with the enemies of liberty has involun-tarily withdrawn my attention from very dif-ferent and more pleasurable pursuits.'

1654–55. *History of Britain,* Books V-VI.

1655.   August. *Defense of Himself* (*Defensio pro Se*),
             a reply to Alexander More, or Morus.
             Supplement to *The Defense of Himself*.
             Salary reduced.

1656.   June. Letter to Henry Oldenburgh: 'Your
             letters which young Ranley brought, found me
             so much employed that I am compelled to be
             more brief than I could wish.'
             12 November. Married Katharine Woodcock.

1657.   Andrew Marvel appointed Assistant Latin Sec-
             retary.
             19 October. Daughter born.
             December. Letter to Peter Heimbach: '[I have]
             little familiarity with those who have favors
             to bestow, since I have more pleasure in keep-
             ing myself at home' . . . .

1658.   February, March. Katharine Woodcock and
             infant daughter died.
             Published with foreword, Sir Walter Raleigh's
             The Cabinet Council.
             3 September. Death of Cromwell.
             Threats of civil war.

1659.   February. *A Treatise of Civil Power in Eccle-
             siastical Causes.*
             15 May. Last letter written as Latin Secretary.
             25 May. Abdication of Richard Cromwell.
             Original Rump Parliament returned to power.
             August. *Considerations Touching the Likeliest
             Means to Remove Hirelings out of the Church.*
             December. Letter to Henry Oldenburgh:
             'My regard for you has, believe me, suffered
             no diminution; but either my studies or my do-
             mestic cares, or perhaps my indolence in writ-
             ing, has made me guilty of this omission of
             duty. . . . I fear with you lest our civil dissen-
             tions, or rather maniacal agitation, should ex-

pose us to the lately confederated enemies of religion and of liberty.'

?1660. Letter to General Monk: 'The Present Means and Brief Delineation of a Free Commonwealth.' *Proposals of Certain Expedients for the Preventing of a Civil War now Feared.*

1660. 3 February. General Monk entered London.
February-March. *The Ready and Easy Way to Establish a Free Commonwealth.*
April. *Brief Notes upon a Late Sermon.*
Second edition, enlarged: *The Ready and Easy Way . . .*
25 April. Convention Parliament.
Milton dismissed from office.
1 May. General Monk proposed the Restoration.
25 May. Charles Stuart landed at Dover.
16 June. Journal of the House of Commons: 'His Majesty should be humbly moved to call in Milton's two books [*Eikonoklastes and Defensio pro Populo Anglicano*], and that of John Goodwin [*The Obstructors of Justice*], written in justification of the murder of the late king, and order them to be burnt by the common hangman; and that the Attorney-General do proceed against them by indictment or otherwise.'
13 August. Proclamation: 'The said John Milton and John Goodwin are so fled, or so obscure themselves, that no endeavors used for their apprehension can take effect, whereby they may be brought to legal trial, and deservedly receive condign punishment for their treasons and offenses.'
27 August. Copies of the condemned books burned.

29 August. The Act of Oblivion and Indemnity.

15 December. Order of the House of Commons: 'That Mr. Milton, now in custody of the Serjeant at arms, attending this House, be forthwith released, paying his fees.'

17 December. Order of the House of Commons: 'A complaint being made that the Serjeant at arms had demanded excessive fees for the imprisonment of Mr. Milton; it was ordered, that it be referred to the Committee for Privileges to examine this business, and to call Mr. Mead the Serjeant before them, and to determine what is fit to be given to the Serjeant for his fees in this case.'

1663.   24 February. Married Elizabeth Minshull. Moved to Artillery Walk, Bunhill Fields.

1665.   During the plague, resided at Chalfont St. Giles, Buckinghamshire.

1667.   Publication of *Paradise Lost*.

The Records of the House of Commons, quoted in the preceding historical table, show that on 16 June, 1660, Milton was among the supporters of the Commonwealth specifically named for punishment. He was sought for during the summer, and in custody 15 December. Scholarly opinion generally disregards the phrase 'the imprisonment of Mr. Milton,' and holds that the poet was subjected to only technical custody. Be that as it may, he stood in personal danger from the middle of June until shortly after the middle of December, 1660. At such a time as this Milton wrote the opening verses of Book VII:

> Standing on earth, not rapt above the pole,
> More safe I sing with mortal voice, unchanged
> To hoarse or mute, though fallen on evil days,

On evil days though fallen, and evil tongues,
In darkness, and with dangers compassed round,
In solitude, yet not alone, while thou
Visit'st my slumbers nightly, or when morn
Purples the east. Still govern thou my song,
Urania, and fit audience find, though few.
But drive far off the barbarous dissonance
Of Bacchus and his revellers, the race
Of that wild rout that tore the Thracian Bard
In Rhodope.

If the poet's words merit acceptance, he began composition of Book VII shortly after the Restoration, within
the months when he stood in personal peril. The first six
books of the epic then belong to pre-Restoration years.

Precisely how long before the Restoration Milton began
the composition of *Paradise Lost*, we can only surmise.
However, both the anonymous biographer and Edward
Phillips agree that he set seriously to work upon the epic
shortly after the autumn of 1655. In his statement, Phillips
wrote that following the second answer to Alexander More:

> Being now quiet from state adversaries and public
> contests, he had leisure again for his own studies and
> private designs; which were his foresaid *History of
> England*, and a new *Thesaurus Linguae Latinae* accord-
> ing to the manner of Stephanus—a work he had been
> long since collecting from his own reading, and still
> went on with it at times, even very near to his dying
> day—but the papers after his death were so discomposed
> and deficient that it could not be made fit for the press;
> however, what there was of it, was made use of for
> another dictionary.
>
> But the height of his noble fancy and invention began
> now to be seriously and mainly employed in a subject
> worthy of such a Muse; that is, a heroic poem, en-
> titled *Paradise Lost*—the noblest in the general esteem

of learned and judicious persons, of any yet written by any either ancient or modern.

With this account and Milton's statement in Book VII, we exhaust all available first hand information regarding the exact periods when he either worked upon or composed the verses of his epic. Fortunately, supplementary data may be had, both from Edward Phillips and other sources. Continuing his description of *Paradise Lost*, Milton's nephew stated:

> This subject was first designed a tragedy, and in the fourth book of the poem there are ten verses, which several years before the poem was begun, were shown to me and some others, as designed for the very beginning of the said tragedy. The verses are these:
> O thou that with surpassing glory crowned!
> Look'st from thy sole dominion, like the god
> Of this new world; at whose sight all the stars
> Hide their diminished heads: to thee I call,
> But with no friendly voice; and add thy name,
> O Sun! to tell thee how I hate thy beams
> That bring to my remembrance, from what state
> I fell, how glorious once above thy sphere;
> Till pride and worse ambition threw me down,
> Warring in heaven, against heaven's glorious King.
> There is another very remarkable passage in the composure of this poem, which I have a particular occasion to remember; for whereas I had the perusal of it from the very beginning—for some years, as I went from time to time to visit him—in a parcel of ten, twenty, or thirty verses at a time, which being written by whatever hand came next, might possibly want correction as to the orthography and pointing. Having as the summer came on, not been showed any for a considerable while, and, desiring the reason thereof, was answered: that his vein never happily flowed but from the autumnal

equinoctial to the vernal, and that whatever he attempted [at another time] was never to his satisfaction, though he courted his fancy never so much, so that in all the years he was about this poem, he may be said to have spent but half his time therein.

His pardon having passed the seal, he removed to Jewin Street. There he lived when he married his third wife [24 February, 1663], recommended to him by his old friend Dr. Paget in Coleman Street. But he stayed not long after his new marriage, ere he removed to a house in the Artillery Walk leading to Bunhill Fields. . . . Here he finished his noble poem, and published it in the year 1666 [*sic*].

Among other important details, Phillips stated that he had known the poem from its very beginning, and that during the early years of its composition Milton dictated his verses to whatever person was at hand. Since the poet dictated the lines, he doubtless was blind, so that the period described by Phillips must have been later than the first months of 1651. It also was in the year 1651 that Phillips returned to London, and became in position to visit his uncle 'from time to time.' In addition to being later than the first half of 1651, the period of which Phillips spoke must have preceded the year 1657. The period obviously was one wherein Milton lacked a regular amanuensis, and, as Mr. James Holly Hanford has shown, he employed Jeremie Picard as a permanent scribe during the years 1657-61. That he dictated poetry to such a scribe, the anonymous biographer confirmed when he said that Milton, 'waking early . . . had commonly a good stock of verses ready against his amanuensis came.' This biographer's implication that the amanuensis came in the morning, John Aubrey supported with the statement that 'his man' read to the poet at four-thirty, and returned at seven for writing and further reading.

If Phillips spoke accurately, the period of composition which he described preceded the year 1657. Nor does this interpretation contradict the statement that about 1655-56 Milton began to be 'seriously and mainly employed' with *Paradise Lost*. Moreover, it is our most probable interpretation. Phillips declared flatly regarding the poem: 'I had the perusal of it from the very beginning—for some years as I went from time to time to visit him.' The expression *for some years* describes a period of time greater than two years. Since Milton had a regular amanuensis in 1657, his nephew necessarily began before 1655 to correct the verses 'written by whatever hand came next.'

The historical table shows that Milton had ample leisure for poetic composition during the years 1652-53. He then had left Whitehall, and published no pamphlets between the *First Defense* of February, 1651, and the *Second Defense* of the spring of 1654. At this time, said Edward Phillips, his uncle had 'some breathing space' from official obligations. The Psalms and the sonnets to Cromwell and Vane evinced an interest in poetry. Moreover, in discussing with Oldenburgh the *Second Defense*, Milton stated that his stand in behalf of liberty had withdrawn his attention from 'more pleasurable pursuits.' As Mr. Tillyard believes, the implicit description of these interrupted pursuits as noble undertakings, definitely suggests work upon such a subject as *Paradise Lost*.

The interpretation that during 1652-53 Milton began composition of the epic does not conflict with any statement made by Phillips. The resulting period of 1652-1663 for the entire work also harmonizes with his reference to 'all the years' his uncle 'was about this poem.' The remaining point made by the biographer said that *Paradise Lost* was first designed a tragedy. 'Several years' prior to his alteration of the 'subject' into an epic, Phillips stated,

Milton wrote Satan's Address to the Sun as the 'very beginning of the said tragedy.' This point I shall touch on later, mentioning now only the fact that during 1648 and again in 1650, both dates 'several years' earlier than 1652-53, the poet had more than sufficient leisure to plan a tragedy and compose the ten verses of Satan's Address.

In addition to Phillips's direct testimony, we have in Aubrey's *Minutes of the Life of Mr. John Milton* two brief passages attributed to the poet's nephew:

> In the ~~second, third,~~ fourth book of *Paradise Lost* there are about six verses of Satan's exclamation to the sun, which Mr. E. Ph. remembers, about fifteen or sixteen years before ever his poem was thought of, which verses were intended for the beginning of a tragedy which he had designed, but was diverted from it by other business.

> From Mr. E. Phillips. . . . All the time of writing his *Paradise Lost*, his vein began at the autumnal equinoctial, and ceased at the vernal (or thereabouts, I believe about May), and this was four or five years of his doing it. He began about two years before the King came in, and finished about three years after the King's restoration.

The second-hand version at times agreed with Phillips's direct account, on occasion added to it, and again partially differed from it. The repetition consisted of the statements that Milton designed a tragedy which opened with Satan's Address, and that he composed poetry during only autumn and winter. The additions state that 'other business' diverted Milton from the tragedy, and, that he spent upon *Paradise Lost* four or five years, completing the poem about the year 1663. The partial differences claim that Milton began the epic about 1658, that Satan's Address contained six verses, and that the Address had been composed 'about fifteen or sixteen years before ever his poem was thought of'—if by the last was meant 'fifteen or sixteen years before Milton thought of *Paradise Lost*.'

Those details wherein Aubrey duplicated Phillips appear unquestionable, as does his statement that 'other business' diverted Milton from the projected tragedy. In 1640, 1648, and again in 1650, Milton was torn from literary pursuits by other affairs. The second addition, which says in effect that he concluded the epic 'about' three years after May, 1660, limits rather than conflicts with the direct account of Phillips. The first variant, according to which Milton began *Paradise Lost* about 1658, must be regarded as an error. It probably resulted either from faulty memory of what Phillips stated orally, or from misunderstanding at the time the information was given. What Phillips said to Aubrey, if his oral account conformed to that which he put into writing, perhaps was this:

About three years after the Restoration, Milton took a house in Artillery Walk, and there completed *Paradise Lost*. His vein never happily flowed from the autumnal equinoctial to the vernal, so that despite all the years he was about this poem, he actually spent but half his time— a total of four or five years—in the doing of it. In the fourth book of *Paradise Lost* are ten verses of Satan's exclamation to the sun which Milton composed fifteen or sixteen years before people knew he had written his noble poem. These verses he originally intended for the very beginning of a tragedy which he had designed, and from which he had been diverted by other business.

That Aubrey was not wholly clear in his mind as to what Phillips had told him is indicated by his writing six instead of ten verses, and by the placing of Satan's Address in both the second and third books before deciding that the fourth was correct. It is improbable Phillips should have said the Address was 'shown to me and some others' fifteen or sixteen years before Milton ever thought of *Paradise Lost*. Seriously and chiefly employed upon it by 1655, to say nothing of the high probability that some writing had been done earlier, he necessarily had thought of the poem before this year. Accepting for discussion 1654 as the last year when Milton had as yet not 'thought of' his epic, 1639 is the latest period when Phillips could have seen the verses. At this time he had not joined Milton, who indeed did not return to England until August, 1639. Nor can we expect a lad of nine to remember for forty-one years that he had read ten verses of poetry, that these verses were the beginning of a projected tragedy, and that his uncle had been diverted from the tragedy by other business.

It may well be that Aubrey substituted his own interpretation of Phillips's 'several years;' or, as I previously suggested, that he garbled his informant's statement that Satan's Address was written fifteen or sixteen years before *Paradise Lost* was published. Fifteen or sixteen years prior to 1666, and this was Phillips's date for publication of the epic, includes the year 1650. This period not only was one wherein Milton had leisure for literary pursuits, but it also was closed by the business of writing the *First Defense*. The precise date, however, is less important than the point made in Chapter XI—that Milton outlined the tragedy subsequent to his work upon *Adam Unparadised*.

I hasten to add that this reconciliation of the accounts of Phillips and Aubrey is not the conventional one. Our conventional interpretation accepts the Phillips-anonymous biographer date of 1655-56 as that when Milton began preliminary work on the epic, and describes Aubrey's date of 1658 as the year when the poet commenced actual composition. Such a solution is of course none. It gives a secondary and obviously confused account equal authority with the first-hand, and disregards completely the dual fact that Phillips said nothing of preparation, but spoke in detail of actual composition. The picture of Milton devoting perhaps three years to concentrated preparation for a subject which he long had considered savors less of the poet than of the embryo scholar developing a dissertation. It ignores in addition a variety of facts. The first is that Milton had a regular amanuensis before, during, and after 1658, so that Phillips's description of the parcels of ten, twenty, or thirty verses composed at the 'very beginning' of composition does not apply to this period. The second fact is the anonymous biographer's statement that Milton read in the evening to store his fancy, and in the morning dictated verses to his amanuensis. This situation scarcely suggests writing after years of preparation. The poet had studied and read consistently throughout his life, and certainly did not require three years to gather ideas well-known to every educated man of his age. As the events of the historical table show, 1658 was not a likely time for Milton to embark upon *Paradise Lost*.

So far as personal and political circumstances are concerned, three periods were available to the poet for relatively uninterrupted work upon his epic—it being borne in mind that he apparently composed its verses during only the fall and winter. These periods include 1652-53, perhaps less than two working half-years; 1655-58, three full half-years; and 1660-63. The last period, at least three half-years in length, and according to Phillips's direct account, apparently a somewhat longer time, may be given as slightly less than three and one-half of the poet's working years.

We should add to the resulting eight and one-quarter half-years of composition, the time probably given to fugitive writing. We then find, as Aubrey said, that Milton spent 'four or five years' in the 'doing of' *Paradise Lost*. That he required such a period again is indicated by the fact that following 1660, he utilized perhaps three and one-half of his six month periods in developing approximately two-fifths of the epic. Should the five years of actual composition have fallen largely within the three eras of 1652-53, 1655-58, and 1660-63, we may expect evidence of disjunctive composition within the poem. As all writers know too well, disjoined composition invites inconsistencies which the greatest care does not always locate. Handicapped by blindness, Milton would have found their detection unusually difficult.

The hypothesis that Milton began *Paradise Lost* about the year 1652 may well appear overly radical, and the related interpretation too forced which regards as a reference to the poem's publication, the *thought of* that Aubrey employed in his 'fifteen or sixteen years before ever his poem was thought of.' If so, I may quote a similar conclusion discovered after I had reached both hypothesis and interpretation. This similar conclusion is the matured opinion which George Saintsbury set forth in the *Cambridge History of English Literature*. Unfortunately, Saintsbury failed to present the evidence upon which he based his considered opinion:

> The present writer has always from internal evidence of a vague but not unsatisfactory kind, been inclined to believe that the poem was actually begun not long after his blindness had become a settled fact with him, which would coincide with the fifteen or sixteen years above mentioned.

The interpretation that during the years 1652-53 Milton was engaged in completing some integrated and fairly extended work also provides one explanation of a fact noted by Mr. Hanford—that the *Second Defense* 'did not appear until the spring of 1654, though it had been ordered by the Council long before.'

Our inquiry is now confronted with a problem untouched by Miltonic scholarship: Did the poet compose
the books and sections of *Paradise Lost* in the order in
which they appeared in his published version? Obviously,
no one may give, or should attempt a final answer to this
question. There stands available however some trustworthy
evidence, all of which suggests that the order of publication was not the order of composition. A major part of this
evidence comes from *Adam Unparadised* and the abandoned tragedy seemingly entitled 'Paradise Lost.'

As I mentioned in the preceding chapter, neither *Adam
Unparadised* nor the three preceding drafts included any
suggestion of Books I and II. The *Adam*, however, and to
a minor degree the third draft, set forth in this order the
principal themes found in these sections of Paradise Lost:
the second fourth of Book IV; the latter two-thirds of
Book VIII; the first and final quarters of Book IV; the
latter third of Book V; and the whole of Book VI. In the
abandoned tragedy, Milton opened with a theme taken
from *Adam Unparadised*—that of Satan entering the Garden, lamenting his overthrow, and bemoaning himself.
This episode he made the *very beginning* of the tragedy,
and with such an episode he opened Book IV of the epic.
To move forward in the plot the entrance of Satan into
Paradise, would necessarily do as much with the subsequent 'discourse of enmity' that followed his discovery
by the angels. Taken in combination, the abandoned tragedy and the *Adam* present in sequence major conceptions
of the first half of Book IV; the final quarter of this book;
the last two-thirds of Book VIII; the latter third of Book
V; and the whole of Book VI. It is with this group of
themes that Milton appears most likely to have begun, and
for the purposes of analysis will be assigned to the initial
period of 1652-53.

Since Milton began Book VII during 1660, and from this point in the epic followed largely the sequence of *Adam Unparadised*, much the greater part of Books VII-XII (originally VII-X), definitely belongs to the period 1660-1663. Book I-III may be assigned to the years 1655-1658, together with those parts of Books IV and V not included in *Adam Unparadised*. As I have implied, this working hypothesis assumes that during both the several periods of composition and relatively inactive intervening years, the poet made minor additions and alterations.

Prior to discussion of the internal evidence which suggests these several periods, I mention the conviction of Mr. E. M. W. Tillyard that Books I-III are closely related in mood and spirit to the great *Second Defense*, published in the spring of 1654. The Hymn to Light at the beginning of Book III, he regards as a poetic version of part of the passage in the *Second Defense* wherein Milton discussed his blindness. Because of these relationships, Mr. Tillyard would place the three opening books immediately before rather than after 1654. However, as Mr. Hanford has observed, Milton could carry mood and idea from prose to poetry as well as *vice versa*. Indeed, as I mention in the chapter preceding, he did carry into *Paradise Lost* ideas employed in earlier works.

It is also true that Milton held in 1658 much the same feeling toward his blindness which we find in Book III. He lamented in his introduction to this book:

> Thus with the year
> Seasons return; but not to me returns
> Day, or the sweet approach of even or morn,
> Or sight of vernal bloom, or summer's rose,
> Or flocks, or herds, or human face divine;
> But cloud instead, and ever-during dark

Surrounds me, from the cheerful ways of men
Cut off.

Similar in mood are lines from the sonnet, 'On His De-
ceased Wife,' evidently composed shortly after Katharine
Woodcock's death in February, 1658:

Methought I saw my late espousèd saint,
Brought to me like Alcestis from the grave,
. . . such as yet once more I trust to have
Full sight of her in heaven without restraint,
Came vested all in white. . . . Her face was veiled. . . .
But, oh! as to embrace me she inclined,
I waked, she fled, and day brought back my night.

Among the indisputable inconsistencies found in *Paradise
Lost*, the most obvious is Milton's use of two radically different mountains for the hill which rose within Eden. As
I point out in Chapter VI, the first mountain of Paradise
derived from the tradition of Spenser, if not from Spenser
himself. The sides of this peak were overgrown with bram-
ble and thicket; the top spread out as a plain; and round the
plain grew high walls of trees:

[On Satan] fares, and to the border comes
Of Eden, where delicious Paradise
Now nearer, crowns with her enclosure green . . .
The champain head of a steep wilderness,
Whose hairy sides with thicket overgrown,
Grotesque and wild, access denied . . . Yet higher . . .
The verduous wall of Paradise up-sprung . . . .
And higher than that wall a circling row
Of goodliest trees.

Forty lines later, in IV, 172 ff., Milton again employed
the wooded mountain as the site of the Garden:

Now to the ascent of that steep savage hill
Satan had journeyed on, pensive and slow;

> But further way found none; so thick entwined,
> As one continued brake, the undergrowth
> Of shrubs and tangling bushes had perplexed
> All path of man or beast that passed that way.

Within a half-hundred verses we again meet the thicket-covered hill:

> Southward through Eden went a river large,
> Nor changed his course, but through the shaggy
> Hill passed underneath engulfed.

Fifty-five lines later, Milton specifically declared that the mountain of Paradise was not the Abyssinian Mount Amara:

> Nor, where Abassin kings their issue guard,
> Mount Amara (though this by some supposed
> True Paradise) under the Ethiop line
> By Nilus' head, enclosed with shining rock,
> A whole day's journey high.

Despite three passages in Book IV which described the mountain of Paradise as a wooded hill, and a fourth which declared it not Mount Amara, a subsequent passage transformed the shaggy hill into the towering rock known to the Seventeenth Century as the Abyssinian mountain. This passage followed exactly two hundred and sixty verses after that which denied Amara was the place of Paradise:

>   The setting sun
> Slowly descended, and with right aspect
> Against the eastern gate of Paradise
> Levelled his evening rays. It was a rock
> Of alabaster, piled up to the clouds,
> Conspicuous far, winding with one ascent
> Accessible from earth, one entrance high;
> The rest was craggy cliff, that overhung
> Still as it rose, impossible to climb.

Having once changed from the Spenserian mountain to Mount Amara, we might expect Milton to retain the latter. However, when Adam subsequently related that after his creation, God carried him to Paradise, the poet used for a fourth time the wooded hill enclosed by trees:

> So saying, by the hand he took me, raised,
> And over fields and waters, as in air
> Smooth sliding without step, last led me up
> A woody mountain, whose high top was plain,
> A circuit wide, enclosed, with goodliest trees
> Planted, with walks and bowers.

Three subsequent and extremely brief references to the mountain of the Garden, two in Book XI and a third in Book XII, employed details drawn from the Amara of Heylyn and Purchas:

> And on the east side of the garden place,
> Where entrance up from Eden easiest climbs . . .
> It was a hill of Paradise the highest . . .
> In either hand the hastening angel caught
> Our lingering parents, and to the eastern gate
> Led them direct, and down the cliff as fast
> To the subjected plain.

In these nine passages and fragments, four have described Paradise as the wooded Spenserian mountain, and one as not Mount Amara. Each and all of these five passages belong to sections of the epic definitely foreshadowed by *Adam Unparadised*. In this early draft, they also are treated as a unit. Stated differently, the passages from IV, 131 ff., 172 ff., 223 ff., 280 ff., and VIII, 300 ff., fall within the divisions of *Paradise Lost* assigned tentatively to the years 1652-53. Those divisions which utilized either Mount Amara or details drawn from its description, belong to the subsequent periods of 1655-58 and 1660-63.

If the argument from similarity of mood carries weight, a further tie connects parts of Books IV and VIII included as a unit within *Adam Unparadised*. I refer to the passages wherein Eve and Adam recorded so delightfully their experiences immediately following creation. In Book IV, Eve confided to the admiring Adam:

> That day I oft remember, when from sleep
> I first awaked, and found myself reposed,
> Under a shade, on flowers, much wondering where
> And what I was, whence thither brought, and how.
> Not distant far from thence a murmuring sound
> Of waters issued from a cave, and spread
> Into a liquid plain. . . . I thither went
> With unexperienced thought, and laid me down
> On the green bank, to look into the clear
> Smooth lake, that to me seemed another sky.
>   As I bent down to look, just opposite,
> A shape within the watery gleam appeared,
> Bending to look on me. . . . There I had fixed
> Mine eyes till now, and pined with vain desire,
> Had not a voice thus warned me: 'What thou seest,
> What there thou seest, fair creature, is thyself;
> With thee it came and goes; but follow me . . .
> He whose image thou art; him thou shalt enjoy. . . .'
>   What could I do, but follow straight,
> Invisibly thus led? till I espied thee,
> Fair, indeed, and tall, under a platan . . . Thy
> Gentle hand seized mine . . . and from that time see
> How beauty is excelled by manly grace
> And wisdom, which alone is truly fair.

Adam's related account in Book VIII likewise made skilful use of the vision motif:

> For man to tell how human life began
> Is hard; for who himself beginning knew?
> . . . As new-waked from soundest sleep,

Soft on the flowery herb I found me laid,
In balmy sweat, which with his beams the sun
Soon dried . . . About me round I saw
Hill, dale, and shady woods, and sunny plains,
And liquid lapse of murmuring streams. . . .
Myself I then perused, and limb by limb
Surveyed, and sometimes went and sometimes ran
With supple joints, as lively vigor led;
    But who I was, or where, or from what cause
Knew not . . . On a green shady bank, profuse of
Flowers, pensive I sat me down. There gentle sleep
First found me, and with soft oppression seized . . .
When suddenly stood at my head a Dream,
Whose inward apparition gently moved
My fancy to believe I yet had being,
And lived. One came, methought, of shape divine,
And said, 'Thy mansion wants thee, Adam; rise. . . .'
So saying, by the hand he took me, raised,
And over fields and waters, as in air
Smooth sliding without step, last led me up
A woody mountain, whose high top was plain.

A second noticeable inconsistency is the impropriety
of describing God as twice exalting the Son, and command-
ing the angels to bow before him. Such a Divine decree
as the Exaltation was as irrevocable as it was eternal. In
Book V, the earliest under the chronology of Milton's narrative, we recall that God decreed to all angels, the good
and those soon to rebel:

Hear, all ye angels, Progeny of Light,
Thrones, Dominations, Princedoms, Virtues, Powers,
Hear my decree, which unrevoked shall stand!
This day I have begot whom I declare
My only Son, and on this holy hill
Him have anointed. . . . Your head I him appoint,
And by myself have sworn to him shall bow
All knees in heaven, and shall confess him Lord.

In Book III, chronologically later in the story, Deity decreed before the angels who remained in heaven after the fall of Satan:

> Here shalt thou sit incarnate, here shalt reign . . .
> Anointed universal King. All power
> I give thee; reign forever, and assume
> Thy merits; under thee, as Head Supreme,
> Thrones, Princedoms, Powers, Dominions, I reduce:
> All knees to thee shall bow of them that bide
> In heaven, or earth, or, under earth, in hell.

When describing in Book VI the victory of Christ over the host of Satan, Milton wrote:

> Yet half his strength he put not forth, but checked
> His thunder in mid-volley.

Book III, however, stated flatly that Christ did not check his thunder:

> [God] by thee threw down
> The aspiring dominations. Thou that day
> Thy Father's dreadful thunder did'st not spare.

This discrepancy is the more suggestive for the reason that in the latter part of Book VII, the angels sang of the creating Christ:

> [Thou art] greater now in thy return
> Than from the giant-angels. Thee that day
> Thy thunders magnified.

As with the mountain of Paradise, the intermediate description differed both with that which had preceded, and with that which followed.

The early draft known as *Adam Unparadised* included 'the battle and victory in heaven,' and made no mention of the themes employed later by Milton in Book III. Book VII, foreshadowed in the draft, we have noted belonged to the 1660-63 group. The result is that on one hand we meet discrepancies between divisions of the epic included in the draft and those not foreshadowed by it. On the other, discrepancies occur between parts of the poem written before 1660, and other parts composed at a later date, both of which developed from *Adam Unparadised*. I mention in passing that had Milton spent three years working out the plans for his epic we should not expect these and other infelicities. Similarly, he probably would have relied less completely on the outline and themes of the *Adam*.

As the preceding chapter pointed out, *Adam Unparadised* omitted a number of conceptions and episodes employed in the previously composed third draft. Without exception, Milton dropped from it every item suggestive of Book III. He also eliminated the evening star, whose appearance he was to paint so effectively in the third quarter of Book IV (598 ff.). This passage, I may add, followed within fifty lines of that which described the hill of Paradise in terms of Mount Amara. In short, these omissions show a trend within Milton's mind at the time he wrote out the *Adam*. Continuation of this trend when he began the epic necessarily would result in non-use, during the first stages of *Paradise Lost*, of themes found both in Book III and in the third quarter of Book IV.

A further point of interest is that without exception the evil angels who participated in the battle in heaven differed either in name, function, or in ascribed characteristics from those found in Books I and II. One might infer that Adramelech, Asmadai, Ariel, Arioch, Ramiel, and Nisroch perished in the conflict, for they were not mentioned among the evil angels who thronged hell. The taunting, gamesome Belial of the battle became in the epic catalog the personification of vices connected with idolatry. In the infernal council he appeared as the suave diplomat who concealed his feeling, and was 'timorous and slothful.' The Moloch who in Book VI 'fled bellowing' before Gabriel, stood in the council as 'the strongest and fiercest spirit that fought in heaven.' In the first two books of the epic, Milton named Beelzebub as the chief lieutenant of Satan, gave much space to him, and described him as having participated actively in the celestial conflict. However, Book V mentioned only an unnamed and unidentified 'next subordinate,' who served as adjutant; and Book VI no subordinate whatsoever. The faithful Abdiel and Zophiel appeared only in these books, and the Gabriel who here ranked next to Michael is nearer in importance to the Gabriel of the manuscript draft than is the officer of the guard posted upon Mount Amara.

The connection which the battle in heaven has with the first two-thirds of Book V is external. In other words, the story of the conflict was related by Raphael and heard by Adam and Eve, the three characters of the first parts of the book. With one exception, Raphael's narrative in this and the succeeding Book VI is in the third person, and could have been presented by the chorus which gave it in the *Adam*. This exception occurs near the middle of Book VI, where Raphael spoke briefly in the first person. In the immediately preceding lines, he had said:

> Uriel and Raphael his vaunting foe,
> Though huge and in a rock of diamond armed,
> Vanquished—Adramelech and Asmadai . . .
> Nor stood unmindful Abdiel to annoy
> The atheist crew, but with redoubled blow
> Ariel, and Arioch, and the violence
> Of Ramiel, scorched and blasted, overthrew.

There was nothing unusual in Milton's employment of Michael and Gabriel, Uriel and Raphael as the important angels of the battle, or in his addition of fictitious characters whose names closed with *el*, 'of God.' However, exclusive of himself, Abdiel, and his three conventional associates, Raphael proved extremely modest for the many spirits who had fought beside him:

> I might relate of thousands, and their names
> Eternize here on earth; but those elect
> Angels, contented with their fame in heaven,
> Seek not the praise of men. The other sort,
> In might though wondrous and in acts of war,
> Nor of renown less eager . . . to glory aspires,
> Vain-glorious and through infamy seeks fame:
> Therefore eternal silence be their doom.

It is at least disconcerting to hear *Raphael* inform Adam of Raphael's valorous deeds, to say nothing of his refusal for modesty's sake to catalog additional comrades in arms. Under such a plan as that of *Adam Unparadised*, where 'the chorus sings of the battle and victory in heaven,' it would be wholly fitting to write:

> Uriel and Raphael his vaunting foe,
> Though huge and in a rock of diamond armed,
> Vanquished.

The passage which produces the impropriety can be omitted from Milton's text without alteration of line, and with improved continuity. Between the verses which immediately precede and follow it, I give in italics the first and last lines of the perhaps interpolated passage:

> But with redoubled blow
> Ariel, and Arioch, and the violence
> Of Ramiel, scorched and blasted, overthrew.
> *I might relate of thousands, and their names . . .*
> *Therefore eternal silence be their doom.*
> And now, their mightiest quelled, the battle swerved,
> With many an inroad gored; deformèd rout
> entered. . . .

Excluding the battle in heaven, where use of his name would be expected, Uriel appeared chiefly in Book III and in the episodes of Book IV not indicated in *Adam Unparadised*. He is mentioned briefly in two other places, early in Book IX, and in IV, 124-30. In the latter passage, which falls within that section of Book IV tentatively assigned to 1652-53, Milton wrote that Satan:

> Yet not enough had practiced to deceive
> Uriel, once warned; whose eye pursued him down
> The way he went, and on the Assyrian mount
> Saw him disfigured, more than could befall
> Spirit of happy sort: his gestures fierce
> He marked, and mad demeanor, then alone
> As he supposed, all unobserved, unseen.

This passage apparently is an interpolation. Uriel had not been 'once warned.' In addition, the fragment is partially incompatible with the verses which precede it. As with the verses spoken by Raphael in the first person, it can be omitted without alteration of line and with improved continuity. I again give in italics the first and last lines of the fragment:

> Whereof he [Satan] soon aware
> Each perturbation smoothed with outward calm,
> Artificer of fraud; and was the first
> That practiced falsehood under saintly show,
> Deep malice to conceal, couched with revenge.
> *Yet not enough had practiced to deceive . . .*
> *As he supposed, all unobserved, unseen.*
>   So on he fares, and to the border comes
> Of Eden, where delicious Paradise,
> Now nearer, crowns with her enclosure green. . . .

There is, I may add, neither allusion to nor use made of astronomical ideas in the divisions of *Paradise Lost* tentatively assigned to the years 1652-53. Flights through the universe occur in Books III and V, allusions to the telescope in I and III, and to the axial rotation of the earth in IV, 592-95—in short, within those sections not indicated in the *Adam*, and dated as 1655-58. These references, at times neutral and on occasion sympathetic toward the new astronomy, contrast markedly with the attitude of the dialogue on celestial motions which opens Book VIII. As Mr. Richard F. Jones, Robert K. Merton, and other scholars have emphasized, the scientific movement of Milton's day drew in England its chief support from the Puritan and Independent. In 1654 and later, Milton was close to Henry Oldenburgh, one of those most active in less speculative phases of the 'new philosophy.' During 1655-58, his associations would have influenced him to take a sympathetic attitude, to say nothing of the interest in the telescope which Miss Marjorie Nicolson has disclosed so effectively. With the coming of the Restoration, Oldenburgh, Wilkins, and the scientifically-minded followers of the Commonwealth generally made peace with the King, and soon petitioned that their organization be chartered as the Royal Society. I do not suggest that Milton wrote the dialogue on celestial motions to attack 'apostates;' rather, that he was a human being who now was untrammeled by considerations which not infrequently have softened the utterances of mankind.

Additional information, in part negative, may be had from the analogues or probable sources of various sections of the epic. In the several parts assigned to the years 1652-53, no fragment has a correspondence later than the first of these years. Indeed, only two details apparently were drawn from a work published in 1652, the *Cosmography* of Peter Heylyn. Both items occur in the poet's declaration that Mount Amara was not true Paradise. In the first of the two, Milton repeated Heylyn's 'a day's journey high,' as 'a whole day's journey high.' In the second instance, he seemingly derived his 'shining rock' from the geographer's, 'the rock so smooth and even . . . that no wall can be more evenly polished.' However, Heylyn had used the first expression in his *Mikrokosmos,* the eighth edition of which appeared in 1639; and the second detail conceivably, although improbably, could have been developed from Purchas. In any event, Milton had sufficient time to have used the *Cosmography* in the 1652-53 period. I mention in passing that Satan's defiant Address to the Sun of Book IV, has a partial analogue in Beaumont's *Psyche,* published in 1648.

Analogues or sources for Books I-III and other sections assigned to 1655-58 belong normally to later dates than those of the 1652-53 group. In fact, this division appears to have drawn more heavily upon seventeenth-century literature than any other, a circumstance which may explain in part its greater interest for the average reader. The *Pansebeia* of Alexander Ross, which I consider a major encyclopedic source for the epic catalog, first appeared in 1653. The *Davidëis,* which described as an army a catalog of devils headed by Moloch—the first character of Milton's band—Cowley published in 1656. According to Todd, Milton's third wife named Cowley as one of his favorite English poets. In the *Chronographia* of Syncellus, published in Paris in 1652, and doubtless available in England by 1653, we find the Uriel of the closing passages of Book III. Equally important is the rare analogue of Milton's description of the daughters of Cain seducing by musical instruments the sons of Seth, set forth in Book XI. As Mr. Denis Saurat pointed out some years ago, the *Chronographia* is the most probable source for Azazel, standard bearer for the devils who marched in the epic catalog of Book I. Since Milton unquestionably utilized two, and ordered at least six other volumes of the Corpus of Byzantine History to which Syncellus's work belonged, he probably knew this edition of the book. With the exception of Caedmon, available in manuscript by 1651 and published in 1655, all other important analogues had appeared before 1650.

So far as the evidence of probable sources or analogues is admissible, it shows that Milton had available in 1652 the subject-matter and themes of the books and sections assigned to the years 1652-53. This evidence also suggests, first, that Book I was not composed during these years, and secondly, that Books I-II and subsequent related sections could have been written during 1655-58. The unusual Cowley analogue, which I regard as a partial source of the epic catalog, dates this enumeration as later than the year 1655. So far as I have observed, Books VII-XII neither use nor echo any work published after 1656. This also is the latest date of any book listed by Todd as a possible source for this part of *Paradise Lost*.

By way of summarizing this discussion, I mention that according to Thomas Ellwood, Milton had completed the epic by 1665. Edward Phillips placed its conclusion sometime after February, 1663, but whether in 1663 or 1664 he does not say. John Aubrey, quoting Phillips, in effect placed the date as 'about' 1663. Under the English calendar then in vogue, 1663 extended until almost the close of March rather than to the end of December. During the latter part of 1660, the poet began the composition of Book VII, and presumably by that time had finished, perhaps in rough draft, the preceding books. Of the high probability of these points we may be confident.

Less clear is the precise time when Milton initiated composition of the epic. Aubrey, citing Phillips, said in effect that he began the poem 'about' 1658. Milton's nephew, whose account has the partial corroboration of the anonymous biographer, wrote that after the autumn of 1655 his uncle began to devote the major part of each fall and winter to *Paradise Lost*. He failed to say definitely when Milton began writing, but his account described a period of some years which must have ended in 1657. Other evidence set the opening of this period as about the year 1651. Milton's varied activities and important political events largely eliminated two periods of approximately two years each, 1653-55 and 1658-60, leaving available for concentrated work the three periods of 1652-53, 1655-58, and 1660-63. We may, I believe, be reasonably certain that during these periods Milton wrote the greater part of *Paradise Lost*. During the intervening years he doubtless did some writing, and perhaps an appreciable amount.

Necessarily conjectural are my conclusions regarding the order in which Milton composed the first three-fifths of the epic. Evidence chiefly internal, but supported by *Adam Unparadised* and the abandoned tragedy, suggests strongly that Books I-III, the third quarter of Book IV, and the first two-thirds of Book V were written later than the remaining parts of Books IV-V, Book VI, and apparently sections of Book VIII. On the basis of Milton's activities and his letter to Henry Oldenburgh, the two provisional periods were set as 1652-53 and 1655-58. Further evidence from probable sources corroborates the data to the extent of setting composition of the epic catalog almost certainly after 1652, and apparently after 1655. As a probability which merits careful consideration, and only as such, I suggest that Milton began composition with sections of Book IV, and that he wrote perhaps four-fifths of *Paradise Lost* during the three periods of 1652-53, 1655-58, and 1660-63.

Chapter XIII

INTERPRETATION AND CONCLUSION

THE knight who rode off in many directions is wholly representative of this concluding chapter. However, the varied characteristics and tendencies of Miltonic criticism which I shall discuss are often fundamental, and on occasion rise in part from a common source. The partial common source is that defensive psychology which has permeated and influenced much of our criticism. Mr. Douglas Bush aptly described the situation when he wrote, 'admirers of Milton have always been, consciously or not, on the defensive.'

An outstanding example of this inferiority complex comes in the replies made to T. S. Eliot, F. R. Leavis, and others of their school. In general, their type of criticism describes Milton as having adversely affected English prosody of the Eighteenth Century, and his poetry either as basically verbal music, or as a collection of words and phrases applied externally. The central method and argument of this school I may illustrate by a few passages from the *Revaluation, Tradition and Development in English Poetry* of Mr. Leavis. The section of *Paradise Lost* under discussion falls within that part which I believe Milton first composed. This fact, if it be a fact, doubtless contributed to making the verses so well-suited to the critic's purpose:

> This [section], for instance, is from the description, in Book IV, of the Garden of Eden, which, most admirers of Milton will agree, exemplifies sensuous richness if that is to be found in *Paradise Lost:*

And now, divided into four main streams,
Runs diverse, wandering many a famous realm
And country whereof here needs no account;
But rather to tell how, if art could tell
How, from that sapphire fount the crispèd brooks,
Rolling on orient pearl and sands of gold,
With mazy error under pendent shades
Ran nectar, visiting each plant, and fed
Flowers worthy of Paradise, which not nice art
In beds and curious knots, but nature boon
Poured forth profuse on hill, and dale, and plain,
Both where the morning sun first warmly smote
The open field, and where the unpierced shade
Imbrowned the noontide bowers. Thus was this place
A happy rural seat of various view:
Groves whose rich trees wept odorous gums and balm;
Others whose fruit, burnished with golden rind,
Hung amiable—Hesperian fables true,
If true, here only—and of delicious taste.

It should be plain at once that the difference [between Shakespeare and Milton] was not exaggerated. As the labored, pedantic artifice of the diction suggests, Milton seems here to be focussing rather upon words than upon perceptions, sensations or things. 'Sapphire,' 'Orient pearl,' 'sands of gold,' 'odorous gums and balm,' and so on, convey no doubt a vague sense of opulence, but this is not what we mean by sensuous richness. The loose judgment that it is a verbal opulence has a plain enough meaning if we look for contrast at the 'bestud with stars' of Comus's speech; there we feel—the alliteration is of a different kind from that of the Grand Style —the solid lumps of gold studding the 'forehead of the deep.' In the description of Eden, a little before the passage quoted, we have:

And all amid them stood the Tree of Life,
High eminent, blooming ambrosial fruit
Of vegetable gold. . . .

It would be of no use to try and argue with any one who contended that 'vegetable gold' exemplified the same kind of fusion as 'green shops!'

It needs no unusual sensitiveness to language to perceive that, in this Grand Style, the medium calls pervasively for a kind of attention, compels an attitude towards itself, that is incompatible with sharp, concrete realization; just as it would seem to be, in the mind of the poet, incompatible with an interest in sensuous particularity. He exhibits a feeling *for* words rather than a capacity for feeling *through* words; we are often, in reading him, moved to comment that he is 'external' or that he 'works from the outside.' The Grand Style, at its best, compels us to recognize it as an impressive stylization, but it functions very readily, and even impressively, at low tension, and its tendency is betrayed, even in a show piece like the description of Eden, by such offenses as:

>   Thus was this place
> A happy rural seat of various view:
> Groves whose rich trees wept odorous gums
>   and balm;
> Others whose fruit, burnished with golden rind,
> Hung amiable—Hesperian fables true,
> If true, here only—and of delicious taste.

If the Eighteenth Century thought that poetry was something that could be applied from the outside, it found the precedent as well as the apparatus in Milton.

A principal rejoinder to this trenchant school has been personal attack. Mr. Eliot, as the chief offender, we have subjected both to abuse and amateur psycho-analysis, deciding from the latter that a phobia acquired in childhood occasioned his animadversions. However, the idea that the poetry of *Paradise Lost* did not spring as the living product of soil and root, sap and leaf, is much older than Mr. Eliot or Mr. Leavis. Among other early critics, Dryden and Johnson set forth much the same conception. The latter said plainly in his *Life of Milton*:

Whatever be his subject, he never fails to fill the imagination. But his images and descriptions of the scenes or operations of nature do not seem to be always copied from original form, or to have the freshness, raciness, and energy, of immediate observation. He saw nature, as Dryden, expresses it, 'through the spectacles of books;' and on most occasions calls learning to his assistance. The Garden of Eden brings to his mind the vale of Enna, where Proserpine was gathering flowers. Satan makes his way through fighting elements, like Argo between the Cyanean rocks, or Ulysses between the two Sicilian whirlpools, when he shunned Charybdis on the larboard. . . . He does not confine himself within the limits of rigorous comparison; his great excellence is amplitude, and he expands the adventitious image beyond the dimensions which the occasion required. Thus, comparing the shield of Satan to the orb of the moon, he crowds the imagination with the discovery of the telescope, and all the wonders which the telescope discovers.

We may argue that Dryden and Johnson, as well as Eliot and Leavis, were unfortunate victims of obsession; perhaps proving this of Johnson by citing his habit of touching the posts which he passed. It might be more rational, however, to note that in much of *Paradise Lost*, the ideas and themes could not grow or flourish as might an independent organism. Tradition had too largely determined not only the idea to be used, but also the place where it should be employed. The chief contribution of the hexameral poet necessarily was addition or amplification. Equally in point is a probability to be discussed later— that we have attributed to Milton a disunity of word and thought perhaps primarily of our own making.

It is not argument to state that Milton affected adversely English poetry of the Eighteenth Century. Had the authors of the century not read Milton, their poetry might well have been worse. Again, the great poet has in the long run profited from reading and early imitation. The Eighteenth Century may have lacked its full quota of such poets. It is quite possible that the 'influence' was more apparent than real. In keeping with Milton, the writers of the era generally were well-educated men. They were interested in ideas and values, not in louse and daffodil; in philosophy, not biology; in the issues which challenged the mature mind, and not in the persistent self-exploitation of the congenital adolescent. Learned poetry, as learned prose, rarely has produced the sparkling brook which tripped blithely to the sea.

For decades Chaucerian and Shakespearian scholarship has welcomed studies in source and analogue. By so doing it achieved a riper and more complete criticism of these men. In apparent disregard of this example, the Miltonic tradition had defended almost vehemently its conception of the poet's originality. If I mistake not, the determined defense has on occasion resulted from our pressing inferiority complex. To be sure, a number of attacks may be disregarded, for the author's actual objective was to substitute sources of his discovery for those previously advanced. Other specific strictures have the justification of fact, although studies of sources have produced no more than their proportional share of nonsense.

Our traditional attitude toward Milton's 'originality,' and one which I believe seriously has handicapped understanding of his work, appears to have expressed itself in three types of thought. The first is that voiced by Mr. Whiting, when he attacked as heresy the conclusion that Milton drew 'the great bulk of his ideas from a few sources, or literally' followed 'one source and then another.' Whether heresy, long since rejected as a plea in science, still has a place in literary scholarship, I shall not debate. However, the magisterial attitude of the heresy hunter is doubly unfortunate in that it leads easily to misrepresentation. The effect which it can have upon accuracy may be illustrated by simple comparison. I give first an 'heretical' conclusion, and secondly the summary used when attack was made upon it. In its several related parts, the offensive analysis had said:

> Regardless of any conclusion which may be reached as to the nature and extent of the poet's indebtedness to Ross, our conventional interpretation of the purpose and nature of the epic catalog should be radically altered, perhaps to read: 'Having assembled the host of Satan, Milton employed such a pattern as that found in the popular *Pansebeia* of his contemporary Alexander Ross, and enumerated and condemned the heathen deities and religions which surrounded and at times seduced the children of Israel.' . . .
>
> The *Pansebeia* was easily available to the poet, and it is the kind of treatise which a man of Milton's interests would have read. Quite naturally, he was *well-informed* [italics added] in the subject-matter of this work, but his knowledge would not preclude use of *Pansebeia* as a guide and partial source for a survey and condemnation of the heathen deities and religions of ancient Palestine, Egypt and Greece. . . .
>
> It is, I believe, quite obvious that Milton knew and used the *Pansebeia* of Ross. . . . With this work as a guide and partial source, he enumerated and condemned the heathen deities and religions which surrounded and at times seduced the children of Israel.

Summarized for censure and refutation, the conclusion became something quite different:

> [This] recent study maintains that in the catalog
> Milton *merely* [italics added] employed the pattern and
> the material found in Ross's widely read *Pansebeia*. . . .
> To accept the recent interpretation. . . . one must as-
> sume that when Milton composed the catalog his mind
> was practically a blank except for the material derived
> directly from Ross.

The second attitude was succinctly expressed by David
Masson, who labelled investigation of Milton's sources
'futile' and 'for the most part laborious nonsense.' This
dogma probably has proved a greater obstacle than the
first—the stigma of heresy might be withstood, but scarcely
that of futile nonsense. The third deterrent is the somewhat more liberal belief which admits that shadowy re-
flections of Milton's reading may be found within his
work. Mr. Hanford presented accurately this interpretation when he wrote:

> [Milton] certainly leaves nothing as he found it.
> That is why the resemblances which I have been dis-
> cussing are in general so shadowy. All is transformed
> to the substance of his imagination. The Miltonic accent
> is everywhere, and when the labors of the source hunters
> are done, *Paradise Lost* remains one of the most original
> works in English or in any literature.

The greater part of this volume stands in complete disagreement with these related conceptions. In addition to
discouraging an essential type of investigation, they make
implicitly or explicitly undemonstrated assumptions regarding Milton and his poetry. So far as the question of
'originality' is concerned, it makes but little difference
whether Milton utilized an idea, a theme, or an episode
drawn from a book, or repeated the idea, theme, or episode
which a powerful tradition ruled should be employed.
That Milton more often than not wrote exactly what a

Christian poet should write, has, I believe, been sufficiently demonstrated. Moreover, his almost scrupulous care in following tradition indicates a conscious desire to do so. His poetic ideal was not the innovator. It was rather the 'interpreter and relater of the best and sagest things.' We do Milton no honor and some discourtesy by seeking to foist upon him a type of originality which he himself rejected.

To say that Milton transformed all material which he used doubtless is true in the limited sense intended. In the broader and more vital sense, however, transformation was not attempted and apparently not sought. Satan played in heaven, hell, and on earth his expected rôles. Adam and Eve conducted themselves according to tradition, and the Garden in Eden was the customary beautiful place. The idea that inclement weather and other evils followed Adam's fall, the exposition of Biblical history, the promise of a Messiah, all these reflected established tradition. In *Paradise Lost*, the originality which Milton both desired and achieved was in part that of doing better the conventional and expected thing. This conception of originality he refers to in the often misquoted passage which concluded Chapter XXIII of *Eikonoklastes*. In charging Charles I with literary theft, Milton stated: 'For such kind of borrowing as this, if it be not bettered by the borrower, among good authors is accounted plagiary.'

In sharp contrast with our doughty defense of Milton's 'originality' stands a broadening attack upon what the poet must have valued inestimably more—his courage and strength of will. I speak of the conclusions advanced by the Pessimistic School. An able representative of this group, Mr. George Whiting, remarked after a study of Burton's early seventeenth-century work on melancholy:

A systematic survey shows that Milton was profoundly influenced by melancholy, the prevailing dis-

order of his age. In fact, it appears that the mood and
a fairly large part of the subject-matter of Burton's
Anatomy of Melancholy are paralleled in Milton's work.
The conditions and the experiences of his life perfectly
illustrate many of the causes of melancholy discussed in
the *Anatomy*.

Other members of this school describe Milton as having
grown dispirited and pessimistic because of the failure of
the Commonwealth. One distinguished scholar, Sir Herbert
Grierson, believed a growing disillusionment not only led
Milton to write *Paradise Lost*, but inferentially based this
interpretation in part upon the emphasis which the epic
gives to the new heaven and earth and the promise of
the Messiah:

To *Paradise Lost* then, Milton came finally in a very
different spirit from that in which he had dreamed of an
historical epic, symbolizing the great achievements of the
English people, a 'song to generations,' a poem in which
great deeds were to be celebrated 'with a suitable majesty.' *Paradise Lost* was to be something very different.
An historical subject was out of the question for Milton
as he sat in silence expiating his offenses. Even parts of
the *History of England* which referred too obviously
to the course of events during the Rebellion, the lamentable failure of the English Parliament and people, had
to be cut out when the *History* was printed. No; Milton
would take up the Biblical story, what the Dutch poet
calls 'the tragedy of tragedies,' and make of it what one
must call an arraignment of mankind from Adam to the
Day of Judgment—Man's fatal weakness, his prone-
ness to subordinate reason to passion, what Mr. Tillyard
calls man's triviality. . . . Milton's mind has passed
through the cycle which Dr. Charles describes in the
progress of Jewish prophetic and apocalyptic literature,
postponing to a remoter and remoter future, and ulti-

mately to the coming of a new heaven and a new earth, the hopes for a Messianic Kingdom.

The thesis that *Paradise Lost* is pessimistic, Mr. E. M. W. Tillyard supported by calling attention to 'Satan's anguished impotence at the beginning, . . . the warning lines at the beginning of Book Four, . . . [and] the description of Paradise, which has in it the hopeless ache for the unattainable.' Continuing, this gifted interpreter of Milton held that pessimism 'comes out strongest of all in the last four books. There is a dreadful sense of the wrongness of things in the approach of action in the Ninth Book: "O much deceived, much failing, hapless Eve." ' In addition, Mr. Tillyard found the first books of the epic stronger than the last, in part for the reason that Milton's pessimism has here penetrated the texture of the verse.

In view of the fact that works of the hexameral tradition frequently closed with prophecy of the Messiah and the new heaven and earth, it is difficult to accept the persuasive argument of Sir Herbert. Indeed, as the Trinity manuscript clearly shows, Milton had planned such an ending for his epic years before the Commonwealth came into being. Moreover, his continued interest in the subject for a quarter of a century questions seriously the conclusion that Milton selected it 'as he sat in silence expiating his offenses.' *Paradise Lost* may well be 'an arraignment of mankind,' but as such it so closely resembles scores of other works that I cannot regard it as biographical. My feeling is rather that Milton stated honestly his objective when he proposed to 'assert Eternal Providence, and justify the ways of God to men.'

There can be little evidence of personal pessimism in the use of such expected commonplaces as Satan's anguish, the idyllic Utopian description of Paradise, or emphasis upon the point that Eve was much deceived. The robust warning against Satan echoed from many seventeenth-century pulpits, and is not unknown today. Tonal shading and treatment of these commonplaces are of course another matter, and may be urged in support of the interpretation that *Paradise Lost* was the pessimistic creation of a writer who had lost both faith and will. It is however in point to recall that where for decades pre-war critics described the literary renaissance of the Sixteenth and Seventeenth Centuries with the word *joyous*, critics of the post-war era frequently have replaced this word with its contraries, *pessimistic* and *despairing*. With the inclusion of Milton among those who fell before despair, the most distinguished hundred years of English literature has become, not the Century of Genius, but the Century of pessimistic Genius. Nor should the fact be ignored that it is our own confused generation which chiefly has stressed the despair and melancholy of the literary era which closed with Milton.

The Satanic School of criticism—that group which regarded Satan as the hero of *Paradise Lost*—has now largely disappeared. It should vanish completely, for Milton's conception and treatment of the Apostate was altogether traditional, and challenges rather than supports the belief that the poet belonged to 'the Devil's party.' A further detail, one previously touched upon, is the attempt to find heresy or unorthodoxy in Milton's idea of 'one first matter.' The doctrine was never condemned, and as the analogues cited suggest, had the approval or sympathy of respected and distinguished writers. A third incidental point involves the belief that we may find the partial source and an explanation of *Paradise Lost* in the prose works, particularly the *Christian Doctrine*. However, repetition of a commonplace does not make it original, with the result that prior use of a theme in a treatise contributes nothing to our knowledge of origins. The *Christian Doctrine* includes many ideas properly Milton's own, but the most cursory reading of the compendiums of Ames and Wolleb will show that Phillips spoke accurately when he described his uncle as preparing this digest chiefly from the works of these men.

The evidence of analogues and apparent sources shows Milton untouched either by intellectual snobbishness or religious prejudice. His themes were those advanced and held sacred by high and low, by Catholic and Protestant. His poem stands as a universal Christian epic. Our practice today of giving credence to an extremely questionable correspondence from Plato or Ariosto, and rejecting a markedly close correspondence from Du Bartas, doubtless would have amused both Milton and his age. I may add that to the extent the poet's thought was Platonic—if there is agreement as to what Platonic thought may be—to such an extent was Platonism to be found in the tradition which chiefly nourished *Paradise Lost*. Contrary to popular conception, Milton did not create from the Bible the expanded paraphrases of Scripture scattered throughout the epic. For the most part, these paraphrases lay at hand within the vast storehouse of hexameral literature.

Perhaps the most pointed criticism recently brought against *Paradise Lost* is that of Sir Herbert Grierson, who considers the poem didactic but not prophetic. Since all Old Testament prophets were didactic, Sir Herbert obviously used prophetic with a special meaning. To him, a prophetic poet is one who puts 'into the language and pattern of poetry his deepest intuitions as these have been evoked by a great political and religious experience. . . . Of intuitive, prophetic poetry the characteristic is' that 'style and thought are inseparable.' Under the first of these definitions, *Paradise Lost* cannot be regarded as prophetic. Milton did not attempt to treat of personal religious ex-

perience; rather, he chose that of Christendom. His justification of God, in keeping with the dominant tradition,
was rational and historical, not emotional and intuitive. The
implicit interpretation that in the epic thought and style
did not fuse into one inseparable unity is, I believe, less
justifiable. Unquestionably, there exist numerous passages
wherein this criticism holds, but certainly as much should
be said of Wordsworth, the prophetic poet. There are also
many sections where the criticism lacks application, as in
that which described the fall of Satan from heaven:

> Him the Almighty Power
> Hurled headlong flaming from the ethereal sky,
> With hideous ruin and combustion, down
> To bottomless perdition, there to dwell
> In adamantine chains and penal fire,
> Who durst defy the Omnipotent to arms.
> Nine times the space that measures day and night
> To mortal men, he, with his horrid crew,
> Lay vanquished, rolling in the fiery gulf,
> Confounded, though immortal.

In discussing the question of Milton's originality, I remarked that in part this consisted of doing better that which
tradition expected should be done. As I conceive it, a
second phase of his originality appeared in his selection and
use of the most striking and compelling themes afforded by
the tradition. He might have placed the creation of the
angels with that of the world. However, he expanded
his canvas by choosing the belief which set their creation
long before the building of the cosmos. Where the battle
in heaven might well have been a conflict between either
Michael and Satan, or Christ and Satan, he again achieved
greater magnitude by pitting both, plus Abdiel, against the
Apostate. The use of two mountains for the Garden in
Eden may not have resulted from a desire for greater

scope, but description of two temptations of Eve undoubt-
edly did. Rather than one or two of the four major divisions of the hexameral tradition, Milton gave all four definite
place.

A third phase of the poet's originality appears in his
organization of the epic. In the dramatic drafts, action began
in heaven; later, it passed to earth; in the epic, it opened
within hell. By beginning the epic in hell, and later using
Raphael as narrator of the battle in heaven, Milton avoided
a disconcerting shift of scene. Use of Raphael, rather than
a chorus, made his revelation more an essential part of the
story. To place Raphael and Adam in familiar dialogue before and after descriptions of the celestial conflict and the
Creation improved greatly the earlier plan. Every change
in organization of which we have record shows Milton's
keen awareness of the important part structure plays in
effective presentation.

Not the least important trait of Milton's inventive genius
may be termed a capacity for expansion. Frequently in
Paradise Lost the inclusion of essentials required by tradition
led to compression inimical to his best work. Such necessitated compression, I believe, affected adversely the story of
the Creation and the recital of Biblical history. In Books I
and II, however, Milton had and probably made space for
expansion; and it was within these books that he wrote
consistently such poetry as he alone could create. The latter
half of both Books III and IV, and the first half of Book V,
set forth more than the required essentials, and at the same
time included many noteworthy passages. These several
sections of the epic, which I believe written shortly after
composition of the *Second Defense*, reflect the creative
expansiveness and fecundity found within Milton's greatest
prose work.

In evaluating the 'originality' of Milton, it is necessary
to recall that he consciously filled his mind with the works

of other men. This he apparently made an open as well as an habitual practice. In quoting entire the anonymous biographer's description of this custom, I again reverse the relative position of the two statements:

> The evenings he likewise spent in reading some choice poets, by way of refreshment after the day's toil, and to store his fancy against morning. And he, waking early (as is the use of temperate men), had commonly a good stock of verses ready against his amanuensis came— which, if it happened to be later than ordinary, he would complain, saying 'he wanted to be milked.'

The minor structural patterns discussed in Chapter X would result naturally from this type of purposive reading. As much probably should be said of many comparable analogues among those considered in Part I. This type of reading also explains the repetition in *Paradise Lost* of key words and phrases found in *Purchas His Pilgrimage* and other prose works.

These varied traits are nothing more than facets of Milton's personality. The love which he held for books, and the inspiration that he drew from them, *Areopagitica* has illustrated well. We cannot doubt that to him a good book represented 'the precious life-blood of a master-spirit, embalmed and treasured up on purpose to a life beyond life.' His pronounced feeling for organization showed itself in the *Commonplace Book*, and his intense love of scope and magnitude in his incessant reading of history.

The fecundity of the poet's nature displayed itself early, the first unmistakable symptoms being the repeatedly expressed desire and promise to create a distinctive work. Of his lack of originality in the modern sense, he doubtless was unaware. In harmony with his age he used liberally all that past and present had spread before him—the Bible, the Classics, religious and secular prose and poetry. He borrowed as instinctively and naturally from Fletcher, as Fletcher had borrowed from Spenser. Similarly, he drew upon Du Bartas as freely as Du Bartas had drawn upon Ambrose, or Tasso upon Basil. What Milton took, he used for the glory of God, and although he did not always transform the idea or substance, he never failed to add some contribution truly his own.

At the opening of this chapter I spoke of the defensive complex endemic among lovers of Milton. In some measure this complex has resulted from consciousness of his continued loss of prestige. The major cause, however, may lie elsewhere—perhaps within those who profess admiration for the poet. Specifically, we find meaningless and often distasteful the religious beliefs to which Milton dedicated his greatest work. The thought rejected, we read primarily his musical word and phrase. Having so divorced word and thought, now as Sir Herbert Grierson, and again as Mr. Eliot, we easily assume that Milton did likewise.

Our present century cannot feel instinctively the unity of Milton's style and thought, especially within those passages which set forth theological concepts. By awareness of the classical and religious background which nourished *Paradise Lost*, we may, however, sense frequently the oneness of phrase and idea. What perhaps is more vital than this, such awareness may bring before us the picture of a noble edifice. Its foundations sink deep into antiquity; its walls show the handiwork of medieval craftsmen; its towers reflect the artistry of the Renaissance. Within this edifice labors a slight, bent figure, blind, and knotted of hand. As he works, his lips repeat the morning's invocation:

> Still govern thou my song,
> Urania, and fit audience find, though few.

BIBLIOGRAPHY

BIBLIOGRAPHY

The scope and limitations of the three divisions which comprise this bibliography are described under the several heads. For the reason that general bibliographies of Milton are easily available, none is given. The non-specialist will find an admirable selected bibliography in the final pages of Mr. James Holly Hanford, *A Milton Handbook*.

I

SUPPLEMENTARY STUDIES BY THE WRITER. The more comprehensive of these articles, particularly the *'Paradise Lost,'* will provide much more detailed citation of evidence than it was possible to include in the text. I am grateful to the several journals for their courtesy in permitting use of the studies in the preparation of this book.

'The Astronomy of *Paradise Lost,'* *Studies in Philology*, XXXIV (1937), 209-247

Campanella, Thomas, *The Defense of Galileo*, edited with Introduction and Notes. *Smith College Studies in History*, XXII, Nos. 3-4 (April-July, 1937).

'The Book of Enoch and *Paradise Lost,'* *Harvard Theological Review*, XXXI (1938), 21-39.

'The Epic Catalogue of *Paradise Lost,'* *ELH, A Journal of English Literary History*, IV (1937), 180-191.

'Macbeth and *Paradise Lost,'* *Shakespeare Association Bulletin*, XIII (1938), 146-150.

'Milton's Ariel,' *Notes & Queries*, CLXXVII (1939), 45.

'Milton's Dialogue on Astronomy: The Principal Immediate Sources,' *PMLA*, LII (1937), 728-762.

'Milton's Golden Compasses,' *Notes & Queries*, CLXXVI (1939), 97-98.

'Milton's Lost Tragedy,' *Philological Quarterly*, XVIII (1939), 78-83.

'Milton's Technique of Source Adaptation,' *Studies in Philology*, XXXV (1938), 61-110.

'Paradise Lost,' *Harvard Theological Review*, XXXII (1939), 181-235.

'Nicolas Reymers and the Fourth System of the World,' *Popular Astronomy*, XLVI (1938), 25-31.

'The Ross-Wilkins Controversy,' *Annals of Science*, III (1938), 153-189.

'The Seventeenth-Century Doctrine of a Plurality of Worlds,' *Annals of Science*, I (1936), 385-430.

II

SECONDARY SOURCES. This group includes contemporary books and articles discussed or cited.

Bailey, Margaret L., *Milton and Jakob Boehme*, New York, 1914.

Bennett, Josephine Waters, 'Milton's Use of the Vision of Er,' *Modern Philology*, XXXVI (1939), 351-358.

Bush, J. N. Douglas, *Mythology and the Renaissance Tradition in English Poetry*, Minneapolis, 1932.

————— *The Renaissance and English Humanism* (The Alexander Lectures in English at the University of Toronto), Toronto, 1939.

Dustoor, P. E., 'Legends of Lucifer in Early English and in Milton,' *Anglia*, LIV (1930), 213-268.

Eliot, T. S., 'A Note on the Verse of John Milton,' *Essays and Studies by Members of the English Association*, XXI (1935), 32-40.

Fletcher, Harris F., *The Use of the Bible in Milton's Prose*, Urbana, 1929.

Gilbert, Allan H., *A Geographical Dictionary of Milton*, New Haven, 1919.

————— 'The Cambridge Manuscript and Milton's Plans for an Epic,' *Studies in Philology*, XVI (1919), 172-176.

————— 'The Outside Shell of Milton's World,' *Studies in Philology*, XX (1923), 444-447.

Greenlaw, Edwin, 'Spenser's Influence on *Paradise Lost*,' *Studies in Philology*, XVII (1920), 320-359.

Grierson, Sir Herbert J. C., *Milton and Wordsworth: Poets and Prophets*, Cambridge, 1937.

Hanford, James Holly, *A Milton Handbook*, 3rd ed., New York, 1939.

————— 'Milton and the Art of War,' *Studies in Philology*, XVIII (1921), 232-266.

————— 'The Rosenbach Milton Documents,' *PMLA*, XXXVIII (1923) 290-296.

Havens, Raymond D., *The Influence of Milton on English Poetry*, Cambridge, 1922.

Jones, Richard F., *Ancients and Moderns*, St. Louis, 1936.

Leavis, F. R., *Revaluation, Tradition and Development in English Poetry*, London, 1936.

Lovejoy, Arthur O., *The Great Chain of Being*, Cambridge, 1936.

————— 'Milton and the Paradox of the Fortunate Fall,' *ELH*, IV (1937), 161-179.

Merton, Robert K., 'Science, Technology, and Society in Seventeenth Century England,' *Osiris*, IV, No. 2 (1938).

Murray, Gilbert, *The Classical Tradition in Poetry*, Cambridge, 1927.

Nicolson, Marjorie H., 'Milton and the Telescope,' *ELH*, II (1935), 1-32.

————— 'Milton's Hell and the Phlegraean Fields,' *University of Toronto Quarterly*, VII (1938), 500-513.

————— 'The Spirit World of Milton and More,' *Studies in Philology*, XXII (1925), 433-452.

Osgood, Charles Grosvenor, *The Classical Mythology of Milton's English Poems*, New York, 1900.

Robbins, Frank E., *The Hexaemeral Literature*, Chicago, 1912.

Saurat, Denis, *Milton: Man and Thinker*, New York, 1925.

Taylor, George C., *Milton's Use of Du Bartas*, Cambridge, 1934.

Thibaut de Maisières, Maury, *Les Poemès Inspirés du Début de la Genèse a l'Epoque de la Renaissance*, Louvain, 1931.

Thompson, E., N. S., 'Milton's Knowledge of Geography,' *Studies in Philology*, XVI (1919), 148-171.

Tillyard, E. M. W., *Milton*, London, 1930.

————— *The Miltonic Setting*, Cambridge University Press, 1938.

Todd, Henry J., *The Poetical Works of John Milton*, London, 1809.

Watson, Foster, 'Alexander Ross: Pedant Schoolmaster of the Age of Cromwell,' *Gentleman's Magazine*, CCXXIX (November, 1895), 464-473.

Whiting, George W., *Milton's Literary Milieu*, Chapel Hill, 1939.

Williams, Arnold, 'Commentaries on Genesis as a Basis for Hexaemeral Literature,' *Studies in Philology*, XXXIV (1937), 191-208.

Woodhull, Marianna, *The Epic of Paradise Lost*, New York, 1907. This study includes valuable digests of such books as Grotius, *Adamus Exsul*, and Vondel, *Adam in Ballingschap*.

III

PRIMARY SOURCES. This bibliography does not list such well-known works as those of Phineas Fletcher, Shakespeare, and Spenser, nor books for which adequate citation is given in the text. The writings of the numerous Greek and Latin Fathers cited in the text, but not included here, will be found in one or both of Migne's editions. I also omit the works of a number of men mentioned in passing, particularly those in the sections which discuss cosmological beliefs, and the conflict between religion and science. Full documentation of these and additional books may be had in the appropriate articles cited in Section I of the bibliography.

Anonymous. *A Discourse of the Nature and Substance of Devils and Spirits . . . A Discourse Concerning Devils and Spirits,* an appendix to the third (1665) edition of Scot's *Discoverie of Witchcraft.*

Anonymous. [?Phillips, John], *The Life of Mr. John Milton,* ed. Helen Darbishire, *The Early Lives of Milton,* London, 1932.

Acevedo, Alonso, *Creacion del Mundo,* Rome, 1615.

Ainsworth, Henry, *Annotations upon the Five Bookes of Moses,* London, 1639.

Ariosto, Ludovico, *Orlando Furioso,* trans. W. S. Rose, London, 1873.

Ashmole, Elias, *The Way to Bliss,* London, 1658.

Aubrey, John, *Minutes of the Life of Mr. John Milton,* ed. Helen Darbishire, *Early Lives,* London, 1932.

Augustine, *The City of God,* trans. Rev. Marcus Dods, New York, 1907.

Avitus, Alcimus, *De Initio Mundi,* Paris, 1545.

Babington, Gervase, *Workes,* London, 1615.

Barlow, William, *A Breife Discoverie of the Idle Animadversions of Marke Ridley,* London, 1618.

Baronius, Caesar, *Annales Ecclesiastici,* Lucae, 1742 (first edition, Rome, 1588).

Basil, *Opera Omnia,* Paris, 1839.

Beaumont, Joseph, *Psyche,* London, 1648.

Bonaventure, *Opera Omnia,* Paris, 1864.

Brahe, Tycho, *Opera Omnia,* ed. J. L. E. Dreyer, Hauniae, 1922.

Buchanan, George, *Poemata,* London, 1686.

?Caedmon, *Metrical Paraphrase of Genesis,* trans. Benjamin Thorpe, London, 1832.

Calvin, John, *Commentaries on the First Book of Moses,* trans. John King, Edinburgh, 1847.

————— *Institutes of the Christian Religion,* trans. John Allen, Philadelphia, 1902.

Campanella, Thomas, *Defense of Galileo,* as cited Section I.

Cedrenus, Georgius, *Compendium Historiarum,* ed. B. G. Niebuhr, Bonnae, 1838.

Junius MS *Christ and Satan*, ed. R. P. Wülker, Grein-Wülker *Bibliothek der Angelsächsischen Poesie*, Leipzig, 1883-1898, Vol. II.

Clavius, Christopher, *In Sphaeram Ioannis de Sacro Bosco, Opera*, Moguntiae, 1611, Vol. II.

Cornish Creation, see William Jordan.

Cowley, Abraham, *Poems*, ed. A. R. Waller, Cambridge, 1905.

Crashaw, Richard, trans. Marini's *Strage degli Innocenti*, in *Poems of Richard Crashaw*, ed. L. C. Martin, Oxford, 1927.

Damascene, John, *Opera Omnia*, Paris, 1712.

Daneau, Lambert, *The Wonderfull Woorkmanship of the World* (*Physica Christiana*), trans. T[homas] T[wyne] London, 1578.

Diodati, Giovanni, *Pious Annotations upon the Holy Bible*, London, 1643.

Donne, John, *Devotions upon Emergent Occasions*, London, 1624.

Du Bartas, Guillaume de Saluste, seigneur du Bartas, *Divine Weekes and Workes*, trans. Josuah Sylvester, London, 1621.

Edward, Earl of Clarendon, *A Brief View and Survey of the . . . Leviathan*, Oxford, 1676.

Book of I Enoch, trans. R. H. Charles, *Apocrypha and Pseudepigrapha of the Old Testament*, Oxford, 1912, Vol. II.

Ephraem Syri, *Opera Omnia Quae Exstant*, Rome, 1737.

Eusebius Pamphilius, *Praeparatio Evangelica*, trans. E. H. Gifford, Oxford, 1903.

Eustathius of Sebaste, *In Hexaemeron*, in Basil, *Opera Omnia*, as cited, I, 909-974.

Fletcher, Joseph, *The Historie of the Perfect-Cursed-Blessed Man*, London, 1629.

Foscarini, Paulo Antonio, *Epistle to Sebastianus Fantonus*, trans. Thomas Salusbury, *Mathematical Collections*, London, 1661.

Fuller, Nicholas, *Miscellaneorum Theologicorum Libri III*, Heidelberg, 1612 (other editions, Oxford, 1616, Leyden, 1622).

Galileo Galilei, *Epistle to her Serene Highnesse Christinia Lotheringa*, trans. Thomas Salusbury, *Mathematical Collections*, London, 1661.

Gilbert, William, *De Magnete*, London, 1600.

————*De Mundo nostro Sublunari Philosophia Nova*, Amsterdam, 1651.

Glanvill, Joseph, *A Blow at Modern Sadducism in some Philosophical Considerations about Witchcraft*. London, 1668.

———— *Plus Ultra,* London, 1668.

Goodman, Godfrey, *The Fall of Man,* London, 1616.

Heath, Robert, *Paradoxical Assertions and Philosophical Problems,* London, 1664.

Heywood, Thomas, *The Hierarchie of the Blessed Angells . . . The Fall of Lucifer,* London, 1635.

Heylyn, Peter, *Cosmography in Four Books,* London, 1674 (first edition, 1652).

———— *Mikrokosmos,* eighth edition, Oxford, 1639.

Hill, Thomas, *The Schoole of Skil,* London, 1599.

Hippolytus, *Philosophumena,* trans. F. Legge, London, 1921.

Jordan, William, *Cornish Creation of the World,* trans. J. Keigwin and ed. D. Gilbert, London, 1827.

Junius, Franciscus, *Testamenti Veteris . . . brevibus scholiis illustrati* ab Immanuele Tremellio et Francisco Junio, Geneva, 1590.

Kepler, John, *Astronomia Nova,* trans. Thomas Salusbury, *Mathematical Collections,* London, 1661.

———— *Dissertatio* (Kepler's preface to his edition of Galileo's *Starry Messenger*), *Opere de Galileo Galilei,* Firenza, 1930, Vol. III, i.

Lactantius, Lucius, *The Divine Institutes . . . The Epitome of the Divine Institutes,* trans. William Fletcher, Edinburgh, 1871.

Luther, Martin, *Colloquia Mensalia, or His Divine Discourses at His Table,* London, 1659 (*Tischreden, Werke,* Weimar, 1912).

Marini, see Richard Crashaw.

Masenius, Jacob, *Sarcotis,* ed. J. Dinouart, Coloniae Agrippinae, 1757.

Melanchthon, Philip, *Initia Doctrinae Physicae,* Vitebergae, 1567.

Mercator, Gerhard, *Atlas sive Cosmographicae Meditationes,* Amsterdam, 1623.

Mercer, John, *Commentarius in Genesin,* Paris, 1598.

Mersenne, Marin, *Quaestiones Celeberrimae in Genesim . . . Observationes et Emendationes,* Paris, 1923.

Mistère du Viel Testament, ed. Rothschild et Picot, Paris, 1878-1891.

More, Henry, *Complete Poems,* ed. Alexander Grosart, Chertsey Worthies' Library, 1878.

Moses Bar Cepha, *Commentarius de Paradiso,* trans. Masius, Antwerp, 1569 (Migne, *Patrologia Greco-Latine,* CXI, 1863).

Murtola, Gasparo, *Della Creazione del Mondo,* Venice, 1608.

Nash(e), Thomas, *Pierce Penniless's Supplication to the Devil*, ed. from the first edition of 1592 by J. Payne Collier, London, 1842.

Old English Hexameron, trans. S. J. Crawford, Hamburg, 1921.

Origen, *The Writings of Origen*, trans. Frederick Crombie, Edinburgh, 1869 (also Migne, *PG*).

Overbury, Thomas, *Works*, ed. E. F. Rimbault, London, 1856.

Pareus, David, *In Genesin Mosis Commentarius*, editio altera, Francofurti, 1615.

Pererius (Pereira), Benedict, *Commentariorum . . . in Genesim*, Moguntiae, 1612.

Peter Lombard, *Libri IV Sententiarum*, studio et cura PP. Collegii S. Bonaventurae, 2nd ed., 1916.

Peyton, Thomas, *The Glasse of Time*, London, 1620, as reprinted by John B. Alden, New York, 1886.

Phillips, Edward, *The Life of Mr. John Milton*, ed. Helen Darbishire, *The Early Lives of Milton*, London, 1932.

Philo the Jew, *On the Account of the World's Creation Given by Moses*, trans. F. H. Colson and G. H. Whitaker (Loeb Library), New York, 1929.

Purchas, Samuel, *Purchas His Pilgrimage*, London, 1626.

Raleigh, Sir Walter, *Historie of the World*, London, 1634.

Ramsey, Andrew, *Poemata Sacra*, Edinburgi, 1633.

Ross, Alexander, *Commentum de Terrae Motu Circulari*, London, 1634.

——————— *The New Planet no Planet: or, The Earth no Wandring Star*, London, 1646.

——————— *Pansebeia: or, A View of all Religions in the World*, 3rd ed., London, 1658 (first edition, 1653).

Rothmann, Christopher, *Letter* to Tycho Brahe, in *Tychonis Brahe Dani Opera Omnia*, ed. cit., VI (*Epistolae Astronomicae*).

Scot, Reginald, *The Discoverie of Witchcraft*, reprinted from the first edition of 1584 by Brinsley Nicholson, London, 1886.

Selden, John, *De Diis Syris*, London, 1617.

Stafford, Anthony, *Niobe, or His Age of Teares*, London, 1611.

Swan, John, *Speculum Mundi*, 2nd ed., Cambridge, 1643.

Syncellus, Georgius, *Chronographia*, ed. W. Dindorf, Bonnae, 1829.

Tasso, Torquato, *Jerusalem Delivered*, trans. Edward Fairfax, London, 1687.

————— *Le Sette Giornate del Mondo Creato*, ed. Angelo Solerti, Bologna, 1891.

Taubman, Friderich, *Bellum Anglicum*, in *Melodaesia*, Lipsiae, 1655.

Tertullian, Quintus, *The Writings of*, Ante-Nicene Christian Library, Edinburgh, 1869-1870.

Thomas Aquinas, *Summa Theologica*, trans. Fathers of the English Dominican Province, London, 1922.

Tostatus (Tostado), Alonso, *Commentaria in Genesim*, Venice, 1728.

Turberville, George, *Eglogs*, London, 1567.

Valmarana, Odorico, *Daemonomachiae, sive de Bello Intelligentiarum Libri XV*, Bononiae, 1623 (Lauder and Newton cited only the revised and enlarged edition of twenty-five books, Vienna, 1627, entitled *Demonomachiae, sive de Bello Intelligentiarum super Divini Verbi Incarnatione*).

Valvasone, Erasmo di, *L'Angeleida*, with preface by Q. Viviani, Undine, 1825.

Vondel, Justus van den, *Lucifer*, trans. Leonard Charles van Noppen, New York, 1898.

Wilkins, John, *The Discovery of a New World*, 3rd ed., London, 1640.

————— *A Discourse Concerning a New Planet*, London, 1640 (bound with the 3rd edition of the *Discovery*, as a second part).

————— *Of the Principles and Duties of Natural Religion*, London, 1675.

Willet, Andrew, *Hexapla in Genesin*, London, 1608.

Wolleb, Johan, *Abridgment of Christian Divinitie*, trans. . . . and in some obscure places cleared and enlarged by Alexander Ross, 3rd ed., London, 1660.

INDEX

INDEX OF WRITERS AND BOOKS

The number which follows immediately the name of an author, or the title of a work, refers to the page of the present volume wherein the writer or work is cited or discussed. The second number or group of numbers, *where given within parentheses*, cites the book, chapter, section, folio, page, column, stanza, or line where the reference may be found. Should no title precede the number within the parentheses, reference is to the work cited in either the text or the preceding parenthesized citation (or citations); or, to a single work by the author given in the bibliography. If documentation is unnecessary, or has been provided in the text, it is omitted here. I do not include some few writers of incidental importance to this inquiry.